A PASSION *FOR* TRUTH

THE INTELLECTUAL COHERENCE OF EVANGELICALISM

Alister McGrath

InterVarsity Press
Downers Grove, Illinois

InterVarsity Press
P.O. Box 1400, Downers Grove, IL 60515
World Wide Web: www.ivpress.com
E-mail: mail@ivpress.com

InterVarsity Press® is the book-publishing division of InterVarsity Christian Fellowship/USA®, a student movement active on campus at hundreds of universities, colleges and schools of nursing in the United States of America, and a member movement of the International Fellowship of Evangelical Students. For information about local and regional activities, write Public Relations Dept., InterVarsity Christian Fellowship/USA, 6400 Schroeder Rd., P.O. Box 7895, Madison, WI 53707-7895.

Cover illustration: Cowgirl Stock Photography

ISBN 0-8308-1591-0 (pbk.)

Printed in the United States of America ♻

Library of Congress Cataloging-in-Publication Data

McGrath, Alister E., 1953-
    A passion for truth: the intellectual coherence of Evangelicalism /
    Alister E. McGrath.
        p.   cm.
    Includes bibliographical references and index.
    ISBN 0-8308-1866-9 (cloth: alk. paper)
    ISBN 0-8308-1591-0 (pbk.: alk. paper)
        1. Evangelicalism.   I. Title.
    BR1640.M42   1996
    230'.046—dc20   96-822
                                                                                                       CIP

16   15   14   13   12   11   10   9   8   7   6   5   4   3

11   10   09   08   07   06

contents

acknowledgments

This book has been many years in preparation. In particular, I wish to acknowledge the kindness of the following in inviting me to deliver lectures which allowed me to develop these ideas, in interaction with others: Oxford University, for the invitation to deliver the 1990 Bampton Lectures; McGill University, Montreal, for the invitation to give the 1992 Anderson Lectures; Wheaton College, Illinois, for invitations to deliver the 1992 Inch Lectures and to provide a keynote address along with Professor George Lindbeck at the 1995 Wheaton Theology Conference on 'evangelicalism and postliberalism'; and Southwestern Baptist Theological Seminary for the invitation to give the Day-Higginbotham Lectures in 1995. The material relating to modernism and postmodernism was developed for an interdisciplinary seminar series at Regent College, Vancouver, in January 1995. I am grateful to Blackwell Publishers for permission to use some sections of material already published in *The Genesis of Doctrine* (1990), which is of direct relevance to the themes of this volume.

I am most grateful to many who have read and commented on earlier drafts of this book, in particular Dr David Bebbington. I have also benefited considerably from the wise editorial advice of Colin Duriez (Inter-Varsity Press, UK) and Rodney Clapp (InterVarsity Press, USA). I myself remain responsible for all errors of fact and interpretation.

introduction

It is now clear that evangelicalism is the largest and most actively committed form of Christianity in the West. The future of the movement has thus been the subject of intense discussion of late, in the light of its continuing successes and expansion. In my earlier work, _Evangelicalism and the Future of Christianity_,[1] I explored a series of questions concerning the identity, strengths and weaknesses of the movement. The present volume seeks to build on this earlier work, by considering the intellectual coherence of evangelicalism with a view to considering what its future might be in a postmodern western world, with its competing ideologies and widely diverging theories of legitimation. Evangelicalism has long since got past the stage where it needs to feel defensive about anything, and is perfectly capable of mounting a sustained bid both for a justified presence within the academic community, and for intellectual respectability as a serious option for thinking people in today's world. Yet evangelicalism has generally not fostered any serious attempt to engage with the life of the mind, by encouraging believers to think within a specifically Christian framework across the entire spectrum of modern learning and culture.

This clearly signals the need for evangelicalism to engage with the leading worldviews of our day, with a view to laying the foundations for the emergence of what Mark Noll has termed 'the evangelical mind'.[2] This can be done only on the basis of a _theological_ vision. While the 'evangelical mind' embraces many aspects of life, including politics and work, its ultimate foundation must be grounded in an understanding of the nature and purposes of God. The formation of an evangelical mind requires confidence in the intellectual coherence and credibility of the evangelical vision in general. Yet despite the fact that evangelicalism has been articulating a coherent theological vision for several hundred years, there is a perceptible reluctance on the part of many evangelical leaders today to become involved in academic theological debate. So how is this reluctance to be explained? What insights does it allow into the nature of evangelicalism itself?

Evangelical hostility towards academic theology

Despite its long history of theological reflection, evangelicalism is widely regarded as the new kid on the academic block. For many, it has not been a welcome arrival. The word 'evangelicalism' continues to evoke images of the anti-intellectualism especially associated with North American fundamentalism during the 1920s and 1930s. Yet evangelicalism has long since moved on from the defensive posturing and over-reactions of this critical period. Since the Second World War, evangelicalism has increasingly shown itself to be concerned about intellectual issues, without in any way weakening or compromising its concern for pastoral and spiritual matters. Yet this new interest in theology has raised a number of issues relating to the identity and goals of the movement.

To refer to the 'intellectual coherence' of evangelicalism is inevitably to talk about evangelical theology. On account of its recent history in North America, a significant constituency within evangelicalism has had a markedly ambivalent attitude towards theology in the last generation. Since its emergence as a major presence in global Christianity after the Second World War, at least a large section of the evangelical movement has not seen sustained theological engagement as a pressing priority on its substantial agenda. Why is this?

Four major reasons may be given, each of which merits further exploration. Three of these are particularly associated with North American, rather than with British, evangelicalism, which accounts to some extent for the very different intellectual ethos associated with the American and British wings of the movement.

1. The fundamentalist heritage of North American evangelicalism distanced it from academic theology for a generation. This factor is of little significance in Britain, where there has been a long history of evangelical involvement in academic theology.[3]

2. Particularly in North America, evangelicalism has come to place emphasis on pragmatic criteria of success, which has led to a retreat from theological engagement on account of its questionable utility for pastoral and evangelistic practice.

3. Academic theology is under an obligation to respond to the secularizing agenda of the professional academy, which distances it from the life and concerns of the Christian churches.

4. Theology is potentially élitist, and thus strongly in tension with the populist character of North American evangelicalism.

We shall explore each of these points in what follows.

I. The fundamentalist legacy

The rise of fundamentalism in North America during the 1920s is of decisive importance in relation to understanding the ambivalent attitude within evangelicalism in this region to theology.[4] The rise of fundamentalism had an impact on the evangelical commitment to scholarship in general which shows distressing parallels with events during the so-called 'Cultural Revolution' in the People's Republic of China. Both divorced a generation from mainline academic engagement, making the subsequent process of reintegration both painful and hazardous. And in the meantime, American universities and colleges have generally drifted still further away from their foundational Christian moorings, making that reintegration additionally problematical.[5] Evangelicalism, which seems to have yet to recover fully from the lingering influence of the fundamentalist insistence that it was exempt on religious grounds from any kind of thinking or cultural engagement,[6] still retains a reputation for intellectual shallowness in some quarters.

The fundamentalist legacy is not, however, totally to blame for evangelicalism's lack of commitment to intellectual engagement. It is arguable that it is the present fixation of the movement on the American therapeutic culture of 'feel-good-ism' which is as much to blame for the intellectual weakness of the movement. We shall explore this in what follows.

2. The dominance of pragmatism in evangelicalism

In a penetrating and important recent study, David F. Wells has argued that evangelicalism has lost whatever grasp it once had of the importance of theology.[7] The strongly pragmatic nature of the movement has, he suggests, led to an emphasis on church growth, feel-good preaching and styles of ministry informed largely by secular psychology. The role of classical theology has become seriously eroded, with evangelical seminaries failing to allot it the place of honour it was once universally acknowledged as possessing. No longer is theology regarded as integral to maintaining and nourishing Christian identity in the world, or as a seminal resource in forging new approaches to ministry. 'The responsibility of seeking to be a Christian in the modern world is then transformed into a search for what [Edward] Farley calls a "technology of practice", for techniques with which to expand the church and master the self that borrow mainly from business management and psychology.'[8] There is a widespread consensus within evangelicalism that Wells has identified a real and worrying trend within the movement, even if his particular presentation of these defects is perhaps somewhat overstated. Wells suggests that the problem lies with evangelicalism, and makes some wise and helpful comments concerning the causes and possible consequences of this neglect.

Although evangelicalism has produced a substantial and sustained theological output since the Second World War,[9] it has tended to focus on a series of more practical issues relating to church growth and evangelism, where theology exercises a less obvious – although arguably important – role. The strongly populist and activist tendency within North American evangelicalism inevitably means that theology is seen as an applied science, orientated towards the practical life of the church. Yet this reflects a wider aspect of American culture as a whole: the 'evasion of philosophy', which can be described as a tendency to address cultural problems, rather than to indulge in philosophical analysis.[10] The 'evangelical evasion of theology' reflects a broader cultural trend which casts doubt on the merits and necessity of theoretical analysis, and prefers to engage directly with the issues of the day.

Yet there are other issues involved, not least the manner in which academic theology is viewed as having become adrift from the life of the Christian community. If evangelicalism has marginalized academic theology, the problem lies at least in part with that theology itself, which has failed to ensure that it understands for itself, let alone communicates to others, its distinctive role within the evangelical community. Theology cannot expect evangelicals to assume that it possesses relevance, given the widespread contempt for academic theology within the church at large. It must *demonstrate* that relevance to a constituency whose very success has rested on its insistence that relevance is an issue.

Evangelicalism has always been aware that no revival in history has ever been born out of a renewed interest in purely academic theology. The renewal of evangelical *theology* depends upon the renewal of *evangelicalism*. It is not theology which brings a revival into being. Theology is what erupts from a self-confident and reflective community of faith, in possession of a vision of why it exists and what it proposes to do. It is the expression, not the cause, of that vision. As Ninian Smart has perceptively pointed out, 'doing theology, in the proper sense, is articulating a faith'.[11] If there is no faith to articulate, theology has nothing to convey or express. Theology may help the evangelical community to judge, reformulate, contextualize and better articulate its vision – but it cannot create that vision in the first place. A vibrant tradition of theological reflection is the outcome, rather than the cause, of a dynamic community of faith.[12]

This point can be seen clearly from the 'Death of God' controversy, which erupted during the 1960s.[13] Much attention was then paid to its theological ideas. However, it is now clear that too little notice was taken of what is now being recognized as a lack of religious vitality within the mainline churches which seems to have occasioned the emergence of this theology.

While most of the philosophy and theology contained in the 'Death of God' literature seems to be very second-rate or worse, it is very necessary to reflect on how absolutely deadly must have been the experience which the writers of this literature must have had, both in the worshipping and in the theological lives of their churches. For example, the God whose death is proclaimed in Thomas Altizer's *The Gospel of Christian Atheism* is a very sick God indeed. But someone must have given him this idea of God. The evidence suggests that it comes from a very sick church.[14]

A church without any sense of vision and purpose, lacking any expectations of what God could do with it, inevitably leads directly to a weary, unfocused and irrelevant theology.

This observation would therefore seem to suggest that the future wellbeing of evangelicalism lies in evangelistic activism, perhaps – but by no means necessarily – coupled with the vigorous pursuit of sustainable spiritualities and an increased engagement with social and political issues. An emphasis on the issue of personal salvation, such as that which lay behind the complex network of regional revivals usually linked together as the 'Second Great Awakening',[15] is therefore widely regarded as integral to evangelical consolidation and expansion. The preaching styles associated with such revivals – populist sermons aimed at an emotional response – reflect the wish to bring audiences to the point where they were prepared to make commitments of personal conversion, on the basis of an immediate existential decision rather than a careful process of reflection.[16] On the basis of the highly pragmatic criteria which evangelicalism has tended to use to measure its successes, theology had little discernible role to play in the serious business of conversion.

The importance of this point cannot be overstated. Evangelicalism has become a mass movement precisely because evangelicals have been concerned to identify and promote its popular appeal. Its activist, immediate and somewhat individualist approach to the Christian faith has ensured that it has maintained a high presence and profile in a culture increasingly tending towards democratic individualism. So who needs theology? There is no place for a version of the Christian faith which has become so cerebralized that it has become the preserve of a small academic élite, and has lost any clear links with the concerns and issues confronting Christians in their everyday lives. And that, in the view of most evangelicals, is where theology takes us.

I am uneasy about this viewpoint. Yet, in offering a criticism of it, I must make it clear that the anti-theological ethos which pervades popular evangelicalism embodies much wisdom and insight. Much theology is irrelevant, arrogant and élitist. The failure or unwillingness of so many academic theologians to concede this point seems to me to be nothing short of scandalous. It reminds me of Hans Christian Andersen's story of the emperor's new clothes, in which nobody was prepared to admit the obvious (on account of cultural pressures) until it became patently obvious that the illusion could no longer be sustained.

When all is said and done, however, this remains a critique of a particular style of theology – what one might loosely call 'academic theology', not in the sense of an informed and thoughtful theology, but a theology whose agenda is dictated by the values and goals of the academy; an academy which is not merely preoccupied with a series of purely 'academic questions' (in the negative sense of this phrase), but which conducts its debates on the basis of a series of non-Christian or anti-Christian assumptions. We shall explore this point in what follows.

3. The secularism of the academy

The days are long since past in which 'the academy' was equated with learning, wisdom and personal integrity. Evangelicals have noted with concern some increasing indications that the modern American academy seems to have more to do with élitism, ideological warfare and rampant anti-religious propaganda than with learning.[17] Especially in the United States, some academic theologians have often seemed to be little more than acolytes to these trends, articulating what often turn out to be profoundly illiberal theologies and firing both their opponents and less than totally enthusiastic colleagues, rather than engaging in the dialogue for which the academy was once noted, honoured and valued.[18] The strongly institutionalized liberal ethos of the modern American university, which is widely perceived to be anti-Christian (although it is arguably hostile to public commitment of any kind, religious or otherwise),[19] has reinforced both the determination of evangelicals to remain faithful to the gospel, rather than the latest cultural trend, and their perception that 'academic theology' is at best an irrelevance to be avoided, conditioned and sustained by a series of secularizing and relativizing assumptions.

These evangelical perceptions may not always be entirely justified, and may occasionally reflect misreadings of complex situations. For example, it is important to distinguish between the social process of 'secularization' (in which functions once associated with the church are taken over by governmental agencies),[20] and the ideology of 'secularism' (which aims to eliminate religion from the public arena). The secularization of the academy does not necessarily imply that it is committed to a secularist ideology. Nevertheless, it is clear that the academy has a substantial way to go before it allays evangelical fears that its agenda is, whether in intent or merely in effect, anti-evangelical.

Yet evangelicalism is not alone in sensing that academic theology now lies on the margins of Christian life. There is a widespread perception within the churches that academic theology has largely lost whatever connections it may once have had with the mission, concerns and life of the church. The relation of academic theology and the Christian church is thus problematical – at least, for theologians. To put it bluntly, nobody seems to want them any more. It is possible to be cynical about much modern theology, and to see it as kept going by academics concerned both to perpetuate themselves and their institutions, and to distract attention from their growing irrelevance and marginalization. The abstracts of the American Academy of Religion all too often reveal items such as the following, which reinforce this increasingly influential perception.

> Taylor's metaphorical 'body', then, is an (ex)tension of the phallocentric and phallocratic technology of modern theology, now confined to a two-dimensional wordplay indifferent to the cries and joys of a richly signed wor(l)d.[21]

This could easily be dismissed as pompous posturing, devoid of any significance except as an example of the felt need to mount obscurity upon obscurity in an endless spiral of self-validation – a classic example of what Charles Newman has called 'the inflation of discourse', in which verbal pretentiousness is deliberately cultivated and any relationship to public utility or relevance is abandoned.[22] But it seems to me that it represents something much more mundane. It is a cry for help. It is a desperate plea to be noticed, a public announcement of one's relevance and significance to a world which has quite obviously lost whatever interest it may once have had in academic religion. On this showing, it is highly unlikely to regain that interest.

A further point of importance concerns the postmodern aversion to questions of truth (see pp. 189–197). Modern western academia occasionally allows its critics to gain the impression that it has lost any concern with issues of truth, and has opted for an easy accommodationism through appeasement of various ideological factions, irrespective of the merits of their cases. Evangelicalism's passion for the truth of the gospel cannot be accommodated within this context. The evangelical critic of the modern academy will point to its failure to address the issue of truth with sufficient seriousness, and argue for the vulnerability of the postmodern outlook in consequence. Evangelicalism recognizes the need for commitment; the academy prefers to stress detachment.

Academic theologians occasionally refer to evangelicalism as 'naïve'. Yet this epithet requires translation. On closer examination, this generally turns out to mean something like 'refusing to acknowledge the *imperium* of the academy', or 'failing to accept the norms of a self-serving and closed academy'. In short, the term has little to do with intellectual ability or scholarly activity; instead, it focuses on the refusal of evangelicalism to become subservient to the ideology of what is coming to be seen as an increasingly marginalized and anti-religious academy.

In this environment of growing scepticism concerning the merits and viability of academic theology, evangelicalism has insights to offer which are of relevance beyond its own boundaries. Theology is the servant of the church. Evangelicalism has always seen theology as part of a greater whole, rather than as a professionalized department which is isolated from the life of the church as a whole. The theologian is not someone who stands above the community of faith, but someone who is deeply involved in its life of worship, prayer, adoration and evangelism.

For evangelicalism, the theologian is one who is called to serve the community of faith from within. Part of that service is criticism of its ideas and outlooks – but it is a loving and caring criticism on the basis of shared Christian beliefs and commitments, rather than the modern criticism of the Christian community by academic 'theologians' on the basis of secular beliefs and values, often radically agnostic or atheistic, which that community feels no pressing reason to share. For evangelicalism, academic theology is as élitist as it is irrelevant; indeed, its irrelevance may have a direct proportional relation to its élitism. In view of the importance of the perceived élitism of the academy, we may turn to deal with this point in more detail.

4. The élitism of academic theology

Academic theology is widely seen as intellectually élitist, and contemptuous of the concerns of ordinary Christian believers. The élitism of theology raises serious concerns for evangelicalism, especially in North America. As we noted earlier, North American evangelicalism is a strongly populist movement, with a genuine heartfelt concern for the issues which are of importance to ordinary Christian believers. It takes seriously the ideas of ordinary people. Nobody has thought that about academics of any kind for a very long time; indeed, the popular stereotype of academia as being an 'ivory tower' detached from – and even contemptuous of – popular culture is too close to the truth for comfort. The detachment of the academy from the realities of everyday life is widely linked, at least in popular perceptions, with the élitism of the academy.

Evangelicalism, then, has little time for the élitism of academic theology, and is primarily concerned with addressing the issues faced by ordinary people. Yet it must be appreciated that 'populism' has its limits. Evangelicalism has ensured that the relevance of the gospel to popular culture is never sidelined through an improper concern for purely academic issues. Popular culture, however, often shows an alarming trend towards shallowness.[23] This intellectual superficiality often means that the ideas of one generation – or even decade – are discarded in the next. Evangelicalism needs to ensure that its concern for popular appeal is never gained or maintained by throwing overboard the deep theological roots of the Christian faith, which provide it with stability and depth across generational divides. A purely 'academic' theology is élitist and irrelevant; a populist theology may well have mass appeal without having any depth. Theology, rightly understood, is about intellectual and spiritual depth and staying power. Given both the widespread contempt for the concern of ordinary Christians by academic theologians and the shallowness of populist theology, evangelicalism would do well to encourage the emergence of sustained serious theological reflection from a committed standpoint within the Christian community, and see the theologians as believers who think for themselves and for others within the community of faith.

A similar approach was advocated by the Marxist writer Antonio Gramsci (1891–1937), who used the sixteenth-century Reformation as a paradigm for his notion of the 'organic intellectual'.[24] This idea is of considerable importance to evangelicalism, as it reflects on the proper place of theology within its ranks. Gramsci argues that two distinct types of intellectuals can be discerned. In the first place, there are those who are imposed upon a community by an external authority. These 'traditional intellectuals' were not chosen by that community, and have influence only in so far as that authority is forced upon the community. In contrast to this, Gramsci notes – and commends – the idea of 'organic intellectuals', understood as thinkers who operate and are respected within a community, and who gain authority on account of their being seen to represent the outlook of that community. Their authority is thus not imposed, but emerges naturally, reflecting the esteem in which the community holds them and its willingness to regard them as its representatives and thinkers. This model of the theologian resonates with the experience of many evangelicals, who have come to regard 'professional theologians' with intense scepticism as a result of the irresponsibility of the 1960s and 1970s, during which much academic theology showed itself to be the willing prisoner of the latest cultural whim and treated the pastoral and spiritual needs and concerns of the churches with a scarcely disguised contempt.

The British evangelical writer John R. W. Stott is an excellent example of an 'organic intellectual' in this respect. He possesses no academic or institutional authority worth speaking of, but rightly enjoys enormous status within the evangelical community (and beyond) on account of his having *earned* that respect. People regarded him as having authority because he had been accepted as being *worthy* of possessing authority. There was an organic and natural relationship between this person and the community for whom he spoke, and to whom he so clearly holds himself responsible. Echoing the outlook of the Reformation, a careful reading of Gramsci's work will encourage evangelicals to look towards the community of faith, to seek and find authority in individuals with a proven record of fidelity to the Christian tradition, a concern for the *consensus fidelium*, a love for the gospel, and a responsible and informed concern to relate it to the world – whether this is recognized by the academy or not. The best intellectuals may exist and operate outside the academy! Evangelical theologians are conscious of a dual responsibility, in that they are writing both for other theologians, yet also on behalf of the evangelical community, with all the responsibilities which this brings.[25]

The past defensiveness of evangelicalism

Evangelicalism has been the subject of much critical and polemical attention within the North American and European establishments. As a result, evangelicalism has often been forced on to the defensive. Where evangelical theologians would rather concern themselves with the positive and critical articulation of the Christian faith, they have instead been forced to defend their particular approaches to the sources of theology, such as Scripture.

The result was perhaps inevitable: instead of demonstrating the implications of revelation for life and thought, evangelicals have been forced to defend the idea of divine revelation itself against its liberal critics; instead of consolidating a biblical theology, evangelicals have found themselves having to defend the use of the Bible in theology against modernists who argue that it is outdated, irrelevant and devoid of authority.

The outcome of this imposed defensiveness has been that evangelical theologians have generally failed to deal with the central themes of the Christian faith to anything like the extent which one would expect.[26] Evangelical theologians thus often appear to have been more concerned with defending the authority of Scripture than with engaging with its contents. Indeed, many of the debates within evangelicalism have centred on issues, such as the 'inerrancy' and 'infallibility' controversy, which may reasonably be argued to have been imposed on them by their opponents.

There is a need for evangelicalism to take time to set out its own ideas without feeling the need to keep looking over its collective shoulder.[27] Being placed on the defensive forces evangelicalism into a reactive posture. In this volume, I have decided not to adopt such a position. Instead, I propose to set out the coherence of the evangelical vision of theology, and engage critically with its contemporary rivals. I fully concede that the critical questions directed against the evangelical vision of the theological enterprise in the modern academic context cannot be ignored. However, I wish to be able to set out an evangelical vision for theology, without constantly being forced on to the defensive, on account of the negative implications this has for the subsequent presentation of that vision.

Evangelicalism has every right to be taken seriously within the scholarly community, despite the attempt to impose an embargo on its doctrines and presence within that community by some of its more threatened members. While evangelicalism is primarily a mass movement within the global Christian community, it is clear that its theology is now being articulated and developed with a degree of sophistication that entitles it to be represented in the academy as well. Its presence there certainly imposes the responsibility of being prepared to give an account of itself, just as it also grants it the privilege of asking those same critical questions of others.

The present study aims to explore the academic credibility of evangelicalism both through a positive exposition of the inherent virtues of the evangelical approach, and through drawing attention to the defects and vulnerabilities of its rivals. In addition to drawing attention to the limitations and inner tensions of such worldviews, I propose to offer critiques of them from an evangelical perspective. Too often, those who ask critical questions of evangelicalism fail to realize that those same critical questions need to be addressed within their own ranks as well. This book thus represents a critical yet positive exploration of the intellectual foundations, coherence and credibility of evangelicalism.

A working definition of evangelicalism

This book cannot be concerned with the fine details of questions relating to the identity of evangelicalism, which have been discussed in detail elsewhere.[28] The debate over evangelical identity is likely to remain a subject of debate and discussion as evangelicalism continues to develop and expand. In part, this reflects the complex historical origins of the movement, in which shifting alliances and emphases have been coupled with the personal influence, often over several generations, of certain individuals. Nevertheless, most evangelicals and well-informed observers of the movement would suggest that evangelicalism is essentially colligatory, in that it finds its identity in relation to a series of central interacting themes and concerns, including the following:

1. A focus, both devotional and theological, on the person of Jesus Christ, especially his death on the cross;

2. The identification of Scripture as the ultimate authority in matters of spirituality, doctrine and ethics;

3. An emphasis upon conversion or a 'new birth' as a life-changing religious experience;

4. A concern for sharing the faith, especially through evangelism.

To use Ludwig Wittgenstein's familiar image,[29] there is thus a sufficiently clear 'family resemblance' between the various styles of evangelicalism to allow a degree of generalization concerning its theological methodology. My intention is to set out the intellectual attraction of evangelicalism, both in terms of its internal coherence and its resilience in the face of its rivals, rather than to enter at length into a debate over its precise identity.

It should be noted that evangelicalism is prepared to tolerate diversity where this does not concern the central issues of the Christian faith. The wise maxim of the great Puritan writer Richard Baxter (1615–91) is of enormous value here: 'in essentials, unity; in non-essentials, freedom; in all things, love (*in necessariis unitas, in non-necessariis libertas, in utrisque caritas*)'.[30] Evangelicals are thus agreed in their affirmation of the authority of Scripture in Christian living and thinking; they would, however, enjoy freedom in the precise manner in which this authority was articulated or conceptualized, allowing the approach associated with Benjamin B. Warfield and Charles Hodge (see pp. 166–174) to be set alongside others, providing that the fundamental and inalienable authority of Scripture was maintained. This study does not attempt to resolve debates of this nature among evangelicals. Rather, it aims to demonstrate the intellectual coherence of the evangelical theological vision as a whole: both its own inner consistency and logic, and also its credibility in terms of the rival approaches to theology in the contemporary world.

The purpose and structure of this book

This work is best understood as a prolegomenon to the formation of an evangelical mind. It is an exploration of the intellectual viability of the evangelical habitat, with a view to establishing the groundwork for the construction and elaboration of a broader and more comprehensive vision for the movement in relation to the life of the mind. The essential precondition for a renewed evangelical engagement with intellectual life is confidence in its own coherence and credibility. This study therefore aims to explore the coherence of evangelicalism by bringing out the inner consistency of the evangelical approach and demonstrating the internal contradictions and vulnerabilities of its contemporary rivals.

The first part of this work focuses particularly on the evangelical emphases on Jesus Christ and Scripture, which are of direct relevance to the intellectual coherence of evangelicalism. The first two chapters explore and defend the distinctively evangelical approaches to the person of Jesus Christ and Scripture. This analysis demonstrates the intellectual dynamics of the evangelical vision, focusing particularly on the person of Jesus Christ and the normative role of Scripture, showing how the various aspects of the evangelical theological enterprise are correlated and inter-connected. Where appropriate, the weaknesses of rival approaches to these issues will be noted.

The second part adopts a significantly different approach. The coherence of evangelicalism can be explored in several manners. Whereas the first two chapters of the work explore the inner intellectual coherence of evangelicalism, the final three address the coherence of its intellectual rivals in the contemporary intellectual and cultural world. While both liberalism and modernism are addressed, in that these remain significant today, particular attention is directed towards postliberalism, postmodernism and pluralism, on account of their growing importance in recent years.

It must be appreciated that these movements are critiqued on a number of grounds, not all of which are specifically evangelical in nature. For example, the argument that there is a fatal internal inconsistency within the postmodern outlook of Michel Foucault or Jean-François Lyotard is not specifically evangelical; however, it is nevertheless of fundamental importance to evangelicals as they seek to demonstrate the coherence of their intellectual vision, and to critique its rivals. It is beyond the scope of this volume to provide an evangelical alternative to the movements thus critiqued; that is part of the task which lies ahead of the evangelical movement, as it prepares to interact more thoroughly and comprehensively with the 'life of the mind' in general.

We therefore proceed directly to an exposition of the place of Jesus Christ in Christian thought from an evangelical perspective.

The uniqueness of Jesus Christ

Christianity is unique among the religions of the world. And the reason for its uniqueness lies in the historical figure who stands at its centre – Jesus Christ.[1] As Stephen Neill, a scholar with vast first-hand experience and knowledge of the religions of India and Africa, once commented, 'the historical figure of Jesus of Nazareth is the criterion by which every Christian affirmation has to be judged, and in the light of which it stands or falls'.[2] For some, any claim to uniqueness is élitist and arrogant. Others, however, see no inconsistency, arrogance or difficulty in any religion, whether Christianity or Buddhism, claiming to be different. As Aloysius Pieris comments, 'that Jesus is unique is obvious even to Buddhists'.[3] The central crucial question, which Christianity has always been obliged to address, is the nature of that uniqueness, and the manner in which it is to be justified and articulated. As we shall see, evangelicalism is emphatic in affirming not merely the *uniqueness* of Christ, but his *definitiveness*; however, the affirmation of the former is an important first step in the defence of the latter.

Evangelicalism has never felt any awkwardness in defending or proclaiming the uniqueness of Jesus Christ.[4] Some have, however, complained of the 'scandal of particularity', arguing on moral grounds that a decisive and definitive knowledge of God must be universally available in space and time. In particular, writers sympathetic to the Enlightenment have promoted the case for a religion based on universally valid and accessible norms or resources, such as 'reason', 'experience' or 'culture'. As we shall demonstrate (pp. 163–177), the strategies adopted by the Enlightenment and its epistemological satellites focus on the need to establish a universally valid and acceptable foundation for any belief-system.[5] Yet, on critical examination, the foundations – such as 'reason', 'culture', 'experience' or 'religion' – which they propose as universal turn out to be strongly ethnocentric and particular. As scepticism concerning the validity of this 'foundationalist' approach gains ground,[6] there is a growing recognition of the importance of returning to the particularities of the Christian worldview. The rise of the movement now generally known as 'postliberalism' (see pp. 131–134) is one of the most obvious indicators of this collapse in confidence in an appeal to 'grand theory' or 'universal foundations'.

Evangelicalism now finds itself to be a significant beneficiary of the anti-foundationalist wave currently sweeping through North American philosophy and theology. Its traditional Christological stance, which has been the object of scorn in the past on account of its uncompromising particularity, is now seen as an asset. Yet this evangelical Christological particularism is not the result of a strategy to make itself acceptable in the new postliberal theological world. It is simply an integral element of evangelicalism's heritage, which evangelicals have always regarded as essential and proper. Now others are beginning to feel the same way.

Evangelicalism has long been committed to the notion of a particular revelation which has universal validity. It has not sought to ground the Christian revelation in some more fundamental entity – whether 'reason' or 'experience' – but has held that its ultimate justification lies in God himself. While some writers have, for ultimately apologetic reasons, sought to stress the continuity between the Christian revelation and human reason,[7] the ultimate authority remains located in God's self-revelation. While justification of the content of that revelation may be made in terms of an appeal to, for example, reason, such appeals are always secondary and confirmatory, rather than primary and foundational. To allow the latter would be to concede that reason was more fundamental than revelation; for the evangelical, there is nothing more fundamental than God. In affirming the *particularity* of the Christian revelation in this way, evangelicalism is now seen to have avoided the epistemological impasse of foundationalism, while maintaining the critically important notion of a universally valid knowledge of God. The particularity of the Christian gospel, and supremely the person of Jesus Christ as saviour and Lord, does not conflict in any manner with its universal scope. Indeed, the evangelical passion for truth is expressed partly in its focus on the person of Christ, in that Jesus Christ *is* the truth.[8]

In this opening chapter, we shall explore the evangelical understanding of the place of Jesus Christ in relation to the Christian faith.

The authority of Jesus Christ

For evangelicalism, Jesus Christ is of constitutive and definitive importance for Christianity, possessing an intrinsic authority which is grounded and focused in his own person and work. His authority is not grounded upon external considerations; were this the case, those considerations would themselves be foundational, in that the authority of Christ would be dependent upon their authority. In the case of the New Testament, the ultimate legitimating authority for Jesus Christ is God himself, who is seen as having vindicated and exalted Jesus through the resurrection, thereby retrospectively validating his ministry.[9]

Christian theology has always been vulnerable to the temptation to ground the authority of Christ in terms of external principles or considerations. Perhaps the most celebrated instance is Immanuel Kant's attitude to the authority of Christ, seen at its clearest in the *Grundlegung zur Metaphysik der Sitten* (1785), in which human moral reason is identified as the criterion by which Christ is to be judged. The authority of Christ is clearly seen to be secondary, deriving from the prior authority of human morality and reason. The British philosopher and novelist Iris Murdoch characterizes this tendency as follows:

How recognizable, how familiar to us, is the man so beautifully portrayed in the *Grundlegung*, who confronted even with

27

Christ turns away to consider the judgement of his own conscience and to hear the voice of his own reason. Stripped of the exiguous metaphysical background which Kant was prepared to allow him, this man is still with us, free, independent, lonely, powerful, rational, responsible, brave, the hero of so many novels and books of moral philosophy.[10]

Similarly, in the Christological writings of the eighteenth-century German rationalist G. E. Lessing, we find a consistent emphasis on the primary authority of reason, which leads to Christ being accorded a partial and secondary authority, to the extent that he endorses what reason commends.[11] The authority of Christ resides in his teaching. That teaching, however, is evaluated in the light of general rational principles: its authority is not inherent, but derives from its correlation with already existing moral principles. Whatever authority he possesses is derivative, rather than inherent.[12]

To suggest that an individual is bound to receive Jesus' teaching on account of who Jesus is, or what status he possesses, is tantamount to an assertion of intellectual heteronomy which is totally unacceptable within an Enlightenment worldview. As the noted New Testament scholar Ben F. Meyer has noted, 'the heritage of Christian belief affirms as indispensable what the heritage of modern culture excludes as impossible'.[13] Leading Christological affirmations are now viewed as strongly counter-cultural, and are hence the source of some embarrassment for those whose agenda is to harmonize Christianity with modern culture, and thus argue that Christology must be reduced to the minimal level acceptable to western culture.

For such culturally enslaved writers, Jesus does not possess authority in that he *establishes* religious or moral values, but to the extent that he *reflects* what modernity endorses as acceptable religious or moral values. Human reason is in itself authoritative: Jesus possesses a derivative authority, to the extent that his words and deeds are perceived to reflect universal human patterns of rationality. It is the autonomous rational individual who is the criterion for the validity of the teaching of Jesus. In this, Lessing reflects the attitude to history particularly associated with the *philosophes* of the French Enlightenment,[14] soon also to become the common currency of the German Enlightenment (usually known as the *Aufklärung*): history is a convenient vehicle for the illustration of non-historical truths, the validity of which is *independent* of the means of their historical disclosure, while totally *dependent* upon their conformity to the human faculty of reason.

The same pattern may be discerned in the period since the Enlightenment. The attribution of authority to Jesus is generally nothing other than a reluctant projection of the authority of an autonomous individual into the past. It is very difficult to read the writings of, for example, the noted German liberal Protestant theologian Adolf von Harnack (1851–1930) without gaining the impression that the Jesus whom he regards as significant is ultimately a construction of his own making, representing an objectification of his own values and feelings. Harnack's approach lacks the crudity of that adopted by Thomas Jefferson. With a highly moralistic eye, Jefferson sifted through the gospels, filtering out those aspects of the teaching and ministry of Christ which he found unacceptable, while holding on to those aspects of Christ's teaching which he deemed to be 'the most sublime and benevolent code of morals which has ever been offered to man'.[15] Harnack may have been more subtle in its application; nevertheless, he deployed the same methodology. For Jefferson and Harnack alike, the prior views of the investigator determine the outcome of the investigation.

On the basis of his investigation, Harnack suggested that the irreducible Christological affirmation was that Jesus was the 'mirror of God's fatherly heart'. But Harnack's critic George Tyrrell (1861–1909) famously objected that the only reflection to be seen in that mirror was not 'God's fatherly heart' but a liberal Protestant face: 'The Christ that Harnack sees, looking back through nineteen centuries of catholic darkness, is only the reflection of a liberal Protestant face, seen at the bottom of a deep well.'[16] For Harnack to attribute authority to *this* Jesus is merely an indirect affirmation of his own authority. As Albert Schweitzer commented, anticipating the results of his mammoth survey of attempts to write a 'life of Jesus':

> Each successive epoch of theology found its own thoughts in
> Jesus; that was, indeed, the only way in which it could make
> him live. But it was not only each epoch that found its
> reflection in Jesus; each individual created Him in accordance
> with his own character. There is no historical task which so
> reveals a man's true self as the writing of a Life of Jesus.[17]

Inherent to this approach to the authority of Jesus Christ is a form
of narcissism – a desire to worship one's own likeness,[18] probably
as a consequence of the fundamentally modernist impulse,
characterized by Nietzsche as the 'will to power', to control the
world and impose one's will upon it. Non-evangelical theology
often gives the impression of being determined to control Christ,
imposing an acceptable façade upon him, or laying down rules of
engagement which severely truncate his authority on account of a
prior set of authoritative and normative assumptions, derived
directly from modern culture.

Evangelicalism argues that authority is inherent in the person
of Christ, and insists that it is of paramount importance to remain
as faithful as possible to the New Testament portrayal of Christ, no
matter how complex and nuanced this may prove to be.[19]
Evangelicalism is strongly counter-cultural at this point; in a
western cultural context in which the right of individuals to create
their own worlds is vigorously asserted, evangelicalism declares that
it is a movement under the authority and sovereignty of Christ. To
understand the significance of this point, we need to explore one of
the leading features of the modernist worldview – the right to
master.

Modernism and mastery

The term 'modernism' is usually taken to refer to the cultural
mood which began to emerge, especially within literature, towards
the opening of the twentieth century. A fundamental theme of
modernism is its desire to control, perhaps seen at its clearest in the
Nietzschean theme of 'will-to-power'. Humanity needs only the

will to achieve autonomous self-definition; it need not accept what has been given to it, whether in nature or tradition. In principle, all can be mastered and controlled. The rejection of tradition is an integral element of this demand to master, and to achieve emancipation from any form of intellectual or social bondage. In part, the particular emphasis placed by modernism upon the autonomy of human reason was a desire to liberate thought from what was seen as the oppression of the past. The ideas of 'authority' and 'tradition' were seen as tantamount to the fettering of the present by a dead past. As Jeffrey Stout points out, 'modern thought was born in a crisis of authority, took shape in flight from authority, and aspired from the start to autonomy from all traditional influence whatsoever'.[20] Human reason was seen as holding the key to emancipation from the discredited political and social systems of the past. This desire for liberation was often linked with the mythical figure of Prometheus, who came to be seen as a symbol of liberation in European literature.[21] Prometheus was now unbound, and humanity poised to enter a new era of autonomy and progress.

A related theme can be seen emerging in the writings of Feuerbach and Marx: the deification of humanity. For Feuerbach, the notion of 'God' arises through an error in the human analysis of experience, whereby experience of oneself is misinterpreted as experience of God.

> Religion is the *earliest* and *truly indirect* form of human *self-consciousness*. For this reason, religion precedes philosophy in the history of humanity in general, as well as in the history of individual human beings. Initially, people mistakenly locate their essential nature as if it were *outside* of themselves, before finally realizing that it is actually within them . . . The historical progress of religion consists therefore in this: that what an earlier religion took to be objective, is later recognized to be subjective; what formerly was taken to be God, and worshipped as such, is not recognized to be something human. What was earlier religion is later taken to be idolatry: humans are seen to have adored their own nature. Humans objectified

themselves but failed to recognize themselves as this object.[22]

In the end, therefore, it is humanity itself which is 'God', not some objective external reality. In the Marxian development of Feuerbach's theme, the origins of the religious experience which is interpreted as 'God' lie in socio-economic alienation.[23] Marx comments thus on the Feuerbachian approach to alienation:

> Feuerbach sets out from the fact of religious self-alienation, the replication of the world in religious and secular forms. His achievement has therefore consisted in resolving the religious world into its secular foundation . . . Feuerbach therefore fails to see that 'religious feeling' is itself a social product, and that the abstract individual who he is analysing belongs to a particular form of society . . . The philosophers have only *interpreted* the world in different ways; the point is to change it.[24]

By changing the world, the human experience which is conceptualized as 'God' will be removed. Socio-economic transformation therefore allows the mastery of religion, which will be eliminated along with its causes. The mastery of religion therefore lies within the grasp of humanity, allowing the Promethean dream to be realized by revolutionary activity.

The same theme of 'mastery' is also associated with the rise of technology in the modern period. In a remarkably astute analysis of the social role of technology, written in 1923, the theologian and philosopher Romano Guardini (1885–1968) argues that the fundamental link between nature and culture has been severed as a result of the rise of the 'machine'. Humanity was once prepared to regard nature as the expression of a will, intelligence and design that are 'not of our own making'.[25] Yet the rise of technology has opened up the possibility of *changing* nature, of making it become something which it was not intended to be. Technology offers humanity the ability to impose its own authority upon nature, redirecting it for its own ends. Where once humanity was prepared to contemplate nature, its desire now 'is to achieve power so as to bring force to bear on things, a law that can be formulated rationally. Here we have the basis and character of its dominion: arbitrary compulsion devoid of all respect.'[26] No longer does humanity have to respect nature; it can dominate and direct it through the rise of technology.

> Materials and forces are harnessed, unleashed, burst open, altered, and directed at will. There is no feeling for what is organically possible or tolerable in any living sense. No sense of natural proportions determines the approach. A rationally constructed and arbitrarily fixed goal reigns supreme. On the basis of a known formula, materials and forces are put into the required condition: machines. Machines are an iron formula that directs the material to the desired end.[27]

This ability to dominate and control nature will inevitably, according to at least some cultural analysts, lead to the deification of technology, resulting in a culture which 'seeks its authorization in technology, finds its satisfaction in technology, and takes its orders from technology'.[28]

The rise of technology may be seen as one aspect of the growing importance of the theme of 'mastery' within western culture. The theme is also reflected within western philosophy, and is stated most explicitly in the writings of Nietzsche. Nietzsche's philosophy has had a major impact on western thought, and has contributed in no small way to the emergence of a cultural environment which is saturated with the ethos of 'I will make things as I please'. For Nietzsche, there were no facts, only interpretations.[29] The interpreter was free to impose any interpretation he or she chose.[30]

This Nietzschean ethos pervades much modern Christology, which can be regarded as an extended attempt to make Jesus of Nazareth conform to the personal norms of individual interpreters, or the ideological tribes to which they belong. The result is a kind of Christological anarchy, controlled – if it can be said to be controlled at all – by ideological norms reflecting the self-interests of the redefining groups. At this point, evangelicalism is strongly counter-cultural, defending the fundamental right of Christianity to be mastered by Christ, rather than to master him in the light of contemporary transient social mores.

Where the theme of 'mastery' exercises a controlling influence within modernity, evangelicalism sets in its place that of 'stewardship', seeing itself as responsible for the articulation and safeguarding of something which, in the end, it does not have the right to master or control. There is a fundamental issue of integrity at stake, in which evangelicalism is unequivocally committed to responding to what Martin Kähler once termed 'the historic, biblical Christ',[31] rather than to some modern construction or reconstruction of him – a reconstruction which all too often turns out to rest on transient contemporary norms. Evangelicalism does not believe it has the right or the resources to reconstruct Christ, and regards modernist Christologies as reflecting both the desire of modernity to force Jesus to conform to its patterns and its refusal to tolerate those who call its presuppositions into question.

To avoid any misunderstanding at this juncture, a point of clarification is needed. A fundamental distinction must be drawn between the correlation of the gospel with cultural trend, and the foundation of the gospel upon a cultural trend. The former represents an entirely proper and responsible apologetic approach, in which the themes of the gospel are expressed in a manner best suited to its contextualization. It is the gospel which is primary; the contextualization is secondary and provisional. Evangelicalism has long recognized the apologetic need to contextualize the gospel in this manner.[32] This is to be contrasted with the liberal strategy of grounding the gospel in cultural trends, which inevitably means that the gospel becomes enslaved to culture, unable to do anything other than reflect its ideas and values.

In part, the evangelical critique of modernist Christologies is theological and scholarly; yet there is also a deeply pragmatic aspect to this critique. Feuerbach declared the divinity of humanity: the human is God. Yet after a century and a half of experience of this 'god', evangelicalism feels it has every right to question the outcome of this affirmation. The rise of Stalinism and Nazism may be regarded as inaugurating two of the most oppressive regimes in human history and as setting in motion programmes of genocide, the extent of which continues to numb the human imagination. As postmodern critics have emphasized, the modernist quest for mastery has led to a culture of illusion and oppression, in which human power has become a controlling influence.

In this situation, the evangelical emphasis on the authority of Jesus Christ *as he is revealed in Scripture* (rather than as he is constructed by human interest groups or power blocks) is profoundly liberating. This foundational evangelical belief was stated with electrifying directness in the Barmen Declaration (1934), as Nazism attempted to strengthen its grip on a culturally conditioned German church:

> 1. Jesus Christ, as he is attested for us in Holy Scripture, is the one Word of God which we have to hear and which we have to trust and obey in life and in death. We reject the false teaching, that the church could and should acknowledge any other events and powers, figures and truths, as God's revelation, or as a source of its proclamation, apart from and besides this one Word of God . . .
>
> 3. The Christian church is the congregation of brothers and sisters in which Jesus Christ acts presently as the Lord in Word and sacrament, through the Holy Spirit. As the church of forgiven sinners, it has to bear witness in the midst of a sinful world, with both its faith and its obedience, with its proclamation as well as its order, that it is the possession of him alone, and that it lives and wills to live only from his comfort and his guidance in the expectation of his appearance. We reject the false teaching, that the church is free to abandon the form of its proclamation and order in favour of anything it pleases, or in response to prevailing ideological or political beliefs.[33]

The evangelical insistence upon the authority of Jesus Christ is thus not about a self-imposed servitude, but upon a liberating commitment to one who frees us from bondage to the oppression of a power-hungry world.

The significance of Jesus Christ

The evangelical understanding of the significance of Jesus Christ is that he is both constitutive and illustrative of the Christian life. In other words, Christian existence is possible only on the basis of the life, death and resurrection of Jesus Christ; and the nature and shape of that existence is itself embodied in his own life, and inspired and informed by it. We can give greater substance to this foundational statement by exploring five seminal aspects of the Christian understanding of the significance of Christ.

1. The revelational significance of Jesus Christ

The New Testament portrayal of Christ includes strongly revelational elements. Some scholars have argued that the language of revelation plays a peripheral role in Scripture.[34] It is important to notice that these judgments are often made on the basis of modern notions of revelation (some highly influenced by Enlightenment presuppositions), without a detailed examination of the nature of the revelational language found in Scripture.[35] For example, the Greek term *apokalypsis* is not found in any Pauline writing; yet the notion of 'revelation in Christ' may be argued to permeate Paul's theology.[36] It is clear that Scripture regards God as making 'knowledge of himself' (to use a richly nuanced phrase) available, through the 'unveiling' of God's person and purposes. In the New Testament, this 'unveiling', 'showing', and 'making known' is focused on the person and work of Christ. To note two of the most forceful New Testament statements on this matter, which must be allowed their full weight in any Christological analysis, Jesus Christ is 'the radiance of God's glory and the exact representation of his being' (Heb. 1:3) and 'the image of the invisible God' (Col. 1:15). These concepts are often eschatological in their orientation: what we now know and possess through Christ will be brought to its fulfilment and full disclosure on the last day.

A fundamental distinction must be drawn here between the notion of a *revelation from God* and a *revelation of God*. This point is perhaps best understood by comparing the Islamic and Christian notions of revelation.[37] In the Qur'an, every sura except one opens with the word '*qul*' – the imperative form of the verb 'to say'.[38] No matter what literary form the passage in question may take – whether it is anecdotal, historical, prescriptive or exhortatory – it is understood to be a revelation from God, dictated by the archangel Gabriel to the prophet Muhammad. Although later Islamic piety developed an interest in the person of the prophet, the foundational Islamic understanding is that of an authoritative revelation in the form of a book, not a person.[39] The contrast between this and the Christian view is brought out clearly by Martin Luther. For Luther, Islam has the Qur'an and Judaism the Torah; yet for Christians,

> God does not want to be known except through Christ; nor can he be known in any other way. Christ is the offspring promised to Abraham; on him God has grounded all his promises. Therefore Christ alone is the means, the life, and the mirror through which we see God and know his will. Through Christ God declares his favour and mercy to us. In Christ we see that God is not an angry master and judge but a gracious and kind father, who blesses us, that is, who delivers us from the law, sin, death, and every evil, and gives us righteousness and eternal life through Christ. This is a certain and true knowledge of God and divine persuasion, which does not fail, but depicts (*depingit*) God himself in a specific form, apart from which there is no God.[40]

For Christians, Jesus is the embodiment and self-revelation of God. At the heart of the Christian faith stands a living person, not a book.

Underlying the revelational language and conceptualities of the New Testament is an affirmation of the human need to be *told* what God is like. God must be allowed the privilege of naming and disclosing himself, rather than being forced to suffer the indignity of having human constructs and preconceptions imposed upon him. Evangelicalism is determined to 'let God be God', and to receive, honour and conceive him as he chooses to be known, rather than as we would have him be. At its heart, evangelicalism represents a relentless and serious attempt to bring all our conceptions of God and ourselves to criticism in the light of how and what God wishes to be known. In this sense, evangelical theology is *responsible*, in the dual sense of being a *response to divine revelation* (rather than a human initiative) and being *answerable to God* for its formulations and conceptions.

For evangelicalism, any responsible concept of God must be a human response to God's self-revelation, a response which is governed and controlled by that revelation. This is not to say that all human concepts of God prior to revelation are without value; rather, it is to note that such concepts are to be evaluated in the light of revelation. For Ludwig Feuerbach, all concepts of 'God', whether Christian or not (Feuerbach declines to distinguish them), are a human invention, a projection or objectification (*Vergegenständlichung*) of human hopes and fears.[41] This was, and continues to be, a valid and penetrating criticism of any theological methodology – such as that originated by F. D. E. Schleiermacher and continued in the writings of A. E. Biedermann and Paul Tillich – which has its starting-point in human experience.[42]

To begin with 'experience' is thus potentially to begin with a human construction, shaped by gender, class and socio-economic forces. To base theology upon such a resource is inevitably to give birth to a 'god' who is a product of the social location of the theologian. As Karl Marx so perceptively noted, this approach to theology suggests that it is merely necessary to alter the socio-economic situation of the thinker to change the resulting concept of God.[43] Any theology which is a response to human society, whether directly or – through culturally-conditioned human experience – indirectly is determined by that culture. This leads to the conclusion that God may be mastered, which, as we shall see, is a central theme of the modernist project (pp. 179–184).

The notion of 'revelation' was deeply offensive to the Enlightenment, which regarded it as a challenge to the autonomy of the thinking individual. The autonomy of the free-thinking individual would be radically compromised if it were necessary to acknowledge that knowledge of God ultimately derived from another source – a source not directly accessible to unaided human reason. Reason was capable of discerning and disclosing all that needed to be known and could be known about God. It was nothing less than heretical to suggest that there was a source of knowledge which could supplement or, still worse, contradict this autonomous knowledge. For the Enlightenment, both salvation and revelation were accessible to the unaided human faculties. The Enlightenment's decisive rejection of Augustinianism was fundamentally a protest against Augustine's insistence that humanity needed to be helped if it was to know God properly or to be saved.

It is fair to argue that the Enlightenment objections to the concept of revelation lay less in any fundamental intellectual difficulties raised by the notion than in the implications for human autonomy. To concede that we needed to be told anything was an admission of heteronomy – dependence on another for knowledge. Jeffrey Stout has correctly characterized the Enlightenment as a 'flight from authority';[44] that flight was often justified on pragmatic rather than theoretical argumentation, in that 'authority' was regarded as virtually synonymous with the political oppression of the *ancien régime*. There is thus a strongly sociological component to the Enlightenment rejection of authority and tradition, linked with a specific historical context.

The notion of revelation poses a direct challenge to human autonomy. It affirms that human beings are perfectly capable of constructing their own ideas about God – but that these ideas require to be supplemented, challenged and corrected in the light of the way God actually is. To affirm the priority of revelation is ultimately to affirm that God is the supreme authority on God, irrespective of how humiliating this may be for self-professed human authorities on the matter. Human discourse about God is provisional, and cannot be regarded as authoritative on the basis of its own inherent credentials. As 'God' does not refer to an object which is available for public scrutiny, human ideas about God will always be subject to challenge, criticism and correction. 'How do you know that? What authority do you have for stating that? What special privilege do you have which permits you to speak in these terms? Why should we listen to you?' These questions cannot be evaded. The fundamental revelational axiom of the Christian faith is that *only God can reveal God*, just as its fundamental soteriological axiom is that *only God can save*. This brings us to a discussion of the soteriological importance of Christ.

2. The soteriological significance of Jesus Christ

The New Testament affirms that salvation is made possible and available through the death and resurrection of Jesus Christ. The Pauline writings are dominated by two themes, often expressed in formulaic terms: that Christ was 'given up' for the salvation of humanity, and that 'Christ died for us'.[45] The difference between Christianity and Islam at this point is clear: the Qur'an uses the root Arabic word for 'salvation' (*najah*) only once. Although the idea (particularly as understood in terms of being delivered from the punishment of hell) is found within Islam, it is not as highly developed as in Christianity. To refer to Muhammad as 'saviour' would do considerable violence to the Islamic tradition concerning the identity and role of the prophet.[46]

In marked contrast, a wide range of soteriological images is deployed within the New Testament to explicate the meaning of the death and resurrection of Christ.[47] There are reasons for supposing that these images are formulated with apologetic considerations in mind, in order to maximize the perceived relevance and significance of the gospel proclamation on the part of its intended audiences.[48] It is not our concern to explore these in detail; our concern is to emphasize that the death and resurrection of Christ are regarded as of fundamental importance to the Christian gospel. Perhaps one of the most distinctive themes of the New Testament is the critical role of the cross in relation to salvation.

The centrality of the cross of Christ has long been a leading theme of evangelical theology and spirituality. In the New Testament, Paul's letters and the gospel of Mark demonstrate a particular focus on the cross, which could be analysed as follows.[49]

1. The cross is seen as the *exclusive ground of salvation*. All other events in the history of salvation (such as the resurrection of Christ, or his coming again in glory) are seen as being set in their

proper context by the cross. Thus, in the case of the Corinthian theology so powerfully criticized by Paul, the resurrection appears to be detached from the cross, and treated as relativizing the crucifixion. The theology of the cross negates this development.

2. The cross is treated as the *starting-point of authentically Christian theology.* The cross is not an individual aspect of theology, but is itself the foundation of that theology. Far from being an isolated chapter in a textbook of theology, the cross both dominates and permeates all true Christian theology, with its thread being woven throughout the entirety of its fabric.

3. The cross is seen as the *centre of all Christian thought,* in that from its centre radiate Christian statements on ethics, anthropology, the Christian life, and so on. The doctrines of revelation and salvation, so easily detached from one another, converge on the cross.

There can be no doubt of the New Testament's emphasis on the emphasis on the uniqueness and finality of the salvation brought by Jesus Christ. Paul Knitter attempts to distinguish between the confession of 'Jesus as saviour' (which is a core belief) and the confession of 'Jesus as *only* saviour' (which he regards as a discardable cultic expression of the former).[50] The high estimation of Jesus found in the New Testament is, according to Knitter, a culturally conditioned way of speaking which is relational rather than metaphysical.[51] Thus the confession 'Jesus is Lord' is an expression of the *specific* importance of Jesus for the believer (in much the same way as a lover might speak of the beloved), rather than a statement of his *universal* significance for all of humanity. Yet this seems to represent a strategy designed with the sole objective of neutralizing the clear thrust of the New Testament proclamation. We shall consider this point further in our discussion of the issues raised by religious pluralism (see pp. 201–240). Our attention now turns to the role of Jesus Christ as an example or embodiment of the life of faith.

3. The mimetic significance of Jesus Christ

Jesus Christ is not only the basis of salvation; he embodies the contours of the redeemed life. This does not mean that Jesus Christ is to be thought of purely as an external example whom believers are required to imitate, as if Christianity was a kind of Christological reworking of the Platonic notion of *mimēsis*.[52]

A purely mimetic or exemplarist view of Christ as a moral example is inextricably linked with a deficient view of human nature, which fails to come to terms with the sheer intractability of the fact of human sin, and the strange and tragic history of humanity in general, and the Christian church in particular. As Charles Gore pointed out incisively a century ago:

> Inadequate conceptions of Christ's person go hand in hand with inadequate conceptions of what human nature wants. The Nestorian conception of Christ . . . qualifies Christ for being an example of what man can do, and into what wonderful union with God he can be assumed if he is holy enough; but Christ remains one man among many, shut in within the limits of a single human personality, and influencing man only from outside. He can be a Redeemer of man if man can be saved from outside by bright example, but not otherwise . . . The Nestorian Christ is the fitting Saviour of the Pelagian man.[53]

An exemplarist soteriology, with its associated understanding of the nature and role of the moral example of Jesus Christ, is ultimately the correlative of a Pelagian view of the situation and abilities of humanity. The ontological gap between Christ and ourselves is contracted, in order to minimize the discontinuity between his moral personality and ours. Christ is the supreme human example, who evinces an authentically human lifestyle which we are alleged to be capable of imitating.

Such a view is not merely inadequate as an exposition of the significance of Jesus Christ, but is unrealistic in its estimation of the capacities and inclinations of human nature. It is an ethic addressed to an idealized humanity, which does not correspond to humanity as we empirically know it, and as we have been taught to view it by the Christian tradition, trapped in its predicament. Perhaps the most characteristic feature of sin is self-deception, a reluctance to accept the tragedy of our situation. If this is the case, the first step in the reconstruction of an authentically Christian ethic must be the elimination of the 'perfectionist illusions' (to use one of Reinhold Niebuhr's characteristic phrases) which have so hindered liberal Christian ethical reflections during the present century.

This 'moral example' theory rests upon a totally unrealistic and un-Christian view of human nature. It also appears to rest upon a deficient view of the person of Christ. The view of his significance we have just outlined ultimately grounds his continuing ethical relevance in his exemplification of allegedly universal moral values. And, as will become clear in our analysis (see pp. 128–131), this notion is now regarded as highly questionable. The death of Socrates in 399 BC directs our attention to virtues, such as courage and integrity, which are not limited to one particular time and place. In that the story of Socrates' death exemplifies these virtues, it may be said to be charged with moral authority. Socrates is of moral importance in that he witnesses to these virtues. They are prior to his existence, and were not established through his death. They are conveyed through it, not established by it. In principle, these and other virtues could be conveyed through other human beings. The moral authority of such a narrative is interchangeable, in that it can be predicated of other subjects – such as, in the view of exemplarism, Jesus Christ.[54] Exemplarism locates the moral authority of the narrative of Jesus of Nazareth in its reflection of previously recognized universal moral values, the validity of which is independent of him. Other witnesses, preferably more recent, might function considerably better in this respect. Jesus thus appears as a moral example, yet there is no real attempt to spell out the fact that there is a radical difference between Jesus and ourselves at this critical juncture.

Evangelicalism avoids this minimalist view of sin and inadequate conception of Christ through an emphasis on 'being conformed to Christ'. Through faith, the believer is conformed to Christ – or, more accurately, the process of conformation to Christ begins. Clear statements of this process of establishing the conformity of the structure of existence of the believer to that of Jesus are already clearly evident in the New Testament itself. Particularly in the Pauline writings, participation in Christ points to a conformity of one's existence to his. Through faith, the believer is caught up in a new outlook on life, a new structure of existence, embodied paradigmatically in Jesus Christ – and both in their proclamation and person, believers reveal this story of Jesus Christ.

Perhaps the most characteristic thought in the Pauline writings concerning the Christian life is that it is *Christomorphic*.[55] The New Testament ethical exhortations, for example, are doubly grounded in Christology, in that Christology provides both the presuppositions of the situation in which the Christian is located, and the pattern for Christian conduct.[56] At several points, Paul indicates that he thinks of his own life as a believer in terms of a recapitulation of the life of Christ himself, in that Jesus Christ is understood both to enable and to embody the distinctively Christian pattern of life.[57] The Christian life is about being enabled to conform to the structure of existence which is established and defined by the history of Jesus Christ, and reflected in the life of Paul. This is of particular importance in relation to suffering, which assumes a new significance for Christians on account of its correlation with the passion of Christ.[58] In particular, Paul appears to view his own sufferings as an extension of the suffering of Christ, or an embodiment of the gospel.

Thus when Paul urges his readers to be imitators of Christ, as he is (1 Cor. 11:1), his words seem to suggest that being a Christian is to enter into so close and deep a relationship with Christ that believers in some way begin to imitate him in consequence of that relationship. Imitation is thus the fruit, not the precondition, of faith. To become a Christian is to begin the process, not so much of *conforming*, as of *being conformed*, to Christ. It is not so much we who are active, as God who is active, in this process.

The New Testament itself clearly presupposes that ethical exhortations are grounded in Christological insights, in that Christology provides both the presuppositions of the Christian's existential situation and the pattern for his conduct. This is especially true of Paul's writings, which frequently suggest that Paul's personal existence is a recapitulation of the life-pattern embodied in Jesus Christ, and further that Paul's experience is paradigmatic for Christian experience in general. Paul's narration of his personal history, interpreted in the light of that of Jesus Christ, is understood as sketching the contours of a model Christian existence. For the Christian to live *ek pisteōs* is to live in accordance with the structure of existence established and defined by the history of Jesus Christ, and reflected in that of Paul.

Evangelicalism thus argues that the life, death and resurrection of Jesus Christ make possible a new form of existence, which is both instantiated by Jesus Christ, and evoked through a God-worked regeneration within believers as they are conformed to Christ.

4. The doxological significance of Jesus Christ

There is the most intimate of connections between Christian theology and the way in which Christians worship and pray.[59] Theology and doxology – that is to say, an understanding of worship and adoration – cannot be permitted to go their separate ways, as if the ways in which Christians worship have no impact on their theological reflections. As James I. Packer has stressed, theology and spirituality have the most intimate of connections:

> I question the adequacy of conceptualizing the subject-matter of systematic theology as simply revealed truths about God, and I challenge the assumption that has usually accompanied this form of statement, that the material, like other scientific data, is best studied in cool and clinical detachment. Detachment from what, you ask? Why, from the relational activity of trusting, loving, worshipping, obeying, serving and glorifying God: the activity that results from realizing that one is actually in God's presence, actually being addressed by him, every time one opens the Bible or reflects on any divine truth whatsoever. This . . . proceeds as if doctrinal study would only be muddled by introducing devotional concerns; it drives a wedge between . . . knowing true notions about God and knowing the true God himself.[60]

Packer's point is that a genuine experience of God, such as that gained through Christian worship and prayer, makes the detached study of God an impossibility. It is like asking the lover to be neutral about the beloved. Commitment is not merely a natural outcome of an authentically Christian experience and knowledge of God; it is the substantiating hallmark of such experience and knowledge.

It is therefore of the utmost importance to note that the New Testament explicity refers to the worship of Jesus Christ.[61] Within a strictly monotheistic culture, in which it was fully accepted that only the God of Israel was to be worshipped, we find explicit reference to Jewish Christians worshipping Jesus Christ. For example, Matthew's gospel employs the Greek verb *proskynein* with reference to the reaction of the disciples to the presence of the risen Christ (Mt. 28:9, 17). This practice was noted by the younger Pliny in his famous letter of AD 112 to the Emperor Trajan, in which he reports that Christians sang hymns to their Lord 'as to a god' (*quasi deo*).[62]

The Christological hymns in the New Testament are a clear indication of the exalted status accorded to the risen Christ within the early Christian communities, indicating that the lordship of Christ had become fully integrated into both the worship and thought of the New Testament communities, with the latter involving taking full account of the high estimation of Jesus which was already established and accepted within Christian devotion.[63] The fact that Paul is prepared to cite pre-Pauline Christological hymns is a sign of their acceptance within the communities to whom he was writing (or from which he was writing), and of the early formulation of a high Christology similar to that endorsed and expounded by Paul. It has been suggested that the use of *kyrios* to refer to Christ and his divinity is to be attributed to the influx of large numbers of pagan Gentiles into Christian circles.[64] However, the evidence for this is somewhat filmsy; the use of the term in this exalted sense seems to have its origins in Jewish Christians originating from Palestine,[65] and cannot be put down to pagan misunderstandings or misrepresentations.

The strongly doxological character of the evangelical estimation of Jesus Christ can probably be seen at its most striking in the great hymns of this tradition, particularly those deriving from Pietist sources.[66] Worship of Christ as the God who humbled himself to redeem humanity is there mingled with sober reflection on the cost of that redemption and the motivation which it offers for authentic Christian living and evangelism. The coherence of the evangelical understanding of the significance of Christ extends to the manner in which he is worshipped and adored, as well as that in which he is understood theologically.

It will also be clear that the evangelical emphasis upon the lordship of Christ has implications for evangelism. Once more, the coherence of the evangelical understanding of Christ becomes clear; the recognition of the identity of Christ leads directly to the proclamation of Christ to the world – better, to *his* world, in that he is its creator, redeemer and lord. We shall explore this point in the final section of this analysis.

5. The kerygmatic significance of Jesus Christ

Jesus Christ is someone who is proclaimed to the world. This strong emphasis on the proclamation (Greek: *kērygma*) of Christ is integral to the evangelical understanding of his person and place. There is a strongly kerygmatic nature to the New Testament, in that Christ is seen as someone who is to be proclaimed and to whom a response is expected. In fact, the kerygmatic character of the New Testament witness to Christ is such that Martin Kähler was led to declare that 'the real Christ is the preached Christ'.[67] The content of the Christian proclamation is Jesus Christ. For example, Paul's proclamation of the gospel focuses on the person of Christ (Gal. 1:16), and more specifically, on Christ crucified and raised from the dead (1 Cor. 1:23; 15:12). In the Corinthian letters, there is only one reference to the 'gospel of God', yet there are five to the 'gospel of Christ'. Indeed, Paul seems on occasion to treat 'preaching Christ' and 'preaching the gospel' as being interchangeable.

The Christological content of the Christian proclamation is minimized in the writings of Rudolf Bultmann, Gerhard Ebeling, and especially Paul Tillich. Tillich's theology sits so loose to the figure of Jesus that he can dispense with his historical existence and personality without making any noticeable difference to his theology.[68] Jesus illustrates a principle, which can be and is illustrated by others. It is the principle which takes priority over the persons who manifest it, one of whom may have been – but need not have been – Jesus. Bultmann understood the proclamation or *kērygma* primarily in terms of an active and effective word, summoning its hearers to an existential decision. There was thus no informational 'content' (concerning, for example, the historical figure of Jesus) to the kerygma.[69] While Gerhard Ebeling showed considerably more interest in the historical figure of Jesus than Bultmann, he defended the notion of faith as trust, rather than 'trust in Christ'. Jesus is here seen as an example of faith, rather than as its object. It is the faith *of* Jesus which is transmitted in the proclamation of the church, not faith *in* Jesus.[70]

However, recent scholarship has decisively undermined the New Testament basis of this trend towards detaching Christian faith from the historical figure of Jesus. The likely use of the Jesus tradition in the Pauline material indicates the potential importance of Christological specifics for Paul.[71] The rigid distinction between *didachē* and *kērygma* is also difficult to sustain; there are, for example, clear indications that *didachē* may designate the content of the *kērygma*, particularly with reference to its Christology.[72] In general, the tenor of early Christian preaching may be summarized as 'a proclamation of the death, resurrection and exaltation of Jesus that led to an evaluation of his person as both Lord and Christ, confronted man with the necessity of forgiveness, and promised the forgiveness of sins'.[73] The kerygmatic dimension of the New Testament thus focuses on Jesus as Lord, Christ and Saviour.[74]

Evangelicalism has integrated these kerymatic insights into its entire worldview.[75] The evangelical insistence on the importance of evangelism is thus an entirely proper and natural outcome of its Christology: if Jesus Christ is indeed Saviour and Lord, then he must be proclaimed to the world as such. There is a Christological foundation and motivation to evangelism, which evangelicalism has never seen as an optional extra for a select few, but as integral to the life and witness of the church. The identity of Jesus Christ is such that evangelism is an essential aspect of the response of believers, both individually and corporately, to his person and work.

These five considerations underlie the decisive Christian affirmation that God has revealed himself in Jesus Christ, who is the foundation and criterion of evangelical theology. If Jesus Christ is God, or is mandated to speak and act on his behalf, then we are both authorized and required to speak of God in terms of him.[76] If he is not, he deserves to be taken with the same seriousness and weight as any other human being, who can speak of the word and will of God only at second hand and indirectly. It will therefore be clear that Christology plays a decisive role in evangelical theological and spiritual reflection, and gives evangelical theology both its intellectual coherence and evangelistic and spiritual focus. The question 'Who is Jesus Christ?' is thus determinative of the entire evangelical theological enterprise.

And for the evangelical, that question can and must be answered only on the basis of Scripture. As John Calvin put it, we do not have to deal with a naked Christ, but with a 'Christ who is clothed with his gospel'.[77] We have to deal both with the person of Christ and with the interpretation of Christ that we find in the New Testament. The importance of Scripture to the theme of 'knowing Christ' cannot be overstated. It is not merely that we have no reliable knowledge of Christ from any source outside the Bible;[78] the distinctively Christian *interpretation* of Jesus Christ – which is, in the end, the gospel – is also mediated primarily in and through Scripture.

There will be those outside evangelicalism and outside Christianity who will want to make other figures, powers, principles and values of foundational importance. Evangelical Christianity, however, is unashamedly Christ-centred. Jesus Christ *is* the gospel. However complex subsequent theological reflection of this may become, evangelicalism affirms that all must be based upon Christ, and all must be judged by Christ – not seeing him simply as a source of ideas, but as the foundation of every aspect of the Christian life. As the great English evangelical John Newton commented:

The love of God, as manifested in Jesus Christ, is what I would wish to be the abiding object of my contemplation; not merely to speculate upon it as a doctrine, but so to feel it, and my own interest in it, as to have my heart filled with its effects, and transformed into its resemblance.[79]

Conclusion

On the basis of this analysis, it will be clear that evangelicalism is strongly Christocentric. This point may not be clear from some evangelical writings written since 1920, particularly those originating from a North American context, on account of evangelicalism's felt need to defend its views on other matters, most notably in relation to the authority of Scripture. Yet, as I pointed out earlier, the defensive posture into which evangelicalism was forced during this period resulted in a reactive emphasis on issues which were arguably not at the core of evangelicalism. In placing a discussion of the person and work of Jesus Christ at the opening of this work, it is my intention to affirm the pivotal place of Christ in the evangelical worldview.

For evangelicals, Christian theology is first and foremost concerned with the identity and significance of Jesus Christ, affirming and acknowledging the *particularity* of his cross and resurrection, and rejecting any temptation to lapse into generalities. Jesus Christ defines the line of demarcation between a true church, which is responsible to God as he has revealed himself, specifically and particularly, in Jesus Christ, and a false church which answers to and acknowledges the pressures of the age. Evangelicalism insists that the place of Christians is in the world; nevertheless, Christians must maintain their distinctive identity if they are to be salt and light to that world. 'The place for the ship is in the sea; but God help the ship if the sea gets into it' (D. L. Moody). One of the most distinctive aspects of evangelicalism is its dual affirmation of the importance of remaining *in* the world while simultaneously remaining *distinct from* the world. And the central resource which distinguishes the church from the world is Jesus Christ.

Evangelicals are thus adamant that Christian theology is grounded in the particularities of the life, death and resurrection of

Jesus Christ, and that it is ultimately responsible to him – responsible to Christ in that it is obliged both to give account *of* him and to give account *to* him. Whatever statements we may choose to make about the character of God or the nature and destinity of human beings is ultimately grounded in and governed by the self-revelation of God in Christ. The evangelical understanding of the intimacy of the relationship between Jesus Christ and Scripture is such that an appeal to Christ is simultanously an appeal to Scripture, just as an appeal to Scripture is an appeal to Christ. This observation brings us to the evangelical emphasis upon the authority of Scripture, to which we may now turn.

2

The authority of Scripture

At the Diet of Worms (18 April 1521), Martin Luther famously declared: 'My conscience is captive to the word of God.'[1] In much the same way, evangelicalism has seen itself as captive to that same word of God. The principle of the sufficiency of Scripture is of central importance to evangelicalism. The declaration of the Westminster Confession summarizes the evangelical consensus on this major issue:

> The whole counsel of God, concerning all things necessary for his own glory, man's salvation, faith and life, is either expressly set down in Scripture, or by good and necessary consequence may be deduced from Scripture; to which nothing at any time is to be added, whether by new revelations of the Spirit, or traditions of men.[2]

It is perhaps at this point that evangelicalism shows most clearly its theological and spiritual continuity with the Reformation, and its concern to ensure that the life and thought of the Christian community was grounded in, and continually re-evaluated in the light of, Scripture.[3] Yet this must not be understood to mean that evangelicalism is 'a religion of a book'. Rather, evangelicalism focuses on the person and work of Jesus Christ, affirming the centrality and sovereignty of Jesus Christ in all matters of faith and life. Yet there is an inextricable and intimate connection between the word of God incarnate and the word of God in Scripture, in that Jesus Christ is made known to us through the witness of Scripture, which in turn centres on his person and work. So important is this point that we may examine it in more detail.

Scripture and Jesus Christ

Scripture centres on and enfolds Christ, who can be known definitively only through its medium. Scripture, when rightly interpreted, leads to Christ; Christ can be known properly only through Scripture. As Luther put it, Christ is 'the mathematical point of Holy Scripture',[4] just as Scripture 'is the swaddling clothes and manger in which Christ is laid'.[5] John Calvin made a similar point: 'This is what we should seek . . . throughout the whole of Scripture: to know Jesus Christ truly, and the infinite riches which are included in him and are offered to us by God the Father.'[6] As the leading Dutch Reformed theologian Abraham Kuyper (1837–1920) declared, the sole object of saving faith is 'Christ in the garments of Sacred Scripture'.[7]

Despite its high view of Scripture, evangelicalism has resisted the temptation to identify the text of Scripture itself with revelation.[8] Scripture is regarded as a channel through which God's self-revelation in Jesus Christ is encountered. Although it is a bearer of that self-revelation in Christ, it is not to be identified directly with that self-revelation. Scripture is not Jesus Christ. Yet as Kuyper so aptly put it, we cannot encounter Christ in any form other than that which we find in Scripture. Faith accepts Scripture as a testimony to Christ, and submits to Christ as the one of whom Scripture speaks.[9] Christ is therefore known only as he is proclaimed in Scripture, and subsequently through the obedient and responsible proclamation of the Christian church. There is a strongly Trinitarian dimension to the evangelical understanding of revelation, which is particularly evident in its affirmation of the distinctive role of the Holy Spirit.[10] Yet the evangelical understanding of the authority of Scripture focuses particularly on the person and work of Jesus Christ.

As we have seen, at the centre of evangelicalism lies the belief that God has made himself known in and through Jesus Christ.

54

This is not a specifically evangelical belief: it is the common heritage of the Christian church. Karl Barth is but one of the great theologians of the Christian church to affirm this point:

> When Holy Scripture speaks of God, it does not permit us to let our attention or thoughts wander at random . . . When Holy Scripture speaks of God, it concentrates our attention and thoughts upon one single point and what is to be known at that point . . . If we ask further concerning the one point upon which, according to Scripture, our attention and thoughts should and must be concentrated, then from first to last the Bible directs us to the name of Jesus Christ.[11]

If evangelicalism is distinctive at this point, it is on account of the emphasis it has chosen to place upon this belief, and the inferences which it draws from it, rather than the substance of the belief itself. It is a vital part of the common faith of the entire Christian church, which evangelicalism has rightly discerned to be of foundational importance in maintaining the distinctive identity of the Christian faith. Full authority on heaven and earth has been given to the risen Christ (Mt. 28:17–20). Authority of any kind is thus primarily invested in the risen Christ; nevertheless, this leads on to a belief in scriptural authority, on account of the most intimate and natural of connections between Scripture, when rightly interpreted, and Christ. In the first place, evangelicals observe that Jesus Christ himself saw Scripture (in his case, the Old Testament) as God-given. This conviction cannot be regarded as something he uncritically accepted from his contemporaries; Christ had little hesitation in criticizing those beliefs and practices of Judaism which he regarded as unacceptable. Nor can it be treated as something that was incidental to his teaching; there are excellent reasons for asserting that it was integral to his own understanding of his mission, and a central component of his authoritative teaching.[12]

Most Christians acknowledge that the teaching of Jesus possesses an inherent normative status; evangelicals insist that allegiance to Christ as Lord includes acceptance of his attitude to Scripture. It is true to note that 'Christians are not those who believe in the Bible, but those who believe in Christ.'[13] While this has some merit as a statement of priorities and emphases, it nevertheless sets up a misleading and unhelpful false dichotomy. It is not a question of *either* the Bible *or* Christ, as if they can or should be separated. There is an organic and essential connection between the two. We honour Christ by receiving both the Scriptures which he received, and those which the church has handed down to us as a divinely inspired witness to Christ.

In the second place, and following on from what has just been said, Christology and scriptural authority are inextricably linked, in that it is Scripture which brings us to a knowledge of Jesus Christ. John Calvin correctly defined this as the whole point of Scripture. The New Testament is the only document we possess which the Christian church has recognized as authentically embodying and recollecting its understanding of Jesus, and the impact which he had upon people's lives and thought. The reports we have concerning Jesus from extracanonical sources are of questionable reliability, and strictly limited value.[14] The same God who gave Jesus Christ also gave Scripture as a testimony to Christ. It is precisely through the written word of Scripture that we, who live after Christ, have access to the living Word of God, given in history.

The authority of Scripture thus rests upon both theological and historical considerations: it is through Jesus Christ that the distinctively Christian knowledge of God comes about, and this knowledge of Jesus is given only in Scripture. Christ is what gives Scripture its unity: as the British evangelical theologian Stephen Neill has emphasized, the central thought and subject which binds all parts of the Bible together, and in the light of which they are to be interpreted, is the person and work of Jesus Christ.[15]

The authority of Scripture

It is a relatively easy matter to find articles and books originating from the western academy declaring that there is a 'crisis in biblical authority'. Yet the paradox is that these articles and books appear at a time when there is substantial numerical growth in biblically grounded Christian communities, such as those western evangelical churches which regard Scripture as authoritative and Latin American grassroots communities which find in Scripture a foundational resource for their social and political programmes.[16] There are excellent reasons for suggesting that there is a serious disjunction between an academy which finds the notion of 'authority' repellent in itself and is committed to creativity, innovation and total freedom of thought; and ordinary Christians, who recognize that Scripture lies at the heart of the normal Christian life, even if they lack the theological framework to identify with any precision how they would conceptualize this distinctive function.

It is a well-established fact of church history that the church has always regarded Scripture as authoritative, both in the sense of being the origin of its foundational ideas and values, and also the critic of those on offer from other sources. As a matter of historical observation, theories of how Scripture possesses such authority are posterior to the recognition of such authority in the first place. For example, theories of biblical inspiration are actually attempts to provide a *de jure* justification of an already existing *de facto* authority. Such theories aimed to explain why Scripture was accorded such authority and respect within the church; they did not establish that authority in the first place. During the Middle Ages, Scripture was regarded as fundamental to the theological enterprise,[17] and, in the hands of skilled preachers and writers such as Bernard of Clairvaux and Thomas à Kempis, became the basis of a highly developed spirituality. Nothing that can really be said to represent a precise theological formalization of this authority was offered. Scripture was at the heart of Christian devotion and thought.[18]

To speak of a modern 'crisis in biblical authority' is thus potentially seriously misleading. As a matter of fact, the number of Christians who regard Scripture as authoritative is increasing; those who, in sympathy with more liberal trends, have moved away from biblically centred forms of Christianity are in decline. If there is a crisis, it concerns the manner in which this authority is *articulated and formalized at the theological level*, with certain older approaches now being seen as conditioned responses to general cultural developments, particularly at the time of the Enlightenment. Benjamin B. Warfield's understanding of the authority of Scripture, for example, is shaped by pressures and influences from the Scottish philosophy of common sense, which became of major importance at Princeton during the nineteenth century (see pp. 168–171). With the waning of the appeal of this philosophy, along with an increasing recognition of the inadequacy of its rationalist foundations, Warfield's distinctive approach to the issue of the authority of Scripture has indeed found itself in 'crisis' – not on account of any waning in evangelical respect for Scripture, but on account of increasing misgivings concerning one particular manner of grounding and expressing that authority.

It must also be stressed that there are those who have difficulties with the 'authority of Scripture' precisely because they have a determinative prior difficulty with the concept of authority itself. As we shall see, a central theme of modernism is a craving for total autonomy of self-definition. As Don Cupitt, a Cambridge theologian whose writings show a strong degree of affinity with this trend, notes, 'modern people want to live their own lives, which means making their own rules, steering a course through life of one's own choice'.[19] The notion of authority, or of any limitations of options, is thus seen as repressive. Modernity (and also, in a somewhat different manner, postmodernity) want to be free to construct their own realities. The idea of one's intellectual options concerning, for example, the nature and purposes of God being limited or controlled by an external norm is potentially in conflict with a worldview which places an emphasis upon autonomy, self-generation and self-validation – a worldview which has gained the ascendancy in most western universities.[20]

The liberating dimension of scriptural authority

The evangelical insistence upon the authority of Scripture reflects a determination not to permit anything from outside the Christian heritage to become the norm for what is truly 'Christian'. Critics of the notion of biblical authority sometimes suggest that we would be liberated if we were to abandon the authority of Scripture. It seems to me that this is simply a covert demand to acknowledge the authority of something – or someone – else. The Christian insistence upon the authority of Scripture reflects a determination not to permit anything from outside the Christian heritage to become the norm for what is truly 'Christian'. Theological history has provided us with many all-too-uncomfortable examples of what happens when a theology cuts itself loose from the controlling influence of the Christian tradition, and seeks norms from outside that tradition.

There is no difficulty about providing examples of the manner in which Christian thought has become captive to a prevailing ideology. A classic example is provided by the 'imperial theology', whose formulation is especially associated with Eusebius of Caesarea, which shackled the exposition of Scripture (especially its messianic passages) to an ideology which saw the Roman empire as the climax of God's redemptive purposes. With the conversion of the Roman emperor Constantine in the fourth century, a new era in Christian history had dawned. Some Christian writers, most notably Eusebius, portrayed Constantine as an instrument chosen by God for the conversion of the empire. Eusebius' 'Rome-theology' appears to have had a deep impact upon Christian thinking in this crucial period, not least in rendering Rome virtually immune from reflective criticism on the part of Christian writers.

Indeed, so intimate was the connection which came to be presupposed between empire and gospel that the sack of Rome (410) endangered the future of western Christianity. The fall of Rome raised a series of potentially difficult questions for the imperial theology. Why had Rome been sacked? Augustine addresses such questions in *The City of God*, partly to discredit a 'theology of history' which had become influential in Christian circles, and to liberate Christianity from this straitjacket which had been imposed upon it. *The City of God* topples Rome from its position in Eusebius' theology of history. No longer is Rome portrayed as God's chosen instrument for the salvation of the world, and the preservation of the gospel. The restrictive (and highly distorting) controlling influence of an imperial ideology upon the Christian exposition of Scripture was thus removed.[21] As a result, the fall of Rome did not entail the fall of the gospel itself. By enslaving itself to a prevailing ideology, the dominant form of Christian thought had ensured its survival – indeed, its ascendancy – in the short term. But when that ideology collapsed, it brought its allies down with it. At least a substantial section of Christian theology had come to depend upon this ideology. Augustine's great contribution was to allow it to rediscover its true legitimation and foundation in Scripture, as read and received within the church.

A more recent example of such a non-biblical controlling influence upon Christianity may be found by looking to the history of the German church under Adolf Hitler, which was obliged to acknowledge the authority of 'German culture'. Some meekly submitted to this ideological straitjacket; others were bold enough to insist that Christianity must remain faithful to itself, by taking its heritage with the utmost seriousness, and refuse to be controlled by anything other than the living Christ, as we find him in Scripture. As we noted earlier (p. 35), the celebrated Barmen Declaration of May 1934 rejected the Nazi doctrine that God was now speaking a new message to humanity through German history, a view which had been openly stated by theologians such as Paul Althaus in 1933.[22] This declaration was rejected by the 'German Christians', a group within the mainline Protestant denominations who were sympathetic to Hitler. The Ansbacher Consultation, issued by the 'German Christians' in June 1934 in response to the Barmen Declaration, declared that theology and the church should take their cues from culture and the state, and argued that the church should adapt itself radically to conform to the new German situation, recognizing that God had given the German people 'a pious and faithful ruler' in the person of Adolf Hitler.[23]

Many forms of theological liberalism invite us to seek norms drawn from human experience and culture, and acknowledge the authority of Scripture where it happens to endorse or resonate with these. The difficulty for liberalism is that its cultural accommodationism simply makes Christian theology a hostage to the dominant cultural ideology, in a manner which shows alarming parallels with the situation which developed in the German church crisis of the mid-1930s.[24] The Barmen Declaration was not so much a protest against Hitler and Nazism (though that it unquestionably was); it also represented a passionate affirmation of the need for Christian faith and theology to avoid entangling themselves in the bonds of a prevailing culture. As Stanley Hauerwas and William H. Willimon comment:

> Nazi Germany was the supreme test for modern theology. There we experienced the 'modern world', which we had so labored to understand and to become credible to, as the world, not only of the Copernican world view, computers, and the dynamo, but also of the Nazis. Barth was horrified that his church lacked the theological resources to stand against Hitler. It was the theological liberals, those who had spent their theological careers translating the faith into terms that could be understood by modern people, and used in the creation of modern civilization, who were unable to say no. Some, like Emanuel Hirsch, even said yes to Hitler.[25]

Hirsch, like so many other German liberal theologians at the time, failed to see the dangers of allowing theology to slide into bondage to the prevailing culture – even when that culture became Nazi.

It should also be recalled here that it was the German academics who lent their full support to the war policy of Kaiser Wilhelm in 1914.[26] It is too easily forgotten – or deliberately suppressed by those sympathetic to a liberal culture-led theology – that it was leading liberal theologians, such as Adolf von Harnack, who supported the aggressive imperial war policy at this time. It was no wonder that Karl Barth felt that his world was shattered, on seeing his revered liberal teachers lining up to support the policy of war in Europe. As Barth later recalled:

> For me personally, one day in the beginning of August of that year stands out as a black day, on which ninety-three German

intellectuals, among whom I was horrified to discover almost all of my hitherto revered theological teachers, published a profession of support for the war policy of Kaiser Wilhelm II and his counsellors. Amazed by their attitude, I realized that I could no longer follow their ethics and dogmatics, or their understandings of the Bible and history, and that the theology of the nineteenth century no longer had any future for me.[27]

And what, one wonders, was the Soviet academy doing throughout the dark night of the Russian soul?[28] All the evidence points to Soviet academics being little more than puppets who lent covert support to the shocking oppression of Stalinism. It is often suggested that the academy is the safeguarder of liberty. The evidence simply does not endorse this. Nazi Germany and the Stalinist Soviet Union are clear instances of an academy which lent support, both passive and active, to oppression. Martin Heidegger's existentialism may have proved invaluable to many, seeking inner peace and a truly authentic existence. However, Heidegger's Freiburg *Rektoratsrede* openly advocated support of National Socialism. The irony of this point cannot be overlooked. The church must look elsewhere than to the academy if she is to maintain her liberty and avoid perennial exile on the edge of a secular culture.

Acknowledging the authority of Scripture is thus something profoundly liberating. It frees us from the slavish demand that we follow each and every cultural trend, and offers us a framework whereby we may *judge* them, as the Confessing Church chose to judge Hitler, rather than follow him – despite the enormous cultural pressure placed upon them to conform to the prevailing cultural climate. Reclaiming the Bible allows us to imitate Christ, rather than the latest whim of a fragmented and confused culture.[29]

There is a lesson here for today's western churches, who often seem to be throwing themselves uncritically at the feet of today's cultural norms. Only by rediscovering norms outside and apart from our culture may we avoid becoming enslaved to what Alasdair MacIntyre has styled the 'Self-Images of the Age'. We criticize German liberal theologians for supporting the imperial war policy in 1914, while turning a blind eye to the fact that they were simply endorsing a general cultural trend. We criticize the German Christians for obeying Hitler in the 1930s, conveniently choosing to overlook that they were simply submitting themselves to the prevailing cultural norms. We are doing the same today, by allowing ourselves and our churches to follow societal norms and values, irrespective of their origins and goals. To allow our ideas and values to become controlled by anything or anyone other than the self-revelation of God in Scripture is to adopt an ideology, rather than a theology; it is to become controlled by ideas and values whose origins lie outside the Christian tradition – and potentially to become enslaved to them.

Such ideas and values may be powerful correctives to lazy and irresponsible theologies, just as Marxism has provided a critique of aspects of Christian social thought and feminism of patriarchal tendencies within the church. But Marxist values and 'women's experience' – to name but two pertinent examples to which others could readily be added – cannot become *foundational* for Christianity, which is grounded in God, as known in Christ. The example of the German church under Hitler is instructive, in that it points to the need for a criterion by which the church can judge the secular world. A theology which is grounded in values, whether radical or conservative, drawn solely from the secular world becomes powerless to criticize that world. If the church permits its leading ideas to become grounded in a set of beliefs or values, it is hardly in a position to criticize those values, in that it would merely undermine its own position. A theology grounded in German culture thus found itself without any credible means to criticize that culture when it turned nasty. What was once believed to be liberating turned out to be decidedly menacing and sinister. It is significant that it was theologians such as Karl Barth and Dietrich Bonhoeffer, who refused to look for God anywhere other than in Jesus Christ, who provided the most serious and thoughtful opposition to the culture wars waged by the Third Reich.

To illustrate how Scripture can be enslaved by those who profess to liberate it, I shall explore the writings of John Shelby Spong, especially his *Rescuing the Bible from Fundamentalism*

(1991).[30] All of us know about the problem of fundamentalism. In 1910, the first of a series of twelve books entitled *The Fundamentals* appeared.[31] By a series of historical accidents, the term 'fundamentalist' took its name from this series of works. Fundamentalism arose as a religious reaction within American culture to the rise of a secular culture.[32] Despite the wide use of the term to refer to religious movements within Islam and Judaism, the term originally and properly designates a movement within Protestant Christianity in the United States, especially during the period 1920–40. The weaknesses of this movement are well known, and do not require documentation here. But if we are to reject fundamentalism, what are we to replace it with? There is a real need to rescue the Bible from fundamentalism; but those who claim to rescue it often shackle it to their own ends.

And this is where Bishop Spong, whose somewhat modest theological competence is vastly exceeded by his ability to obtain media attention, comes in. In his *Rescuing the Bible from Fundamentalism* – a work which would probably have been dismissed as utterly inconsequential were its writer not a bishop (a fact heavily emphasized on its front cover) – Spong offers to liberate the Bible from a fundamentalist stranglehold. But it soon becomes clear that the Bible is to be 'liberated' only to be enslaved to the latest cultural norms prevailing among the Greater New England liberal élite. This work is as aggressive in its modernity as it is selective and superficial in its argumentation and intolerant and dismissive of the views of others.

For example, at one point, Spong tentatively advances the idea that Paul might have been a homosexual. A few pages later, this seems to have become an established result of New Testament scholarship, leading Spong to the conclusion that one of the church's greatest teachers was a 'rigidly controlled gay male'.[33] The hard historical evidence for this dramatic assertion? Nil. One cannot help wondering if the New Testament is being less than subtly massaged here, to fit the sensitivities of a retrospective liberal conscience.

Much the same thing can be seen in his *Born of a Woman* (1992),[34] in which we learn that Mary, far from being a virgin, was actually a rape victim. The hard historical evidence for this? Nil. Yet Spong apparently expects his readers to take his views on board as the assured findings of New Testament scholarship, and reconstruct their vision of the Christian faith and life as a result. One cannot help but feel that reasoned argumentation has here been replaced by a special pleading and petulant assertion, more characteristic of the fundamentalist groups to which Bishop Spong takes such exception.

Bishop Spong recognizes that his views are unpopular, and believes that this is because they are thoroughly up to date and intellectually respectable. Sadly, they are just unpopular. Spong constructs a fantasy world, in which his own vision of a politically correct culture leads him to impose political and social stereotypes upon the New Testament with a fierce and uncritical dogmatism and a lack of scholarly insight and responsibility which many had assumed were only associated with the likes of Jerry Falwell. The pseudo-scholarly character of Spong's approach has been pointed out by N. T. Wright.[35] Commenting on Spong's attempts to cast himself as a persecuted hero, standing for the truth in the midst of a fundamentalist ocean, Wright remarks:

> [Spong] rushes on, constructing imaginary historical worlds and inviting us to base our faith and life upon them. If we refuse this invitation he will, no doubt, hurl his favourite abuse-word at us again. But if everyone who disagrees with Spong's book turns out to be a fundamentalist, then I suppose that all the fundamentalist churches in the world would not be able to contain the new members who would suddenly arrive on their doorsteps.[36]

My point is that it is not enough to argue for the need to wrest Scripture free from those who imprison it within the severe limitations of a fundamentalist approach. Too often, the professed liberators of Scripture proceed immediately to imprison it within their own worldview. This is no liberation; this is merely a change in dictators, similar to that experienced by those unfortunate enough to live in the eastern regions of Germany in 1945, who found themselves liberated from Hitler only to discover that they had been rescued by Stalin.

Rival approaches to authority

For some writers, the notion of 'the authority of Scripture' is unacceptable on account of a prior commitment to the authority of something else. In part, the evangelical commitment to the authority of Scripture represents a careful and critical assessment of rival approaches to authority, and an affirmation that Scripture must be regarded as carrying greater theological and spiritual weight than them. In what follows, we shall explore four rival approaches, and subject them to critical evaluation. Each of these concepts is complex, and worthy of extended discussion in their own right; sadly, such a book-length analysis lies beyond the scope of the present study, with the result that the four areas to be discussed cannot be engaged with to the extent that those with a particular concern for methodology would regard as satisfactory. The four areas in question are:

1. Culture
2. Experience
3. Reason
4. Tradition

The first two are characteristic of 'liberal' approaches to theology, which, distressed by the particularity of the Christian faith, attempt to found theology on allegedly 'universal' foundations. We begin by considering what authority can be accorded to culture.

1. Culture

Some liberal writers have argued that theology is to seek its public legitimation and justification by engaging with western culture. An excellent example of this approach can be found in the works of Gordon Kaufman, who argues as follows:

> The roots of theology are not restricted to the life of the church or to special dogmas or documents venerated in the

church, nor are they to be found in something as inchoate as 'raw experience'. They are to be found, rather, in the ordinary language(s) of Western culture at large.[37]

Yet this statement raises fundamental questions of such magnitude that this approach to theology founders before it leaves the harbour. Why *western* culture? What can conceivably justify this ethnocentricity? Something alarmingly like a crude cultural imperialism nestles within this affirmation, which writes off the remainder of global culture as theologically insignificant. Just as nineteenth-century British liberals believed that the best way to improve the world was to bring it all under British rule,[38] so theological liberalism seems to assume that only a western liberal outlook has any global viability. Asian and African Christianity will just have to learn from their western superiors. This approach cannot be taken seriously in today's world, in which the failings and limitations of western culture are evident, even to those who live within its bounds.

Furthermore, the naïve appeal to 'western culture' in the singular cannot be sustained in a modern pluralist culture. The liberal approach is unquestionably at its most credible within a context in which there is a single outlook characteristic of society as a whole – such as that which appears to be presumed by the disarmingly simplistic phrase 'western culture'. Sociologist Peter L. Berger notes that 'every human society has its own corpus of officially credited wisdom, the beliefs and values that most people take as self-evidently true'. There was a point when western society was both culturally homogeneous and professedly Christian. In such a context, liberalism had considerable appeal. But this neat and tidy approach has become virtually unworkable through the chronic intellectual and moral pluralism of modern western society. In the past – for example, in sixteenth-century England – there may have been only one set of beliefs and values in a culture; now, there are many competing beliefs and values on offer, encouraged by a polity which has come to regard the tolerance and fostering of plurality as a national goal in itself, consonant with the pursuit of individual liberty.[39]

An excellent example of a significant work to illustrate this western cultural imperialism while claiming to establish universal norms may be found in Lawrence Kohlberg's analysis of the development of moral stages from infancy to adulthood.[40] Kohlberg believed that he had uncovered a universal cultural pattern; his many critics made the point that his 'moral stages' related only to white males in western post-Enlightenment culture.[41] The same fundamental fallacy underlies the liberal attempt to globalize or totalize on the basis of western culture; allegedly 'universal' judgments or truths are adduced on the basis of highly ethnocentric and particular values and beliefs. Western liberalism has thus been forced to concede its own cultural particularity, and abandon its pretensions to universality. The theological implications of this development for any kind of appeal to 'culture' as a foundational theological resource will be painfully obvious.

A theological liberalism of this kind thus finds itself increasingly adrift, having lost what was once its confident and secure ideological moorings. What is the sense in making a universal appeal to 'culture' when there is no universal culture to appeal to? Berger comments thus on the enormous difficulties facing the liberal theological enterprise in a modern western pluralist culture:

> The various efforts by Christians to accommodate to the 'wisdom of the world' in this situation becomes a difficult, frantic and more than a little ridiculous affair. Each time that one has, after an enormous effort, managed to adjust the faith to the prevailing culture, that culture turns around and changes . . . Our pluralistic culture forces those who would 'update' Christianity into a state of permanent nervousness. The 'wisdom of the world', which is the standard by which they would modify the religious tradition, varies from one social location to another; what is worse, even in the same locale it keeps on changing, often rapidly.[42]

Berger's sociological analysis makes it clear that some views will be 'the accepted wisdom in one social milieu and utter foolishness in another'. Or, to put it another way, it is not a universal way of thinking or set of values; it is socially located, in a specific class or social group. Earlier, we noted how 'fundamentalism' is often linked with a sociological address that would look something like 'lower middle class from the deep South'. Liberalism has traditionally occupied a rather different sociological address: that of the cultural élite. Berger's perceptive comments here merit close study:

> *The wisdom of the world today always has a sociological address.* In consequence, every accommodation to it on the part of Christians will be 'relevant' in one very specific social setting (usually determined by class), and 'irrelevant' in another. Christians, then, who set out to accommodate the faith to the modern world should ask themselves which sector of that world they seek to address. Very probably, whatever *aggiornamento* they come up with will include some, exclude others. And if the *aggiornamento* is undertaken with the cultural élite in mind, then it is important to appreciate that the beliefs of this particular group are the most fickle of all.[43]

It is thus potentially meaningless to talk about 'making Christianity relevant to the modern world' or to 'western culture'. This implies a theoretical universality to 'the modern world' and 'western culture' which is absent in reality. Every attempt to accommodate Christianity to the beliefs of one social grouping proves to make it irrelevant to another. The paradox underlying the entire liberal enterprise is that for everyone for whom the gospel is made 'relevant', there is someone else for whom it is made irrelevant.

A more fundamental problem, however, relates to the traditional liberal insistence that Christian theology relate to 'modern ways of thinking' or 'values acceptable to our culture'. In a monolithic culture, this strategy is fairly straightforward, whatever its theological deficiences may be. However, in an society which is openly committed to pluralism, these demands degenerate into empty platitudes. *Which* ways of thinking? *Which* values? Philosopher Alasdair MacIntyre, reacting against naïve rhetoric about 'rationality' and 'justice', provocatively entitled his celebrated book, severely undermining liberalism's intellectual foundations, *Whose Justice? Which Rationality?* Furthermore, the rapid pace of cultural change in the West results in cultural accommodation having an inbuilt outdatedness; today's prevailing wisdom rapidly becomes tomorrow's discarded whim.

To the historian of Christian theology in the last fifty or so years, the same pattern may be seen to emerge consistently: the 'spirit of the age' turns out to be remarkably ephemeral, leading to a correspondingly brief window of credibility for theologies which ground themselves in contemporary social mores. It was this observation which prompted the wise comment of William Inge, a former Dean of St Paul's Cathedral, London: 'If you marry the spirit of your own generation, you will be a widow in the next.'[44] Thus the seemingly assured radical positions of the 1960s came to be overturned during the 1980s, just as the rise of postmodernism reflects the seriously eroded credibility of a universal rationality once regarded as central to 'liberal' theological method. The noted Jewish liberal writer Eugene B. Borowitz is a perceptive critic of this fatally vulnerable trend in liberal theology. Surveying the ruins of liberal religious thought, both Jewish and Christian, Borowitz points out the vulnerability – indeed, the *indefensibility* – of its central beliefs:

> Liberalism lost its cultural hegemony largely because of the demythologization of its allies, universal rationalism and science. At one time we thought them not only our finest sources of truth but our surest means to human ennoblement. Today the sophisticated know that they deal only in possible 'constructions of reality', and the masses sense that they commend ethical relativism more than necessary values and duties.[45]

But perhaps the most fundamental criticism of all here concerns the 'givenness of culture'. As we have seen, German culture became dominated by National Socialism during the 1930s. Those who argued that theology should take its cues or seek its foundations in culture soon found themselves arguing that Christian theology should respond to the totally new situation created by the rise of National Socialism by taking on board Nazi ideas and values (see pp. 60–61). Thus Emanuel Hirsch argued that, since 'National Socialism, based on the right of historical change, is becoming the self-evident and normative form of live for all Germans', Christianity in Germany was under obligation to incorporate these norms into its life and doctrine.[46] Much the same point has been made in subsequent situations, with demands that Christianity conform to the latest cultural trend, on the assumption that whatever direction culture takes is somehow the outcome of divine providence, and of binding importance. As the rise of Nazism and Stalinism have made abundantly clear, cultural trends need to be criticized. They cannot be allowed to be normative. And that demands that Christianity ground itself on something which transcends cultural particularities – namely, the self-revelation of God.

2. Experience

'Experience' is an imprecise term. The origins of the English word are relatively well understood: it derives from the Latin term *experientia*, which could be interpreted as 'that which arises out of travelling through life (*ex-perientia*)'. In this broad sense, it means 'an accumulated body of knowledge, arising through first-hand encounter with life'. When one speaks of 'an experienced teacher' or 'an experienced doctor', the implication is that the teacher or doctor has learned her craft through first-hand application. Yet the term has developed an acquired meaning, which particularly concerns us here. It has come to refer to the inner life of individuals, in which those individuals become aware of their own subjective feelings and emotions.[47] It relates to the inward and subjective world of experience, as opposed to the outward world of everyday life. A series of writings, including William James's celebrated study *The Varieties of Religious Experience* (1902), have stressed the importance of the subjective aspects of religion in general, and Christianity in particular. Christianity is not simply about ideas; it is also about the interpretation and transformation of the inner life of the individual. This concern with human experience is particularly associated with existentialism, which has sought to restore an awareness of the importance of the inner life of individuals to both theology and philosophy.[48]

Two main approaches may be discerned within Christian theology to the question of the relation of experience to theology:

1. The approach which has become especially associated with liberal writers, which argues that experience provides a foundational resource for Christian theology.

2. The traditional approach, associated with evangelicalism, which argues that Christian theology provides an interpretative framework by which human experience may be interpreted.

We shall begin our analysis of these options by considering the first position, which regards human experience as *explicans*, something which possesses explanatory or revelatory significance.

The idea that human religious experience can act as a foundational resource for Christian theology has obvious attractions. It suggests that Christian theology is concerned with human experience – something which is common to all humanity, rather than the exclusive preserve of a small group. To those who are embarrassed by the 'scandal of particularity' the approach has many merits. It suggests that all the world religions are basically human responses to the same religious experience – often referred to as 'a core experience of the transcendent'. Theology is thus the Christian attempt to reflect upon this common human experience, in the knowledge that the same experience underlies the other world religions. We shall return to this point later in dealing with the question of the relation of Christianity to the other religions.

This approach also has considerable attractions for Christian apologetics, as the writings of many recent American theologians, especially Paul Tillich and David Tracy, make clear. In that humans share a common experience, whether they chose to regard it as 'religious' or not, Christian theology can address this common experience. The problem of agreeing upon a common starting-point is thus avoided; the starting-point is already provided, in human experience. Apologetics can demonstrate that the Christian gospel makes sense of common human experience. This approach is probably seen at its best in Paul Tillich's sermons *The Courage to*

Be, which attracted considerable attention after their publication in 1952. It seemed to many that Tillich had succeeded in correlating the Christian proclamation with common human experience.[49]

But there are difficulties here. The most obvious is that there is actually very little empirical evidence for a 'common core experience' throughout human history and culture. The idea is easily postulated, and virtually impossible to verify. This approach has found its most mature and sophisticated expression in the 'Experiential-Expressive Theory of Doctrine', to use a term employed by the distinguished Yale theologian George Lindbeck. In his volume *The Nature of Doctrine* (1984), Lindbeck provides an important analysis of the nature of Christian doctrine.[50] One of the many merits of this book is the debate which it has initiated over this unjustly neglected aspect of Christian theology, which has assumed new importance recently on account of the impact of the ecumenical movement.

Lindbeck suggests that theories of doctrine may be divided into three general types. The cognitive-propositionalist theory lays stress upon the cognitive aspects of religion, emphasizing the manner in which doctrines function as truth claims or informative propositions. The experiential expressive theory interprets doctrines as non-cognitive symbols of inner human feelings or attitudes. A third possibilty, which Lindbeck himself favours, is the cultural-linguistic approach to religion. Lindbeck associates this model with a 'rule' or 'regulative' theory of doctrine. It is Lindbeck's criticism of the second such theory which is of particular interest to us at this point.

The 'experiential-expressive' theory, according to Lindbeck, sees religions, including Christianity, as public, culturally conditioned manifestations and affirmations of pre-linguistic forms of consciousness, attitudes and feelings. In other words, there is some common universal 'religious experience', which Christian theology (in common with other religions) attempts to express in words. Experience comes first; theology comes in later. As Lindbeck argues, the attraction of this approach to doctrine is grounded in a number of features of late twentieth-century western thought. Thus a contemporary preoccupation with inter-religious dialogue lends plausibility to the view that the various religions are diverse expressions of a common core experience, such as an 'isolable core of encounter' or an 'unmediated awareness of the transcendent'.

The principal objection to this theory, thus stated, is its obvious gross phenomenological inaccuracy. As Lindbeck points out, the possibility of religious experience is shaped by religious expectation, so that 'religious experience' is conceptually derivative, if not vacuous. 'It is difficult or impossible to specify its distinctive features, and yet unless this is done, the assertion of commonality becomes logically and empirically vacuous.'[51] The assertion that 'the various religions are diverse symbolizations of one and the same core experience of the Ultimate'[52] is ultimately an axiom, an unverifiable hypothesis – perhaps even a dogma, in the pejorative sense of the term – not least on account of the difficulty of locating and describing the 'core experience' concerned. As Lindbeck rightly points out, this would appear to suggest that there is 'at least the logical possibility that a Buddhist and a Christian might have basically the same faith, although expressed very differently'.[53] The theory can only be credible if it is possible to isolate a common core experience from religious language and behaviour, and demonstrate that the latter two are articulations of or responses to the former.

Attempts to evaluate this theory are totally frustrated by its inherent resistance to verification or falsification. While conclusive empirical evidence is not available to allow us to evaluate the suggestion that religious language and rites are a response to prior religious experience, the possibility that religious language and rites *create* that experience (for example, through arousing expectation of such experience, and indicating in what manner it may arise, and what form it might assume) is at least as probable on both the empirical and logical levels.[54]

Equally, the suggestion that the experience of individuals is to be placed above, or before, the communal religion itself seems to invert observable priorities. Thus Schleiermacher, who might be taken as the archetype of such an experientially grounded approach to theology, does not understand 'experience' to designate the undifferentiated and idiosyncratic emotions or existential apprehensions of each individual believer; rather, he understands 'experience' to be grounded in the memory, witness and celebration of the community of faith.[55] The theological significance of the Christian experience is articulated at the communal, not the individual, level.

The notion of a common core experience which remains constant throughout the diversity of human cultures and the flux of history, while being articulated and expressed in an astonishing variety of manners, remains profoundly unconvincing. Empirically, this notion is highly questionable: thus Lonergan wisely concedes that religious experience varies from one culture, class and individual to another,[56] while apparently being reluctant to draw the conclusion his concessions suggest, however tentatively – that it varies from one *religion* to another. While the doctrinal tradition of the church is publicly available for analysis, however, allowing its allegedly 'unchangeable' character to be assessed critically, religious experience remains a subjective, vacuous and nebulous concept, the diachronic continuity and constancy of which necessarily lie beyond verification or – as seems the more probable outcome – falsification.[57]

The main lines of Lindbeck's critique of experiential theories of doctrine which treat doctrine as dealing with ubiquitous prereflective private experience common to all religions are timely and persuasive. Three further criticisms of such theories may be added, as follows.

In the first place, we must note the emphatic insistence within at least one strand of the Christian tradition that experience and reality are, at least potentially, to be radically opposed. Doctrine does not necessarily express or articulate experience, but may contradict it. Perhaps the most celebrated instance of such an attitude may be found in Martin Luther's 'theology of the cross',[58] in which emphasis is laid simultaneously upon the importance of religious experience in the authentic Christian life, and its unreliability as a theological resource. The 'experience seeking expression' in the writings of a 'theologian of glory' and a 'theologian of the cross' (to use Luther's expressions) gives every appearance of being very different – yet both require to be subsumed under the same 'experiential-expressivist' model.

In the second place, there is an apparent assumption that the *present* experience of an individual, whatever that may be, constitutes the primary datum of religion. This emphasis appears to suggest that no fundamental distinction may be made between the experience of an individual who has deliberately and consciously determined to reject a religion, and one who has equally deliberately and consciously determined to embrace one. Consider, for example, an occurrence which is increasingly common within the global religious situation, but with important roots in the formative stages of the Christian tradition – conversion.[59] Take the case of an individual, brought up within a purely secular environment and disposed towards a materialist atheism, who subsequently discovers Christianity and becomes a 'born-again Christian'. Is the experience of this individual in these two very different situations the same? It is, surely, inconceivable that they should be identical, or even similar, particularly if one of the more experientially orientated Christian traditions is implicated in the conversion experience. Further, empirical psychological studies have indicated that 'committed' religious individuals have markedly different psychological qualities and social attitudes from those who assume a merely 'consensual' position.[60] In other words, those who have actively chosen to commit themselves to faith are quite distinct in their outlooks from those who simply acquiesce in social attitudes and trends, of which religion is one. Such differences are expressed at both the experiential and cognitive level – for example, the manner in which prayer is experienced and interpreted.[61] Yet the experiential-expressivist approach to religion appears to lack the conceptual framework to distinguish these situations, on account of what Lindbeck terms the 'homogenizing tendencies associated with liberal experiential-expressivism'.[62] 'Experience' is thus treated by liberalism as something which is homogeneous, common and unchanging, unaffected by alterations in religious affiliations – in short, something *universal*, upon which theology may contruct itself in the public arena.

The transition from unbelief to faith would thus be held to involve a degree of existential reorientation, obliging an experiential-expressivist theory of religion to account for this change. In that conversion is a highly significant element in human religious experience, past and present, the need to differentiate between 'believing' and 'unbelieving' experience would seem to be a sufficiently important aspect of religion to require theories of religion and doctrine to be able to account for it.

In the third place, a serious issue demands attention concerning the 'content' or 'referent' of an experience. How can we know that – how, in fact, can we even begin to enquire whether, and in what manner – the experience we are attempting to capture in a verbal moment or symbol really is an experience *of God*?[63] What grounds do we have for suggesting that human experience is in some way related to a reality, traditionally designated 'God'? On what grounds are we entitled to identify a moment or moments as charged with the fragrance of divinity, and not simply an experience which is human and mundane? The great dilemma of the young Karl Barth, preparing his Sunday sermon at Safenwil, becomes our dilemma. For Barth, the crucial question concerned the words he would preach: how could he rest assured that these words in some way embodied or conveyed the word *of God*, rather than his own words? In what sense could he claim that he was proclaiming the word *of God*, and not merely lending a spurious legitimacy and unmerited authority to the words of Karl Barth? How can the 'experience seeking expression' be identified as an experience of God, and not as an experience of a secular and godless world, or an eccentric existential solipsism? And what of non-theistic religions? Doubtless an experiential-expressive account of Theravada Buddhism would insist that this tradition gives access to religious experience – but can it be regarded as an experience *of God*, when that tradition itself explicitly repudiates such a suggestion? Experience may indeed seek expression – but it also demands a criterion by which it may be judged.

This point could be developed further, particularly in the light of the trend towards secularism in western society. The 'experiential-expressive' approach to religion and doctrine asserts the primacy of present experience as the medium of God's revelation. The implicit presupposition of this approach is that there is some experience to express – for example, Schleiermacher's notion of piety as a sense of absolute dependence, Otto's category of the numinous, and Tillich's experience of the unconditioned. But what if there is no experience to express? If God is experienced as absent from his world – which Bonhoeffer suggests is the inevitable result in a 'world come of age'[64] – in what sense can we affirm that he is *present*? Luther, taking the event of the crucifixion as a paradigm, argues that experience is *corrected* by doctrine; that experience is properly interpreted, even to the point of being contradicted, by and within a theological framework. Experience, in other words, is the *explicandum*, rather than the *explicans*; it is what requires to be interpreted, rather than the interpreting agent itself. God is experienced as absent; doctrine affirms that God is present in a hidden manner.[65] Theology engages with human experience; yet experience often needs to be criticized and radically reinterpreted. This is a major theme of Luther's 'theology of the cross'.[66] For Luther, the cross mounts a powerful attack on another human resource upon which too much spiritual weight is often placed, especially in modern western thought. The experience of the individual is singled out as having revelatory authority. 'What I experience is what is right.' 'I don't experience it that way.' Luther suggests that individual experience is often seriously unreliable as a guide to matters of faith. The way we experience things is not necessarily the way things really are.

It is this potential *tension* between theology and experience which raises such difficulties for liberal writers such as David Tracy and Schubert Ogden. As has often been pointed out, the model offered by such theologians systematically minimizes both 'the historical particularity of the [Christian] tradition as well as the force of its conflict with experience'.[67] For such reasons, the second approach outlined above to the understanding of the relation between experience and theology has regained a hearing.

According to this approach, experience is an *explicandum*, something which itself requires to be interpreted. Christian theology provides a framework by which the ambiguities of experience may be interpreted. Theology aims to interpret experience. It is like a net which we can cast over experience, in order to capture its meaning. Experience is seen as something which is to be interpreted, rather than something which is itself capable of interpreting. Christian theology thus aims to *address, interpret* and *transform* human experience. In what follows, I propose to explore these themes with particular reference to the writings of Martin Luther and C. S. Lewis. European theology, with its long tradition of wrestling with experience within a cognitive framework, has an important contribution to make to this global discussion, of especial relevance in an experience-centred age.[68] Three points may be made.

First, theology addresses experience. Christian theology cannot remain faithful to its subject matter if it regards itself as purely propositional or cognitive in nature. The Christian encounter with God is transformative. As Calvin pointed out, to know God is to be changed by God; true knowledge of God leads to worship, as the believer is caught up in a transforming and renewing encounter with the living God. To know God is to be changed by God.[69] As Søren Kierkegaard pointed out in his *Unscientific Postscript*, to know the truth is to be known by the truth. 'Truth' is something which affects our inner being, as we become involved in 'an appropriation process of the most passionate inwardness'.[70]

This is in no sense to deny or to de-emphasize the cognitive aspects of Christian theology. It is merely to observe that there is more to theology than cerebralized information. A theology which touches the mind, leaving the heart unaffected, is no true Christian theology – a point stressed by both Luther and Calvin. Although Luther is critical of the role of experience in spirituality, he does not dismiss it as an irrelevance. Indeed, Luther insists that there is one experience which is basic to being a theologian. He describes this briefly in one of his most quoted (and most difficult!) statements. 'It is living, dying, and even being condemned which makes a theologian – not reading, speculating and understanding.'[71] To be a *real* theologian is to wrestle with none other than the living God – not with ideas about God, but with God himself. And how can a sinner ever hope to deal adequately with this God?

If you want to be a real theologian, Luther insists, you must have experienced a sense of condemnation. You must have had a moment of insight, in which you realize just how sinful you really are, and how much you merit the condemnation of God. Christ's death on the cross spells out the full extent of God's wrath against sin, and shows us up as ones who are condemned. It is only from this point that we can fully appreciate the central theme of the New Testament – how God was able to deliver sinners from their fate. Without a full awareness of our sin, and the dreadful gulf this opens up between ourselves and God, we cannot appreciate the joy and wonder of the proclamation of forgiveness through Jesus Christ. In a letter to his colleague Philip Melanchthon, dated 13 January 1522, Luther suggested that he ask the so-called 'prophets' who were then confusing the faithful at Wittenberg the following question: 'Have they experienced spiritual distress and the divine birth, death and hell?' A list of spiritual sensations is no substitute for the terror that accompanies a real encounter with the living God. For these modern prophets, Luther wrote, 'the sign of the Son of man is missing'. Just about anyone can read the New Testament, and make some sort of sense of it. But, Luther insists, the *real* theologian is someone who has experienced a sense of condemnation on account of sin – who reads the New Testament, and realizes that the message of forgiveness is good news for him or her. The gospel is thus experienced as something liberating, something which transforms our situation, something which is relevant to us. It is very easy to read the New Testament as if it were nothing more than any other piece of literature. And Luther reminds us that it is only through being aware of our sin, and all its implications, that we can fully appreciate the wonder of the electrifying declaration that God has forgiven our sins through Jesus Christ.

Secondly, theology interprets experience. It is a consequence of the Christian doctrine of creation that we are made in the image of God. There is an inbuilt capacity – indeed, we might say, an inbuilt *need* – to relate to God. To fail to relate to God is to fail to be completely human. To be fulfilled is to be filled by God. Nothing that is transitory can ever fill this need. Nothing that is not itself God can ever hope to take the place of God. And yet, on account of the fallenness of human nature, there is now a natural tendency to try to make other things fulfil this need.

Sin moves us away from God, and tempts us to substitute other things in his place. Created things thus come to be substituted for God. And they do not satisfy. And like the child who experiences and expresses dissatisfaction when the square peg fails to fit the round hole, so we experience a sense of dissatisfaction. Somehow, we are left with a feeling of longing – longing for *something* undefinable, of which human nature knows nothing, save that it does not possess it.

This phenomenon has been recognized since the dawn of human civilization. In one of his dialogues,[72] Plato compares human beings to leaky jars. Somehow, we are always unfulfilled. We may pour things into the containers of our lives, but something prevents them from ever being entirely filled. We are always partly empty – and for that reason, experience a profound awareness of a lack of fullness and happiness. 'Those who have endured the void know that they have encountered a distinctive hunger, or emptiness; nothing earthly satisfies it' (Diogenes Allen).[73] This well-documented feeling of dissatisfaction is one of the most important points of contact for the gospel proclamation. In the first place, that proclamation interprets this vague and unshaped feeling as a longing for *God*. It gives cognitive substance and shape to what would otherwise be an amorphous and unidentified subjective intuition. And in the second, it offers to fulfil it. There is a sense of divine dissatisfaction – not dissatisfaction *with* God, but a dissatisfaction with all that is not God, which arises from God, and which ultimately leads to God. Sartre is right: the world cannot bring fulfilment. Here he echoes the Christian view, which goes on to affirm that here, in the midst of the world, something which is ultimately beyond the world makes itself available to us. We do not need to wait for eternity to experience God; that experience can begin, however imperfectly, now. Perhaps the greatest statement of this feeling, and its most exquisite theological interpretation, may be found in the famous words of Augustine of Hippo: 'You have made us for yourself, and our hearts are restless until they rest in you.'[74] There is a sense of homesickness for somewhere we have never visited, an intimation of a far-off land, which attracts us despite the fact we do not know it.

Throughout Augustine's reflections, especially in the *Confessions*, the same theme recurs. We are doomed to remain incomplete in our present existence. Our hopes and deepest longings will remain nothing but hopes and longings. The resolution of this bitter-sweet tension remains real, even for the Christian, who becomes increasingly aware of the wonder of God, and of the inadequacy of our present grasp of that wonder. There is a sense of postponement, of longing, of wistful yearning, of groaning under the strain of having to tolerate the present, when the future offers so much.[75] The grand themes of creation and redemption there find a creative reworking which deserves careful attention. Because we are created by God in his image, we desire him; because we are sinful, we cannot satisfy that desire ourselves – either by substituting something for God, or by trying to coerce him to come to us. And so a real sense of frustration, of dissatisfaction, develops. And that dissatisfaction – but not its theological interpretation – is part of common human experience. Perhaps the finest statement of this exquisite agony is found in Augustine's cry that he 'is groaning with inexpressible groanings on my wanderer's path, and remembering Jerusalem with my heart lifted up towards it – Jerusalem my home land, Jerusalem my mother'.[76] We are exiled from our homeland – but its memories return hauntingly.

Augustine finds one of his finest recent apologetic interpreters in the Oxford literary critic and theologian C. S. Lewis. Perhaps one of the most original aspects of C. S. Lewis's writing is his persistent and powerful appeal to the religious imagination, in developing Augustine's maxim *desiderium sinus cordis* (longing makes the heart deep). Like Augustine, Lewis was aware of certain deep human emotions which pointed to a dimension of our existence beyond time and space. There is, Lewis suggested, a profound and intense feeling of longing within human beings, which no earthly object or experience can satisfy. Lewis terms this sense 'joy', and argues that it points to God as its source and goal (hence the title of his celebrated autobiography, *Surprised by Joy*). Joy, according to Lewis, is 'an unsatisfied desire which is itself more desirable than any other satisfaction . . . anyone who has experienced it will want it again'.[77]

To understand Lewis at this point, the idea of 'joy' needs to be explained in some detail. From the windows of his home in Belfast, Northern Ireland, the young Lewis could see the distant Castlereagh Hills. Those distant hills seemed to him to symbolize something which lay beyond his reach. A sense of intense longing arose as he contemplated them. He could not say exactly *what* it was that he longed for; merely that there was a sense of emptiness within him, which the mysterious hills seemed to heighten, without satisfying. Lewis describes this experience (perhaps better known to students of German Romanticism as *Sehnsucht*) in some detail in his autobiography. He relates how, as a young child, he was standing by a flowering currant bush, when – for some unexplained reason – a memory was triggered off.

> There suddenly rose in me without warning, as if from a depth not of years but of centuries, the memory of that earlier morning at the Old House when my brother had brought his toy garden into the nursery. It is difficult to find words strong enough for the sensation which came over me; Milton's 'enormous bliss' of Eden . . . comes somewhere near it. It was a sensation, of course, of desire; but desire for what? Not, certainly, for a biscuit tin filled with moss, nor even (though that came into it) for my own past . . . and before I knew what I desired, the desire itself was gone, the whole glimpse withdrawn, the world turned commonplace again, or only stirred by a longing for the longing that had just ceased. It had only taken a moment of time; and in a certain sense everything else that had ever happened to me was insignificant in comparison.[78]

Lewis here describes a brief moment of insight, a devastating moment of feeling caught up in something which goes far beyond the realms of everyday experience. But what did it mean? What, if anything, did it point to?

Lewis addressed this question in a remarkable sermon entitled

'The Weight of Glory', preached before the University of Oxford on 8 June 1941. Lewis spoke of 'a desire which no natural happiness will satisfy', 'a desire, still wandering and uncertain of its object and still largely unable to see that object in the direction where it really lies'. There is something self-defeating about human desire, in that what is desired, when achieved, seems to leave the desire unsatisfied. Lewis illustrates this from the age-old quest for beauty, using recognizably Augustinian imagery:

> The books or the music in which we thought the beauty was located will betray us if we trust to them; it was not *in* them, it only came *through* them, and what came through them was longing. These things – the beauty, the memory of our own past – are good images of what we really desire; but if they are mistaken for the thing itself they turn into dumb idols, breaking the hearts of their worshippers. For they are not the thing itself; they are only the scent of a flower we have not found, the echo of a tune we have not heard, news from a country we have not visited.[79]

Human desire, the deep and bitter-sweet longing for something that will satisfy us, points beyond finite objects and finite persons (who seem able to fulfil this desire, yet eventually prove incapable of doing so) towards their real goal and fulfilment in God himself.

Pleasure, beauty, personal relationships: all seem to promise so much, and yet when we grasp them, we find that what we were seeking was not located in them, but lies beyond them. There is a 'divine dissatisfaction' within human experience, which prompts us to ask whether there is anything which may satisfy the human quest to fulfil the desires of the human heart. Lewis argues that there is. Hunger, he suggests, is an excellent example of a human sensation which corresponds to a real physical need. This need points to the existence of food by which it may be met. Simone Weil echoes this theme, and points to its apologetic importance when she writes: 'The danger is not lest the soul should doubt whether there is any bread, but lest, by a lie, it should persuade itself that it is not hungry. It can only persuade itself of this by lying, for the reality of its hunger is not a belief, it is a certainty.'[80]

Lewis's less perceptive critics – sadly, more numerous than one might have hoped – argued that his argument rested upon an elementary fallacy. Being hungry did not prove that there was bread at hand. The feeling of hunger did not necessarily correspond to a supply of food. Yet this objection, Lewis replies, misses the point.

> A man's physical hunger does not prove that man will get any bread; he may died of starvation in a raft in the Atlantic. But surely a man's hunger does prove that he comes of a race which repairs its body by eating and inhabits a world where eatable substances exist. In the same way, though I do not believe (I wish I did) that my desire for Paradise proves that I shall enjoy it, I think it a pretty good indication that such a thing exists and that some men will. A man may love a woman and not win her; but it would be very odd if the phenomenon called 'falling in love' occurred in a sexless world.[81]

In all this, Lewis echoes a great theme of traditional Christian thinking about the origin and goal of human nature. We are made by God, and we experience a deep sense of longing for him, which only he can satisfy. Although Lewis's reflections on the desire he calls 'joy' reflect his personal experience, it is evident that he (and countless others) consider that this sense of longing is a widespread feature of human nature and experience. An important point of contact for the proclamation of the gospel is thus established.

Lewis's insights also bring new depth to familiar biblical passages concerning human longing for God. 'As the deer pants for streams of water, so my soul pants for you, O God. My soul thirsts for God, the living God' (Ps. 42:1–2). Note the great sense of *longing* for God expressed in this verse – a sense of longing which assumes added meaning if Lewis's reflections on 'joy' are allowed. Note also the biblical parallel between a sense of need – in this case, animal thirst – and the human need and desire for God.

Thirdly, theology offers to transform experience. Christian theology does not simply address the human situation; it offers to transform it. We are not simply told that we are sinners, in need of divine forgiveness and renewal; that forgiveness and renewal are offered to us in the gospel proclamation. If the negative aspect of the Christian proclamation of the crucified Christ is that we are far from God, the positive side is that God offers to bring us home to himself through the death and resurrection of his Son. Theology, then, does not simply interpret our experience in terms of alienation from God. It addresses that experience, interprets it as a sign of our global alienation from God through sin, and offers to transform it through the grace of God.

One of the many merits of the writings of C. S. Lewis is that they take seriously the way in which words can *generate* and *transform* experience. For Lewis, words have the ability to evoke an experience we have not yet had, in addition to describing an experience we are familiar with. That which is known functions as a signpost to that which is yet to be known, and which lies within our grasp. In his essay *The Language of Religion*, Lewis made this crucial point as follows.

> This is the most remarkable of the powers of Poetic language: to convey to us the quality of experiences which we have not had, or perhaps can never have, to use factors within our experience so that they become pointers to something outside our experience – as two or more roads on a map show us where a town that is off the map must lie. Many of us have never had an experience like that which Wordsworth records near the end of *Prelude* XIII; but when he speaks of 'the visionary dreariness', I think we get an inkling of it.[82]

At its best, Christian theology shares this characteristic of poetic language (not *poetry* itself, incidentally, Lewis stresses, but the *language used in poetry*), as identified by Lewis – it tries to convey to us the quality of the Christian experience of God. It attempts to point beyond itself, to rise above itself, straining at its lead as it rushes ahead, to point us to a town beyond its map – a town which it knows is there, but to which it cannot lead us.

Theology is able to use words in such a way as to offer some pointers for the benefit of those who have yet to discover what it feels like to experience God. It uses a cluster of key words to try and explain what it is like to know God, by analogy with words associated with human experience. It is like forgiveness – in other words, if you can imagine what it feels like to be forgiven for a really serious offence, you can begin to understand the Christian experience of forgiveness. It is like reconciliation – if you can imagine the joy of being reconciled to someone who matters very much to you, you can get a glimpse of what the Christian experience of coming home to God is like. It is like coming home after being away and alone for a long time, and perhaps fully expecting never to be able to return. Apologetics uses analogies like these to try and signpost – like roads leading off Lewis's map to an unseen town – the Christian experience of God, for the benefit of those who have yet to have this transforming experience.

In this section, I have argued that there is no rightful place in Christian theology for any approach that is purely cognitive or purely experiential. Experience and understanding are like two sides of the same coin, which reinforce and enhance one another. The liberal appeal to pure uninterpreted global experience is widely regarded as discredited, partly on account of the considerations noted by George Lindbeck and others, and partly on account of a new awareness of the implications of the philosophy of Ludwig Wittgenstein. As Stanley Hauerwas remarked, 'Wittgenstein ended forever any attempt on my part to try to anchor theology in some general account of human experience.'[83]

Yet this widespead disenchantment with experience as a theological resource must not allow us to reject a significant experiential component in theological reflection. Furthermore, as I have argued elsewhere, experience is a vital 'point of contact' for Christian apologetics in a postmodern world.[84] Rather, we must insist that experience is to be addressed, interpreted and transformed in the light of the gospel proclamation of redemption through Christ, as this is made known to us through Scripture. By thus anchoring theology in the bedrock of divine revelation, while linking it up to the world of human experience, we may ensure that Christian theology remains both authentic and relevant in the years that lie ahead. Theology can address experience, without becoming reduced to the level of a mere reiteration of what we experience and observe.

3. Reason

With the rise of the Enlightenment came the demand that knowledge must be universally accessible. The idea of a 'privileged' knowledge of God, mediated only by revelation, was rejected on moral grounds. As revelation was not universal, it was argued, God was causing moral problems by limiting revelation to the person of Jesus Christ, the text of Scripture, or the domain of the church. The Enlightenment argued that any such suggestion was to be rejected as constituting a 'scandal of particularity'.[85] Such knowledge had to be universally accessible, in all cultures, historical contexts, and geographical regions. For the Enlightenment, reason provided exactly such a universally valid resource. Everyone had a rational faculty; therefore everyone could use it, and thereby gain access to knowledge of God.

The eighteenth-century rationalist writer G. E. Lessing thus dismissed any idea that Jesus Christ could be of determinative status for Christian theology on account of his conviction that human reason alone could assume such a normative role. His famous declaration that 'accidental truths of history can never become the proof of necessary truths of reason'[86] rests on the characteristic Enlightenment assumption that the only significant form of knowledge consists of the 'necessary truths of reason'. A similar outlook can be shown to undergird the writings of Spinoza, who argued that it was possible to establish fundamental rational truths as axioms, and then to deduce an entire ethical or theological system on their basis, in much the same way as Euclid deduced an entire geometric system from fundamental axioms. As Stephen Toulmin pointed out, the attraction of mathematical logic to writers such as Descartes and Spinoza lay partly in the fact that it was seen to be 'possibly the only intellectual activity whose problems and solutions are above time'.[87]

Yet this approach is now widely regarded as fatally flawed. The 'necessary truths of reason' now turn out to mean little more than 'tautologies', or 'things that are true by definition'. Indeed, precisely this point lay at the heart of Ludwig Wittgenstein's critique of the philosophy of Bertrand Russell. As was pointed out in 1895 by Lewis Carroll, every attempt at rational justification by deduction turns out to be circular, in that the application of the process of deduction presupposes that this process of deduction is itself valid.[88]

Furthermore, discovery of non-Euclidian geometries during the nineteenth century destroyed the parallel between geometry and theology. It turned out that there were other ways of doing geometry, each just as internally consistent as Euclid's. Euclid laid down one set of axioms; others chose to lay down a different set, each giving rise to a different geometric system. But which set of axioms is right? Which system is valid? The question cannot be answered. They were all different, each with their own especial merits and problems.[89] Where once there was only geometry, there were now geometries.

The same criticisms were directed against ethics. Spinoza believed that the systematic application of pure reason would lead to an acontextual universally valid ethical system, independent of space and time. Enlightenment writers believed that this rational morality was accessible to human reason, relativizing all other ethical norms, including the moral example and teaching of Jesus Christ. Even as late as the 1950s, R. M. Hare could speak of 'the language of morals' as if there were only one such language.[90] But not any more. It is now widely accepted that there is a variety of ethical systems, each with its own vision of the nature and destiny of humanity. The Enlightenment dream of a universal morality is over.

In a similar manner, the Enlightenment assumption that there was only one 'rationality', independent of time, space and culture, is no longer regarded as having any credibility. Where once it was argued that there was one single rational principle, it is now conceded that there are – and always have been – many different 'rationalities'. As Stephen Toulmin pointed out, 'the exercise of rational judgement is itself an activity carried out in a particular context and essentially dependent on it; the arguments we encounter are set out at a given time and in a given situation, and when we come to assess them they have to be judged against this background'.[91] Many Enlightenment thinkers appear to have been shielded from this disconcerting fact by the limitations of their historical scholarship, which remained firmly wedded to the classical western tradition. But this illusion has now been shattered. At the end of his brilliant analysis of rational approaches to knowledge and ethics, Alasdair MacIntyre concludes:

> Both the thinkers of the Enlightenment and their successors proved unable to agree as to precisely what those principles were which would be found undeniable by all rational persons. One kind of answer was given by the authors of the *Encyclopédie*, a second by Rousseau, a third by Bentham, a fourth by Kant, a fifth by the Scottish philosophers of common sense and their French and American disciples. Nor has subsequent history diminished the extent of such disagreement. Consequently, the legacy of the Enlightenment has been the provision of an ideal of rational justification which it has proved impossible to attain.[92]

Reason promises much, yet fails to deliver its benefits. It is for such reasons that Hans-Georg Gadamer wrote scathingly of the 'Robinson Crusoe dream of the historical Enlightenment, as artificial as Crusoe himself'.[93] The notion of 'universal rationality' is a fiction, a dream, and a delusion. Philosopher of science Paul Feyerabend takes the consequences of the collapse of belief in a single, universal rationality to its obvious conclusion in his famous comparison between the primitive tribe and the rationalists: 'There is hardly any difference between the members of a primitive tribe who defend their laws because they are the laws of the gods . . . and a rationalist who appeals to objective standards, except that the former know what they are doing while the latter does not.'[94] The comparison has alarmed many; it has, however, yet to be refuted by a philosopher of science.

At this point, we need to stress the difference between 'reason' and 'rationalism', which may appear identical to some. *Reason* is the basic human faculty of thinking, based on argument and evidence. It is theologically neutral, and poses no threat to faith – unless it is regarded as the only source of knowledge about God. It then becomes *rationalism*, which is an exclusive reliance upon human reason alone, and a refusal to allow any weight to be given to divine revelation. Classical Christian theology, including all responsible evangelical theology, makes full use of the human faculty of reasoning – for example, in thinking through the implications of certain aspects of God's self-revelation. For example, consider the role of reason in exploring the relation between a functional and ontological Christology: if Jesus is our Saviour, yet only God can save, reason suggests that Jesus must (in some sense of the word) be God. Yet here reason is reflecting upon revelation, and seeking to explore further its implications. Rationalism declares that all thinking about God must be based upon human reason, thus immediately locking theology into the fallen human situation, with no possibility of being extricated from our confusion and distortion by God himself.

How did this remarkable – and, it must be said, totally misplaced – confidence in reason in matters of religion develop? Three stages can be identified, each leading naturally into that which follows.

1. Initially, it was argued that, as the gospel was rational, it was entirely proper to demonstrate that Christianity made sense, and rested upon thoroughly reasonable foundations. For example, Aquinas argued that Christian belief in God did not involve some kind of intellectual suicide, by providing five lines of reasoning which showed that this belief was entirely reasonable. But Aquinas, and the Christian tradition which he represented, did not for one moment believe that Christianity was limited to what could be ascertained by reason. Faith goes beyond reason, having access to truths and insights of revelation, which reason could not hope to fathom or discover unaided.

The noted historian of medieval Christian thought, Etienne Gilson, made a delightful comparison between the great theological systems of the Middle Ages and the cathedrals which sprang up throughout Christian Europe at this time: the systems were, he remarked, 'cathedrals of the mind'. Christianity is like a cathedral which rests upon the bedrock of human reason, but whose superstructure rises beyond the realms accessible to pure reason. It rests upon rational foundations; but the building erected on that foundation went far beyond what reason could uncover. Thus Aquinas argued that Christianity was based upon a knowledge which, although rational, transcended human abilities, and was thus mediated solely through revelation.[95] John Calvin, a later representative and interpreter of this approach, suggested that reason was perfectly capable of arriving at a knowledge of God the creator. But real knowledge of God – *saving* knowledge of God – could be had only through revelation. Knowledge of God the redeemer was a matter of revelation, not reason. This knowledge did not contradict knowledge of God the creator; it brought it to perfection, by showing that the God who once created the world subsequently acted to redeem it.

2. By the middle of the seventeenth century, especially in England and Germany, a new attitude began to develop. Christianity, it was argued, was reasonable. But where Thomas Aquinas understood this to mean that faith rested securely upon rational foundations, the new school of thought had different ideas. If faith is rational, they argued, it must be capable of being deduced in its entirety by reason. Every aspect of faith, every item of Christian belief, must be shown to derive from human reason.

An excellent example of this approach may be found in the writings of Lord Herbert of Cherbury, especially *De veritatis religionis*, which argued for a rational Christianity based upon the innate sense of God and human moral obligation. This had two major consequences. First, Christianity was in effect *reduced* to those ideas which could be proven by reason. If Christianity was rational, then any parts of its system which could not be proved by reason could not be counted as 'rational'. They would have to be discarded. And second, reason was understood to take priority over Christianity. Reason comes first, Christianity comes second. Reason is capable of establishing what is right without needing any assistance from revelation; Christianity has to follow, being accepted where it endorses what reason has to say, and being disregarded where it goes its own way. So why bother with the idea of revelation, when reason could tell us all we could possibly wish to know about God, the world, and ourselves? This absolutely settled conviction in the total competence of human reason underlies the rationalist depreciation of the Christian doctrine of revelation in Jesus Christ and through Scripture.

This approach to Christianity (or, more accurately, this form of Deism tinged with faintly Christian hues) treats God as an idea, a construction of the human mind. God is something which is posited, an idea which we generate within our minds, and then choose to call 'God'. We have created this idea. It is the work of our own minds. But traditional Christianity argued that God could not simply be posited in this crudely rationalist manner. God has to be experienced, he has to be encountered. He is one who engages us and, by engaging us, forces us to re-evaluate our ideas concerning him. Yet the God of pure reason is trapped within the limits of human minds. And small minds make for a small God.

3. Finally, this rationalist position was pushed to its logical outcome. As a matter of fact, it was argued, Christianity includes some beliefs which are inconsistent with reason. And as reason must be regarded as having final authority in matters of faith, where Scripture is in disagreement with reason, it is to be regarded as mistaken or misleading. God, having been posited by human reason, is thus now deposited by its own creator.[96]

As a result of the sociological deconstruction of the notion of 'universal reason', the appeal to 'the authority of reason' is made with much less conviction today.[97] A fundamental belief in the rationality of the Christian faith remains intact and justified; the Enlightenment attempt to establish unaided human reason as the sole normative foundation for all insight is now seen as seriously flawed. In part, this recognition stems from the realization of the limitations placed on reason; in part, however, it also arises from the postmodern awareness of the potentially authoritarian consequences of an appeal to the 'totalization of reason' (see pp. 179–189). 'Being reasonable' is not reducible to a single method, and can easily lead to the 'tyranny of rationality' through the assertion that only *this* way of thinking, or only *this* type of argument, has any validity. And, as postmodern writers have stressed (see pp. 189–196), 'being reasonable' all too often amounts to a demand to 'accept *my* way of thinking'.

The recognition that frameworks of rationality are not universal, but are socially and historically located, is of considerable importance to Christian theology, particularly in assessing the significance of Enlightenment rationalism. For example, consider the Enlightenment criticism of the traditional Christian notion of the revelation of God in Jesus Christ. For Lessing, this notion was unacceptable, in that it denied access to such 'revelation' to those whose historical location was, for example, chronologically prior to the birth of Jesus of Nazareth. The force of this objection, one assumes, is primarily moral, in that the *accessibility* of truth has no direct bearing upon its accuracy. For Lessing, this point served to highlight the moral superiority of rational religion, which was able to make an appeal to the universal truths of reason.

With the advent of the insights of the sociology of knowledge, the advantages of Lessing's position are seriously eroded, probably to the point of rendering them specious. 'Universal truths of reason' may indeed be found within the somewhat restricted confines of logic and mathematics, even if they amount to nothing more than tautologies – restatements masquerading as explanations or new levels of insight. Patterns of rationality in general, however, are socially and historically located and conditioned. 'Reason' must be taken to refer to those frameworks of rationality and preconceived notions of self-evident truths appropriate to specific social groupings at specific moments in history, rather than some universal and perennial feature of human ratiocination. Precisely the same criticism directed by Reimarus against Christianity may be laid against Lessing's appeal to the fictitious notion of universal reason: the social location of an individual determines the intellectual options open to him or her. 'Reason' and 'revelation' are both subject to the limitations of historicity.

4. Tradition

For some writers, 'tradition' has considerable authority. Tradition would here be understood to designate a traditional doctrine or belief, which has binding force on account of its antiquity. Yet this can easily degenerate into an uncritical sentimentality. 'We've always believed this' can simply mean 'We've always been wrong.' As the third-century writer Cyprian of Carthage pointed out, 'an ancient tradition can just be an old mistake'. Tradition is to be honoured where it can be shown to be justified, and rejected where it cannot. This critical appraisal of tradition was an integral element of the Reformation,[98] and was based on the foundational belief that tradition was ultimately an interpretation of Scripture which had to be justified with reference to that same authoritative source.

Yet the idea of 'tradition' is of importance to modern evangelicalism. Evangelicals have always been prone to read Scripture as if they were the first to do so. We need to be reminded that others have been there before us, and have read it before us. This process of receiving the scriptural revelation is 'tradition' – not a source of revelation in addition to Scripture, but a particular way of understanding Scripture which the Christian church has recognized as responsible and reliable. Scripture and tradition are thus not to be seen as two alternative sources of revelation; rather they are *coinherent*. Scripture cannot be read as if it had never been read before. The hymnodies and liturgies of the churches constantly remind us that Scripture has been read, valued and interpreted in the past. James I. Packer, one of the most influential evangelical writers of recent years, stresses this point:

> The Spirit has been active in the Church from the first, doing the work he was sent to do – guiding God's people into an understanding of revealed truth. The history of the Church's labour to understand the Bible forms a commentary on the Bible which we cannot despise or ignore without dishonouring the Holy Spirit. To treat the principle of biblical authority as a prohibition against reading and learning from the book of church history is not an evangelical, but an anabaptist mistake.[99]

'Tradition' is thus rightly understood (for example, by the Reformers such as Luther) as a history of discipleship – of reading, interpreting and wrestling with Scripture. Tradition is a willingness to read Scripture, taking into account the ways in which it has been read in the past. It is an awareness of the communal dimension of Christian faith, over an extended period of time, which calls the shallow individualism of many evangelicals into question. There is more to the interpretation of Scripture than any one individual can discern. It is a willingness to give full weight to the views of those who have gone before us in the faith, providing forceful reminders of the *corporate* nature of the Christian faith, including the interpretation of Scripture.

At first sight, this emphasis on the importance of the community of faith might seem to be in tension with the belief that it is Scripture alone which is authoritative. But this principle was never intended by writers such as Luther or Calvin to mean that Scripture is read *individualistically*. It was not meant to elevate the private judgment of an individual above the communal judgment of the church (although it was interpreted in this way by certain radical reformers, outside the mainstream of the Reformation). Rather, it affirms that every traditional way of reading Scripture must, in principle, be open to challenge. As the study of church history makes clear, the church may sometimes get Scripture wrong: the sixteenth-century reformers believed that Scripture had been misunderstood at a series of junctures by the medieval church, and undertook to reform its practices and doctrines at those points. This, however, is a case of a tradition being criticized and renewed from within, in the light of the biblical foundations upon which it ultimately rests, and is recognized to rest. The Reformers did not regard themselves as founding a new tradition; their concern was to reform a tradition which already existed, but which appeared to have become detached from its scriptural foundations.

The principle of the authority of Scripture over even its most prestigious interpreters is vigorously upheld by the Lutheran Formula of Concord (1577):

We believe, teach and confess that there is only one rule and norm according to which all teachings and teachers are to be appraised and judged, which is none other than the prophetic and apostolic writings of the Old and New Testaments . . .

Other writings, whether of the fathers or more recent theologians, no matter what their names may be, cannot be regarded as possessing equal status to Holy Scripture, but must all be considered to be subordinate to it, and to witness to the way in which the teaching of the prophets and apostles was preserved in post-apostolic times and in different parts of the world . . . Holy Scripture remains the only judge, rule and norm according to which all doctrines are to be understood and judged, as to which are good or evil, and which are true or truly false. Certain other creeds (*symbola*) and writings . . . do not themselves possess the authority of judges, as in the case of Holy Scripture, but are witnesses of our religion as to how [the Holy Scriptures] were explained and presented.[100]

For in part, the authority of Scripture rests in the universal acceptance of that authority within the Christian church. To recognize Scripture as authoritative is not the judgment of a group of individuals; it is the witness of the church down the ages. Among the many reasons which may be given for trusting the Bible (including the vitally important fact that it is inherently worthy of trust) must be included the simple fact that Scripture is trusted by the church.

In ascribing authority to Scripture, we are thus not merely recognizing and honouring God's decision to reveal himself to us, or only the specific form which this took in Jesus Christ; we are also honouring a living tradition, which has remained faithful to the modes of faith and life made known and made possible through Christ, and mediated through Scripture. There is thus a natural connection between the word of God and the people of God, and – whether this is recognized or not – a strongly ecclesiological element to our understanding of the identity of Jesus Christ.[101]

Biblical authority and biblical criticism

In our analysis thus far, considerable emphasis has been placed on the difficulties attending the utilization of theological authorities other than Scripture. Nevertheless, the evangelical appeal to Scripture as the leading theological source is not without its difficulties. For non-evangelicals, the rise of biblical criticism has raised a series of difficulties which render the notion of the 'authority of Scripture' problematical. These difficulties cannot be dismissed as artificial, arrogant or irrelevant. What, then, does the evangelical make of modern biblical criticism? How does an evangelical reconcile the view of Scripture as the word of God with the views of the critics?

The biblical critical movement has focused attention on the Bible as a human book written by human authors. It has asked, and attempted to answer, many questions concerning the authorship and origins of biblical texts. These questions are recognized as perfectly valid by evangelicals; the answers given by some critics have, however, sometimes been extremely embarrassing, not only to evangelicals, but to others of an orthodox persuasion. The reason for this embarrassment is not difficult to discern: some of the critics' findings have often seemed to be irreconcilable with the view that the whole Bible is the inspired and trustworthy Word of God. Some critics have argued that the Bible is historically inaccurate, internally contradictory, and theologically mistaken. The English liberal critic David Edwards thus speaks of 'innumerable passages' which are 'contradicted either by other passages in the Christian Bible or by the proofs or probabilities of modern historical knowledge'.[102]

Evangelicals have responded in various ways to this challenge. Some have concluded that the critical argument does indeed compel us to abandon the traditional Christian and evangelical view of Scripture, and that we must recognize Scripture as a fallible (though inspired) witness to divine revelation. Others have dismissed criticism as irresponsible and irrelevant, retreating into a dogmatic and simplistic fundamentalism. The one reaction represents the triumph of criticism over tradition, and the promotion of reason at the expense of revelation; the other represents a retreat from reason and from serious engagement with modern thought.

Many evangelicals, rightly in my view, have trodden a path between these two views, welcoming the critical method in principle, yet denying that its implementation necessarily undermines, in theory or practice, the historic Christian conviction concerning the divine authority of Scripture.

The method is to be welcomed, because it takes seriously the incarnational principle, noted earlier, that God has chosen to reveal himself not in some timeless ahistorical form, or in abstract propositions, but in particular historical contexts and through real historical people. To understand God's self-revelation in history it is therefore necessary to understand those contexts and those people; the critical exploration of the human side of Scripture is a means to that end. Evangelical scholars have therefore embraced the method themselves, and contributed significantly to the critical enterprise.[103] The method has its limitations, as will be pointed out below; indeed, some scholars have recently been quite negative about the potential of the historical approach to Scripture. However, although it is correct to recognize that all understanding of Scripture is partial and to some degree provisional, this cannot be interpreted to mean that the historical enterprise is dispensable or impossible. It is not dispensable, on account of the historical nature of Scripture itself; nor is it impossible, as has been shown by the fruitfulness of the method when applied – for example, an understanding of ancient near-eastern law and legal forms has illuminated enormously the meaning and distinctiveness of the Old Testament law codes; form criticism has contributed significantly to our appreciation of the Psalms; recent sociological approaches have opened up new ways of understanding both Old and New Testaments. Evangelicals have welcomed many of these insights.

But what of the critical findings that have appeared to contradict the divine authority of Scripture? Evangelicals have responded to these findings in two manners. *Negatively*, they have noted the limitations of the critical method; *positively*, they have reconsidered aspects of their own understanding of scriptural authority.

Negatively, some evangelicals have argued that all critics are influenced by their own cultural, philosophical and theological presuppositions, and that much of the criticism that has seemed to undermine the authority of Scripture has reflected a deep-rooted prejudice against the miraculous, which rests upon rationalist rather than Christian presuppositions. Even scholars whose work has been in other ways especially illuminating have sometimes found it hard to come to terms with biblical miracles and prophecy.[104] Evangelicals rightly reject criticism based on such prejudice as, in the first place un-Christian, and in the second as based upon a flawed methodology, in which a secular worldview is imposed upon the biblical material.

Evangelicals have also pointed out that many critical conclusions are actually quite tentative and uncertain. Theories that were once regarded as 'assured results of criticism' – such as the JEDP theory of pentateuchal origins, the two-source solution to the synoptic problem, or the controlling belief that Jesus' parables make only one simple point – are now seen to be at best questionable, and at worst definitely mistaken.[105] Biblical critics often appear to overlook the sheer *provisionality* of scholarship.

Both these tendencies are noted and criticized by New Testament scholar Walter Wink, who points out how, in the past, scholars were notoriously dogmatic about what could *not* have happened in the New Testament:

> Historians still can demand that adequate warrants or evidence be produced for believing that something unusual has happened . . . They can provide invaluable checks on superstition by casting a critical eye on extraordinary claims that have a tendentious bent. But to go beyond this to dogmatic assertions that faith healing, or clairvoyance, or resuscitation of the dead is impossible, is to go beyond one's competence as a historian to the faith assertions of a person caught in the narrow confines of a particular world view – or what Paul Ricoeur has called 'the available believable'.[106]

Too easily, the critics' approach to Scripture can become trapped within the rigid and narrow worldview of an ideology, which refused to contemplate that anything beyond its own experience of the world could ever have taken place, or that any ideas alien to its outlook could be correct. At such points, criticism would seem to have overstepped its proper limits; Scripture is here being judged on the basis of a transient and provisional understanding of reality, the limitations and provisionality of which appear to remain unacknowledged. The evangelical is no more free of presuppositions than the liberal, rationalist or secularist. Nevertheless, evangelicals insist that they are concerned to approach Scripture on its own terms, rather than imposing a modernizing straitjacket upon it, and that this approach leads to a sympathetic and intellectually satisfying reading of Scripture.

Yet evangelicals, while pointing out the limitations of biblical criticism, have also responded positively to some of its findings. There is an increased recognition of the need to distinguish issues of *hermeneutics* and issues of *authority*. For example, is the authority of 2 Peter ultimately dependent upon Petrine authorship? Such issues are being given increasing attention within evangelicalism. A total commitment to biblical authority need not, some would argue, commit a scholar to a particular approach to biblical interpretation. An important and potentially difficult debate is emerging within an evangelicalism which no longer feels the need to be defensive over its commitment to either biblical scholarship or biblical authority.

Biblical authority and personal experience

A final element in any account of biblical authority is that of its subjective conviction – an idea expressed in quite different manners as 'the ring of truth' (J. B. Phillips) or 'the internal testimony of the Holy Spirit' (John Calvin). When the Bible is received and taught as the word of God, it speaks to people's needs and situations with a power and relevance that confirm its inherent God-given authority. The gospels describe how Jesus electrified his audiences through his authoritative preaching; that authority was something that was in the first instance *experienced*, and only in the second *explained*, by his followers. The evangelical testimony is that Scripture comes to us as the self-authenticating and convincing word of God. A leading Scottish evangelical writer of the last century put this kind of sentiment into words as follows:

> If I am asked why I receive Scripture as the Word of God . . .
> [I answer] . . . Because the Bible is the only record of the
> redeeming love of God, because in the Bible alone I find God
> drawing near to us in Jesus Christ, and declaring to us in him
> his will for our salvation. And this record I know to be true by
> the witness of his Spirit in my heart, whereby I am assured that
> none other than God himself is able to speak such words to my
> soul.[107]

Inevitably, this runs a risk of subjectivism. Yet, as Søren
Kierkegaard reminded us, 'subjectivism' is not entirely a negative
notion. In its deepest sense, 'subjectivism' means that something has
inward relevance and applicability; in short, it has existential
relevance. In his *Unscientific Postscript*, Kierkegaard stressed the
need for 'an appropriation process of the most passionate
inwardness'.[108] Scripture, as we have seen, possesses a strongly
objective dimension, in that it tells us about the way things are; it
also possesses a subjective component, through which it offers to
transform our inner lives – an offer which, in the evangelical
experience, is more than justified, and leads to an emphasis upon
evangelism as the means by which others might share in this same
'transforming friendship' (James Houston).[109] As Luther put it, we
read Scripture not simply to learn of the 'commands of God'
(*mandata Dei*) but to encounter the 'God who commands' (*Deus
mandantus*), and to be transformed as a result.

The relation between Scripture and systematic theology

Our analysis so far has indicated the enormous importance which
evangelicalism attaches to Scripture. But how is the relationship
between Scripture and theology to be understood? What is the
relation between biblical reflection and systematic theology? In this
concluding section, we shall consider the complex interaction

between Scripture and theology from an evangelical perspective. We begin by exploring the notion of 'biblical theology'.

The notion of 'biblical theology'

The term 'biblical theology' has become problematical for evangelicals. The problem, however, lies primarily in the *associations* of the term within modern theology. The modern understanding of the term derives from the inaugural address delivered by Johann Philip Gabler in March 1787 at the University of Altdorf, in which he argued for the radical separation of 'biblical theology' and 'dogmatics'.[110] It is significant that this address was delivered at the high tide of the Enlightenment; this is particularly evident in relation to Gabler's assumption that the universal truths of reason are to be given precedence over the particularities of Scripture. According to Gabler, 'biblical theology' was to be understood as a purely historical and descriptive discipline, whereas 'dogmatics' was a normative or prescriptive discipline.

Although Gabler's approach was initially ignored by his contemporaries, it began to achieve widespread acceptance in the 1830s, so that 'biblical theology' rapidly came to be understood as a purely historical and descriptive discipline, with no necessary connection with Christian life or belief.[111] To study 'biblical theology' became an exercise in Christian history, examining the theology of biblical writers in much the same way as one might study the theology of early patristic or second-temple Judaism. It was a disinterested exercise in the study of the history of the religion of Israel and the early church, with no direct bearing on the life and thought of Christianity today. Evangelicalism has no place for such an understanding of 'biblical theology'. Yet, despite all the unhelpful and misleading associations which are now attached to the term, evangelicalism must retrieve it and re-establish it.

So what would an evangelical biblical theology be like? For some evangelicals, such a theology would merely repeat what Scripture affirms, perhaps by providing a collection of texts relating to given topics. Yet the essential difficulty with such a 'theology of repetition' is that it fails to interpret, contextualize and correlate.

In the end, repetition is the last resort of those who are intellectually lazy and spiritually complacent. It is all very well to affirm, with Paul, that we are 'justified by faith' (Rom. 5:1). But what does this *mean?* The fundamental statements of Scripture need to be explained. A parrot is perfectly capable of repeating 'We are justified by faith'; repetition is, however, no substitute for understanding. A biblical systematic theology is concerned with the explication of the distinctive vocabulary and conceptualities of Scripture, in order that their meaning may be understood and proclaimed in the living world of today. The theologian is thus required to correlate – that is, to allow biblical affirmations to impact on the contemporary situation.

The history of evangelicalism suggests that the success of the movement rests upon its willingness to correlate Scripture with the context in which it finds itself, rather than mechanically repeating biblical quotations, or simply reaching backwards into evangelical history to draw out past correlations, such as the way in which a text was applied by Calvin in his sixteenth-century Genevan context. The issue is that of applying Scripture to new and hitherto unexperienced contexts, rather than slavishly repeating interpretations of Scripture originally developed with a very different cultural context in mind.[112] David F. Wells, one of evangelicalism's most significant and respected contemporary exponents, comments thus on the task of evangelical theology:

> It is the task of theology, then, to discover what God has said in and through Scripture and to clothe that in a conceptuality which is native to our own age. Scripture, at its *terminus a quo*, needs to be de-contextualized in order to grasp its transcultural content, and it needs to be re-contextualized in order that its content may be meshed with the cognitive assumptions and social patterns of our own time.[113]

Further, the various statements within Scripture require to be correlated – that is, their mutual relation within a greater overall framework needs to be established. Scriptural affirmations concerning the divinity of Jesus Christ require to be set alongside those affirming his humanity, and correlated. How can both these sets of statements be true? And what are their implications for our understanding of the identity of Jesus Christ, the nature of God, and our own identity? Systematic theology is not concerned with merely repeating biblical statements or themes, but with uncovering the overall pattern of thought to which they individually bear witness.

Scripture and narrative

We end this analysis of the role of Scripture in evangelical thought by focusing on an issue which has been of considerable importance in recent biblical scholarship: the recognition of the primacy of the narrative genre within Scripture. How can a narrative serve as the basis of theology?[114] In what way can one speak of a narrative possessing 'authority'? In view of the importance of this issue in contemporary theological analysis, we shall proceed directly to a consideration of the implications for evangelicalism of the predominantly narrational character of Scripture.

In his classic study of biblical interpretation since the Reformation, Hans Frei shows how the rise of rationalism led to a gradual rejection of the 'narrative' character of Scripture.[115] For precritical writers, the interpretation of Scripture concerned 'an interpretation of stories and their meanings by weaving them together into a common narrative referring to a single history and its patterns of meaning'.[116] The Enlightenment, however, adopted a network of approaches to biblical interpretation which reflect the rationalism and anti-supernaturalism of the movement. As Brevard Childs implies, the resulting application of 'common historical critical tools' failed to do 'full justice to the unique theological subject matter of Scripture as the self-revelation of God.'[117] Part of this process of interpretation, evident from the eighteenth century onwards, was a rejection of the 'narrative' character of Scripture.

Earlier evangelicalism was fully aware of the importance of narrative. Martin Luther is an excellent example of an earlier evangelical approach to this matter. He neither (to anticipate the Enlightenment) regarded narrative as something to be eliminated, in order to get at the 'points' it was making; nor (to anticipate

Romanticism) did he regard 'story' as the unique vehicle of truth.[118] Yet despite all its criticisms of the theological and exegetical programmes of the Enlightenment, evangelicalism seems to have chosen to follow it in this respect. The narrative character of Scripture has been subtly marginalized, in order to facilitate its analysis purely as a repository of propositional statements, capable of withstanding the epistemological criteria of the Enlightenment. As Frei points out, the theme of 'narrative' remained present within evangelicalism, but was transferred from Scripture to the believer's personal spiritual journey.[119] It was seen as proper for evangelicals to speak of 'their story' (meaning 'the account of how they came to faith, and are progressing in the Christian life'). But the fact that much of Scripture itself relates a narrative has been overlooked. Why?

The reasons for this are complex, and not that well understood. One factor which seems to be of especial importance in this respect is the way in which evangelicalism is responsive to its intellectual context. Throughout its history, evangelicalism has shown itself to be prone to lapse into a form of rationalism. There is ample evidence that this took place in the Netherlands during the later sixteenth century, as evangelicals became increasingly influenced by the prevailing rationalist worldview.[120] In the United States, the trend towards rationalism within evangelical circles was accelerated during the late eighteenth and early nineteenth centuries by the widespread adoption of what has come to be known as 'Scottish realism' or 'common-sense' philosophy[121] – an issue to which we shall return presently (see pp. 168–171). In particular, evangelicalism has responded to the types of theology of revelation associated with neo-orthodoxy, particularly that of Emil Brunner, which treated revelation purely as a 'personal presence', by stressing the informational content of revelation. Yet, on reflection, this has been an over-reaction; the proper response to Brunner is to affirm the informational content of revelation, not to deny its personal aspects. The result is that forms of American evangelicalism which have been especially influenced by rationalism, such as that associated with Carl Henry, have laid too much emphasis upon the notion of a purely propositional biblical revelation.

But it need not do so. Indeed, as the pressure to defend evangelicalism by stealing the clothes of the Enlightenment diminishes, evangelicals are once more free to rediscover and recover the distinctive features of a more biblical approach to theology, which stresses that God's actions in history, recounted and interpreted in Scripture, form a narrative.[122] Any view of revelation which regards God's self-disclosure as the mere transmission of facts concerning God is seriously deficient, and risks making God an analogue of a corporate executive who disperses memoranda to underlings. Revelation is God's self-disclosure and self-involvement in history, and supremely God's decision to become incarnate in Jesus Christ, so that whoever has seen Jesus Christ has seen the Father. Revelation concerns the *oracles* of God, the *acts* of God, and the *person and presence* of God.

To reduce revelation to principles or concepts is to suppress the element of mystery, holiness and wonder to God's self-disclosure.[123] 'First principles' may enlighten and inform; they do not force us to our knees in reverence and awe, as with Moses at the burning bush, or the disciples in the presence of the risen Christ. For understandable reasons, evangelicalism has in the past chosen to focus on the propositional or cognitive element of the complex network of divine revelation – an element which allowed evangelicalism to maintain its credibility and integrity during a period of rationalist assault. But the ensuing understanding of 'revelation' was itself dangerously deficient, verging on the aridity and sterility which were the hallmarks of the same rationalism which evangelicalism was seeking to oppose.

Recognizing the narrative quality of Scripture allows the fullness of biblical revelation to be recovered. In no way does this strategy involve the abandoning or weakening of an evangelical commitment to the objective cognitive truth of divine revelation. It is simply to recognize that revelation involves more than this, and to commend the wisdom of avoiding reductionist approaches to the issue. Two theologians who have been concerned to recover the importance of narrative in this respect are Karl Barth and H. Richard Niebuhr. For Barth, the Bible related a narrative which identified the 'God of Jesus Christ'.[124] For Niebuhr, the biblical witness, itself narrative in form, illumines our self-understanding and enables us to make sense of 'the story of our life'.[125]

Evangelicalism has always been concerned to demonstrate the close connection between Scripture and doctrine. For reasons which ultimately reflect the dominance of Enlightenment ideas at Princeton during the nineteenth century, evangelicalism was prone to minimize the narrative elements in Scripture, in order to secure the intimate relationship between Scripture and doctrine, often regarding the former as a doctrinal source-book. Yet, rightly understood, there is an equally intimate and interactive connection between the Scriptural narrative and doctrinal affirmations. In what follows, I propose to explore this issue, in order to bring out clearly the connection between narrative and doctrine.[126]

Scripture does not primarily take the form of credal and doctrinal statements, although these are unquestionably interwoven within its structure. Its primary – although by no means its *exclusive* – concern is with narrating what happened at moments held to be of particular importance to the self-definition of the community of faith – moments such as the exodus from Egypt or the resurrection of Jesus of Nazareth. Scripture presents us with a narrative, which purports to tell of God's dealings with humanity, culminating in – but not ending with – the history of Jesus of Nazareth.[127] Where doctrine is concerned with what should be (or is) believed, Scripture appears preoccupied primarily with narrating what happened.[128] (While the New Testament includes much material that is not narrational in character, this can be argued to represent the outcome of engagement with the narrative of Jesus of Nazareth). In that Christianity is centred on the figure of Jesus of Nazareth, a mode of discourse capable of structurally expressing that history is required. Scripture does not articulate a set of abstract principles, but points to a lived life, a specific historical existence, as in some sense embodying and giving substance to some such set of principles.

In the New Testament, the narrative of Jesus is thus interpreted as a story which grounds Christian existence, which gives some shape and specification to those human outlooks on life and those ways of thinking that are appropriate expressions of our own sharing in the life of Christ. Narratives are based in history, in actions, enabling us to avoid thinking of Christianity in terms of universal abstractions, and instead to ground it in the contingencies of our historical existence. Our vision is shaped and informed by the story of Jesus of Nazareth, recalled in the eucharistic celebration of his death and resurrection and the benefits which these are understood to bring us, which we recognize as embodying the shape or pattern of our lives and communities as Christians.[129]

Scripture, then, provides a narrative of a real historical existence, affirmed to be of foundational significance to the community of faith, incarnating both values and ideas. But how is the transition from narrative to doctrine to be effected? The importance of this question in relation to the genesis of doctrine may be illustrated with reference to two examples drawn from the history of Christian doctrine, which illuminate the difficulties encountered in this transition.

The so-called *Christus Victor* theory of the Atonement, prominent in the patristic period, is essentially narrative in its structure.[130] The soteriological markers and metaphors of the New Testament are expanded and reconstructed, to yield a narrative account of the drama of the redemption of humanity. This narrative has certain presuppositions – for example, that humanity is in bondage to tyrants or hostile powers. Nevertheless, these presuppositions are identified by the narrative itself, in the course of recounting the manner in which the death and resurrection of Jesus of Nazareth represent the divine conflict with and victory over the evil powers of bondage.

Our concern is with the structure, rather than the content, of what Gustaf Aulén refers to as the 'classical theory of the Atonement'. The narrative proved to raise more questions than it answered. Why was humanity held bondage to demonic forces? In what way do the cross and resurrection represent a *divine* conflict and victory? Why could not God just have eliminated or bypassed the devil? And, faced with these difficulties, the proponents of the theory were obliged to provide a conceptual substructure in the light of which the narrative might be interpreted. The concept of the *ius diaboli* was thus developed as an attempt to make sense of the narrative at its more perplexing points.[131] A substructure of doctrinal formulations thus began to emerge, as a means of interpreting the drama narrated by the *Christus Victor* theory. With the theological renaissance of the late eleventh and early twelfth centuries, this substructure came under intense critical scrutiny from theologians such as Anselm and Abelard, eventually to be rejected as unsatisfactory and replaced with a doctrine – rather than a *narrative* – of redemption.[132] Our point, however, concerns the structure of the *Christus Victor* theory, which may be seen as an intermediate stage between the scriptural narrative and doctrinal formulations. The narrative required the presupposition of a set of axioms if it was to be meaningful: those axioms were identified and elaborated, in the process of the genesis of doctrine. What narrative lacked, or could plausibly be argued to presuppose, was provided by a doctrinal substructure.

A second example is provided by the Arian controversy of the fourth century. This controversy focused on the identity of Jesus Christ. Was Christ merely a human being, supreme among all of God's creatures, but a creature nevertheless? Or was Christ none other than the divine Son of God? The basic difficulty was that the narrative of Jesus could be read in two quite different ways: as the account of an outstanding human being, or as the account of the incarnation of the Son of God. But which corresponded more precisely to the biblical witness? How was the narrative of Jesus Christ to be understood? The need for a conceptual framework by which the various aspects of the narrative could be interpreted became painfully obvious. The framework offered by Arius was based on the belief that Jesus was supreme among God's creatures; that offered by Athanasius rested on the belief that he was the Son of God incarnate.

At the heart of this dispute lay a tension within the Origenist Christological tradition, in which a narrative and various frameworks of conceptualities demanded correlation.[133] How could the scriptural narrative be related to such an interpretative framework? And which of the various frameworks available (or conceivable) was most appropriate? The Arian controversy illuminates this tension between differing interpretative frameworks as they bear upon a common narrative tradition: both Arius and Athanasius claim to be interpreters of the same narratives. Although Arius was no philosopher, it is clear that his reading of the scriptural narrative required a conceptual framework in which God was totally transcendent and absolute;[134] the scriptural narrative thus centred upon a creature, not the creator. For Athanasius, as we saw, the same narrative centred upon the incarnation of the Son of God.

This controversy illustrates a crucial phase in the development of Christian doctrine: the need to test the adequacy of doctrinal formulations as interpretative frameworks for the scriptural narrative. The frameworks proposed by both Arius and Athanasius were sufficiently internally consistent to necessitate their evaluation on other grounds; those grounds included the degree of correlation with the scriptural narrative itself, and the evaluation of that narrative within the community of faith as expressed in its prayer, worship and adoration. Athanasius' insistence upon the significance of the maxim *lex orandi lex interpretandi* (which can be roughly translated as 'the way we pray establishes the way we interpret') sets him apart from Arius at this point: for Athanasius, worship is the crucible within which theological statements are refined; for Arius, theology provides a framework for the criticism of worship.[135]

The Christological doctrine of the 'two natures' affirms two vital insights: 'Jesus is God' and 'Jesus is man'. Whatever metaphysical or ontological implications may be suggested by these claims, it is important to appreciate that *initially* they refer to the interpretation of the narrative of Jesus of Nazareth. Within the context of this narrative, Jesus may be discerned as playing two roles – the human and the divine. Two roles which had hitherto been regarded as mutually exclusive, demanding different actors, are held by the narrative to be intimately related and focused on the single person of Jesus. Within the context of the narrative, Jesus acts as God (for example, by forgiving sin: Mk. 2:5–7), as well as assuming the more conventional role of a human actor. The doctrine of the two natures thus provides a means of interpreting the scriptural narrative, and of ensuring its internal consistency.

Similarly, the doctrine of the Trinity may be regarded as an interpretation of the Christian narrative. 'Father, Son and Holy Spirit' is an identifying description of God, as he is perceived to act in the New Testament. 'Father', 'Son' and 'Spirit' are identified as related roles within the New Testament narrative.[136] The doctrine of the Trinity provides a hermeneutical key to the correct interpretation of the Old and New Testament narratives, which might otherwise be understood to concern three different deities. Trinitarian discourse is an attempt to identify the God at the centre of the scriptural narrative. In common with doctrine as a whole, it neither explicitly makes, nor explicitly precludes, metaphysical statements. It is initially concerned with interpreting a narrative.

There is thus a dynamic relationship between doctrine and the scriptural narrative. That narrative possesses an interpretative substructure, hinting at doctrinal affirmations. It is evident that there are conceptual frameworks, linked to narrative structures, within Scripture: these function as starting-points for the process of generation of more sophisticated conceptual frameworks in the process of doctrinal formulation. On the basis of these scriptural hints, markers and signposts, doctrinal affirmations may be made, which are then employed as a conceptual framework for the interpretation of the narrative. The narrative is then re-read and re-visioned in the light of this conceptual framework, in the course of which modifications to the framework are suggested. There is thus a process of dynamic interaction, of *feedback*, between doctrine and Scripture, between the interpretative framework and the narrative. One might describe this dialectical relationship in Piagetian terms, as one of assimilation and accommodation: the narrative is assimilated to concepts, and the concepts are accommodated to the narrative. In the course of this hermeneutical spiral, new levels of interpretation are achieved through a progressive interactive oscillation between the generative narrative of Scripture and the interpretative framework of doctrine.

This process of interpretation involves a continuous interaction between scriptural narrative and doctrinal formulations, in an attempt to find an interpretative framework, or range of such frameworks, already hinted at within the New Testament, on the basis of which the narrative of Jesus of Nazareth might be viewed at enhanced levels of meaning. The doctrinal framework which embraces the concept of incarnation was arrived at with some hesitation, on account of its evident implications for Jewish monotheism, and has been subjected to the most sustained criticism in the Enlightenment and post-Enlightenment period. Nevertheless, it remains nothing more than a tentative hypothesis that there is any kind of radical discontinuity between the narrative of Jesus of Nazareth and the primitive interpretative frameworks contained within the New Testament on the one hand, and the doctrine of the incarnation on the other.

We may summarize our analysis of the relation between the biblical narrative and doctrine as follows. Narratives need to be interpreted correctly; Christian doctrine provides the conceptual framework by which the scriptural narrative is interpreted. Narratives demand interpretation. The scriptural narrative is no exception. The Old Testament may be read as a story of the quest for identity among a nomadic people of the ancient near east, just as the synoptic gospels may be read as the story of a misguided Galilean revolutionary or a frustrated Jewish rabbi. Doctrine articulates the particular interpretation, or range of interpretations, of the scriptural narrative appropriate to the self-understanding of the Christian community, calling others into question. Thus the assertion 'Jesus is the Christ' is a doctrinal affirmation which allows the narrative of Jesus of Nazareth to be viewed in a particular light. This assertion is not, however, arbitrary: it is held to be legitimate in the light of that narrative itself. Romans 1:3–4 legitimizes Paul's claim that Jesus is the Christ with reference to the narrative of Jesus of Nazareth, just as a narrative substructure may be detected in the case of other Pauline theological or ethical affirmations.[137]

Doctrine thus provides the conceptual framework by which the scriptural narrative is interpreted. It is not an arbitrary framework, however, but one which is suggested by that narrative, and intimated (however provisionally) by scripture itself. It is to be discerned within, rather than imposed upon, that narrative. The narrative is primary, and the interpretative framework secondary. The New Testament includes both the narrative of Jesus of

Nazareth and interpretation of the relevance of that narrative for the existence of the primitive Christian communities; doctrine represents the extension of the quasi-doctrinal hints, markers and signposts to be found within the New Testament.

The transition from a narrative to a conceptual framework of thinking would have potentially destructive effects for Christian theology if the narrative concerning Jesus of Nazareth, having being allowed to generate a specific framework of conceptualities, were forgotten. Had a conceptual approach to Christianity (such as that associated with the concept of incarnation) been regarded as self-sufficient and autonomous, the narrative which originally precipitated it might have disappeared into the mists of history. Had this occurred, serious anxiety would necessarily have resulted concerning the propriety and adequacy of this framework. It would have been left suspended without visible support. No criteria, save those imposed from outside by rival ideologies, could be adduced by which it could be evaluated. However, the foundational narrative has been preserved by the community of faith, and accorded primary status in doctrinal reflection (particularly within the churches of the Reformation, which remain historical landmarks for an evangelical self-understanding).

The *sola Scriptura* principle is ultimately an assertion of the primacy of the foundational scriptural narrative over any framework of conceptualities which it may generate. The Reformation could reasonably be interpreted as an overdue re-examination of the medieval catholic framework of conceptualities in the light of their generative narrative; similarly, the Reformation slogan *ecclesia reformata, ecclesia semper reformanda* could be interpreted as an affirmation of the need continually to correlate the generating narrative and the resulting concepts. We do not have access to the history of Jesus in its entirety. We do not possess the totality of traditions concerning Jesus. Nevertheless, we do have access to the part of that history and those traditions which the first Christian communities regarded as foundational and identity-giving, along with hints of possible interpretative frameworks, allowing us to evaluate any resulting conceptual representations of the gospel – past, present and future. We retain possession of the criteria by which any proposed framework of conceptualities may be generated or evaluated. In the end, Christian doctrine stands or falls in relation to Scripture, not any particular set of concepts.

The relation of narrative and metaphysics may be further explored by considering Luther's 'theology of the cross', perhaps one of the most theologically acute accounts of this theme.[138] Luther's theology is often incorrectly described as 'anti-metaphysical', which has led to a cluster of unhistorical judgments concerning his theology. Luther's fundamental point, however, is that the narrative of the crucified Christ must be interpreted on the basis of a framework established by that narrative itself, rather than upon the basis of an imposed alien framework. Luther's hostility towards Aristotelian metaphysics is based on his conviction that it imposes upon the scriptural narrative an interpretative framework which leads to serious distortion of the narrative.

Luther's particular concern centres upon a cluster of divine attributes, such as the 'glory of God', the 'power of God', and the 'righteousness of God'. If these attributes are defined on the basis of prior metaphysical presuppositions (including an uncritical use of the principle of analogy), the gospel is distorted. How can the revelation of the 'righteousness of God' (*iustitia Dei*) (Rom. 1:16–17) be good news for sinful humanity, when (on the basis of an Aristotelian analysis of *iustitia*) this revelation can only imply condemnation? Luther's theological breakthrough (to be dated at some point in 1515) centred upon his realization that it is the narrative of Jesus of Nazareth, focusing upon the crucified Christ, which defines the meaning of such terms as 'the righteousness of God'.[139] The 'theologian of the cross' is one who generates a conceptual framework on the basis of the scriptural narrative; a 'theologian of glory' is one who interprets the scriptural narrative on the basis of a predetermined conceptual framework.

Luther thus has no objection to metaphysics, as even a cursory reading of his writings in the period 1515–21 demonstrates; his concern is to allow the scriptural narrative of Jesus of Nazareth, as it is focused upon the crucified Christ, to generate its own framework of conceptualities. Luther's assertion of the autonomy of the scriptural narrative does not involve the rejection of metaphysics; it merely denies to any preconceived metaphysics the right to impose its interpretative framework upon Scripture. To concede the existence of logically prior interpretative categories or frameworks for biblical interpretation is ultimately to undermine radically the authority of Scripture.

For Luther, however, conceptualities such as 'the righteousness of God' are defined by the scriptural narrative, not imported from outside sources. Even 'God' is defined in this manner, as may be seen from Luther's celebrated reference to the 'crucified and hidden God' (*Deus crucifixus et absconditus*). Aristotle's definition of 'God' has, according to Luther, no direct bearing upon the interpretation of Scripture, which identified a somewhat different God as its chief agent.[140] It is possible to regard Luther's axiom *crux sola nostra theologia* as a sophisticated statement of the *sola Scriptura* principle, which asserts the priority of a historically based narrative – rather than abstract concepts of divinity – in theological reflection.

From the above analysis, it will be clear that allowing a narrative to become the foundation of evangelical theological reflection poses no fundamental problems. Indeed, it offers an invaluable catalyst for the cathartic process of purging evangelicalism of the lingering influence of the Enlightenment, and reaching behind the Enlightenment to recover more authentically evangelical approaches to the role of Scripture in Christian life and thought.

Conclusion

In the present chapter, we have argued that the evangelical appeal to the authority of Scripture is coherent and informed. The current rhetoric concerning a 'crisis in biblical authority' is profoundly misleading, in that it confuses secondary issues (how biblical authority is to be articulated and formalized theologically) with the primary issue of the foundational role of Scripture. Increasingly, evangelicals are expressing misgivings concerning the approaches to biblical authority associated with the Old Princeton school,[141] seeing the continuing use of the ideas of this school as contributing to the lingering bondage of evangelicalism to the ideas and outlooks of Enlightenment rationalism.

This, however, cannot be interpreted as representing a retreat from or dilution of the traditional evangelical emphasis on the authority of Scripture; it merely represents an integral part of the continuing evangelical agenda to ensure that every aspect of its theological agenda is grounded in Scripture. There is a growing realization within evangelicalism that the Princeton position is ultimately dependent upon extrabiblical assumptions and norms.[142] In view of evangelicalism's determination not to allow anything from outside the biblical material to assume a normative or foundational role in Christian thinking, it has therefore proved necessary to call into question this particular mode of expressing and defending the authority of Scripture – but *not* to call that authority itself into question. In the end, therefore, evangelicalism is simply in the process of replacing one approach to biblical authority (which is now seen to be based on philosophical axioms) with another (based on more biblical considerations). The commitment to biblical authority remains; it is merely the mode of its articulation which is changing.

In the first two chapters, we have been concerned with the internal coherence of evangelicalism. Our attention now turns to a broader issue: the cohesion and resilience of evangelicalism in the face of its intellectual and theological rivals in the contemporary world. We begin this analysis by considering the relation of evangelicalism to the movement in recent theology which is now becoming widely known as 'postliberalism'.

3

Evangelicalism and postliberalism

In the first part of this work, the inner dynamics of evangelical theology were explored, focusing particularly on the evangelical emphasis on the person and work of Jesus Christ and the normative role of Scripture. Having set out the coherence of the evangelical theological vision in relation to these central issues, I now propose to assess rival approaches of significance within contemporary western culture. My intention is not to present an evangelical alternative to such approaches, but to indicate the grounds upon which they may be critiqued. The first major approach to be considered is 'postliberalism', which emerged in the aftermath of the general disillusionment with liberal theology since the 1960s.

The reaction against liberalism

The general reaction against liberalism in both the academy and the church has now reached such proportions that it may seem pointless to engage with it. As one of my colleagues once asked me, why should modern evangelicalism enter into a dialogue with the dead? However, I believe that it is important to continue to interact with the liberal tendency within Christian theology – or, more accurately, with the cluster of approaches to theology which show liberal 'family resemblances', most notably an appeal to the 'universals' of culture, experience or religion and a retreat from the affirmation of the particularity of the Christian faith. To understand the grounds of the recent reaction against liberalism is to gain a deeper appreciation of the inherent distinctives and strengths of evangelicalism itself.

Evangelicalism has long regarded liberalism as a serious threat to Christian integrity and identity.[1] The liberal strategy of acknowledging norms and sources of theological authority deriving from outside the Christian revelation is seen as something of a Trojan horse, allowing the ideas and values of the world to gain an unmerited and unwelcome presence and influence within Christianity. The sustained evangelical critique of liberalism at both the pragmatic and theoretical level has now been supplemented by other voices from outside evangelicalism, reinforcing the growing consensus within the Christian churches that liberalism is intellectually flawed and tainted. Of these voices, the most significant is the movement known as postliberalism. In view of the importance of this development and the growing influence of postliberalism within both the churches and the academy, the present chapter will present a detailed evangelical assessment of and response to this movement, indicating the areas of convergence and disagreement between these two movements.

The emergence of postliberalism is widely regarded as one of the most important aspects of western theology since 1980. The movement had its origins in the United States, and was initially associated with Yale Divinity School, and particularly with theologians such as Hans Frei, Paul Holmer, David Kelsey and George Lindbeck.[2] While it is not strictly correct to speak of a 'Yale school' of theology, there are nevertheless clear 'family resemblances' between a number of the approaches to theology to emerge from Yale during the late 1970s and early 1980s.[3] Since then, postliberal trends have become well established within North American and British academic theology,[4] indicating that it is likely to have a considerable impact on evangelicalism, at least in the next decade, as the latter increases its presence within the academic community. The relation between evangelicalism and postliberalism is therefore of major importance to the agenda set by the present study.

The distinguishing feature of postliberalism may be located in its rejection of the totalizing projects of modernity, whether this takes the specific form of an Enlightenment-style appeal to universal reason, or a liberal appeal to 'religion', 'culture' or an unmediated religious experience common to all of humanity. Each of these is now recognized as a false universal, a fictitious construction of a totalizing mindset. In the stead of such pseudo-universals, postliberalism places religious communities and their traditions, particularly as mediated through narrative.[5] Thus William C. Placher has helpfully identified the following three fundamental features of postliberal thought:[6]

1. The primacy of narrative as an interpretative category for the Bible;

2. The hermeneutical primacy of the world created by the biblical narratives over the world of human experience;

3. The primacy of language over experience.

It will be clear that this critique of the foundational role of experience represents a decisive move away from the liberal strategy of an earlier generation.

The philosophical roots of this movement are complex. Within the movement, particular appreciation can be discerned for the style of approach associated with the philosopher Alasdair MacIntyre, which places an emphasis on the relation between narrative, community and the moral life.[7] In this respect, postliberalism reintroduces a strong emphasis on the *particularity* of the Christian faith, in reaction against the strongly homogenizing tendencies of liberalism, in its abortive attempt to make theory (that all religions are saying the same thing) and observation (that the religions are different) coincide. We begin our engagement with postliberalism by considering liberalism itself.

Defining liberalism

In one sense, 'liberalism' can simply be defined as the theological position, hitherto characteristic of much of western culture, which has now been displaced by postliberalism. However, there is a need to attempt to explore the foundations of the movement in a little more detail.[8] Perhaps the most distinctive feature of the movement is its accommodationism – that is, its insistence that traditional Christian doctrines should be restated or reinterpreted in order to render them harmonious with the spirit of the age. Considerable emphasis was placed on the need to be open to the new insights afforded by philosophical, social and religious advancement, rather than being tied to the dogmas of the past. Liberalism was especially hostile to any form of particularism, such as the notion of a special divine revelation. For liberalism, religion must be based on universal human resources, such as human culture or common experience. The anti-particularist stance of liberalism is especially evident in its antipathy to evangelism or mission, which are often deprecated as 'theological racism' or 'Christian imperialism'.

To understand theological liberalism, it is necessary to explore the origins of liberalism in general. The term 'liberal' is French in origin, dating from the Napoleonic era. The great sense of liberation which had accompanied the French Revolution of 1789 had given way to a sense of despair, as Napoleon's military machine crushed everything that lay in its path. Both the Jacobin and Bonapartist regimes extended the powers of the state in the name of 'personal liberty', on the basis of the assumption that the liberty and the sovereignty of the people were identical. The origins of this belief probably lay in Jean-Jacques Rousseau's transference of classical Roman and Greek ideas of public virtue to the modern France, without due account of the fundamentally different nature of these contexts.[9]

In reaction against this development, movements arose which stressed the need to safeguard individual liberty against state and social control, chiefly through limiting the power of the state. The term 'liberal' was first used in this political sense by writers such as Madame de Staël and Chateaubriant in 1807, referring specifically to those prepared to oppose Napoleonic totalitarianism.[10] The word makes its appearance in Spanish in 1811, to refer to reforming elements concerned to defend the freedom of the press and individual liberties. Hints of the foreign origins of the word in the English language can be seen in the diary of Walter Scott, who referred to a 'party of *libéraux*'. By the 1830s, the word was firmly established in the English language, being used to refer to a cluster of values which embraced the ideal of political liberty, the inevitability of progress, the virtue of toleration, and the power of reason.[11]

By the 1830s, the term 'liberal' was in fairly regular use, referring especially to a political attitude which celebrated the cult of personal liberty. In his *Prometheus Unbound*, Shelley wrote of human nature as 'free, uncircumscribed, equal, unclassed, tribeless and nationless'. Human nature was subject to none, and totally free in its choices. The strong sense of optimism which pervaded the movement, particularly at the religious level, can be seen in John Morley's (1838–1923) famous declaration 'that human nature is good, that the world is capable of being made a desirable abiding place, and that the evil of the world is the fruit of bad education and bad institutions'.[12]

This sentiment can be found in much liberal English thinking of the early twentieth century, and was often attributed, on the basis of the rather naïve historical positivism which characterized that period, to Jesus himself. An excellent example is provided by the liberal theologian James Franklin Bethune-Baker, who declared that 'human society has in it the immortal germs of progress towards its perfection and the conditions of its perfectibility were described by such sayings as are collected in the Sermon on the Mount'.[13] This illustrates both his perfectionist view of human nature and the general liberal tendency to project thoroughly modern views on to Jesus – a trend devastatingly caricatured by George Tyrrell, with particular reference to Adolf von Harnack: 'The Christ that Harnack sees, looking back through nineteen centuries of catholic darkness, is only the reflection of a liberal Protestant face, seen at the bottom of a deep well.'[14] For many, these progressive social ideas were left in tatters in the aftermath of the First and Second World Wars, especially as the horrors of the Nazi extermination camps became widely known.

Given this foundational liberal commitment to liberty, it is probably one of the greatest tragedies of our times that in recent years 'liberalism' has, in the view of many observers, degenerated from a commitment to openness and toleration into an intolerant and dogmatic worldview, which refuses to recognize the validity of any views save its own. Liberalism was prepared to tolerate or encourage a variety of views, provided that these related to the private world of individuals, and had no social or public significance. In effect, liberalism represents an attempt to control – whether through marginalization or appeasement – different worldviews within strictly imposed bounds, defined and structured on the basis of its own perception of the nature of reality. In effect, liberalism adopted a paternalist approach to differences, tolerating them so long as they did not threaten its own hegemony. It is for this reason that the phrase 'liberal tyranny' is increasingly being applied to the movement.[15] Although it might initially seem to be an oxymoron, the phrase accurately depicts the liberal desire to control differences according to its own worldview. This is as true in the religious field as it is in the political arena. As the British theologian John Macquarrie has commented:

> What is meant by 'liberal' theology? If it means only that the theologian to whom the adjective is applied has an openness to other points of view, then liberal theologians are found in all schools of thought. But if 'liberal' becomes itself a party label, then it usually turns out to be extremely illiberal.[16]

The deeply disturbing paradox of much modern theology is that some of the most dogmatic of its representatives lay claim to be liberals. Despite the strictures noted in the previous paragraph, liberalism is traditionally thought of as implying an inalienable respect for and openness to the views of others. The new dogmatism within liberalism is itself a sure indication of a deep sense of unease and insecurity, and an awareness of its growing isolation and marginalization within mainline Christianity.[17]

Liberalism is now increasingly dismissed as an irrelevance by both conservative and mainline Christian writers, impatient with its easy accommodation to contemporary western culture and its apparently uncritical abandonment of much that is seen to be of vital importance to Christianity. Stanley Fish is one recent writer to draw attention to the fact that political liberalism is 'basically a brief against belief and conviction';[18] this anti-commitment stance is inevitably carried over into its religious embodiments. Yet in the event, liberalism turned out to have just as many certainties and dogmas as orthodoxy, even if this point was initially overlooked, perhaps because those few who bothered to study it had a vested interest in its survival. Its critics charge it with playing to a secular gallery, and giving encouragement to an increasingly self-confident anti-Christian tendency in western culture. The writings of John Shelby Spong are often singled out as a case in point, allegedly demonstrating the intellectual vacuity, the shallow scholarship, and the cultural puritanism of this committed and self-consciously liberal approach. The obvious inadequacy of these writings makes the charges of irrelevance and irresponsibility temptingly easy to endorse. Rather than indulge in such a pointless pursuit, I propose to try to identify what it is about liberalism that has caused such a loss of confidence to emerge within the movement. To begin with, however, we may return to the issue of the identity of liberalism.

In recent American liberal theology, two distinctive (although admittedly related) strategies can be discerned, each of which is concerned to avoid the particularities of the Christian tradition, and ground itself in the commonalities of universal human existence. This may be related directly to the general liberal attempt to 'emancipate individuals from the contingency and particularity of tradition' (Alasdair MacIntyre).[19] The strongly foundationalist approach of classic western liberalism results in its undertaking a programmatic search for a universal basis of such socially significant matters as morality and religion.[20] Schubert Ogden may be taken as a representative of the tendency to ground theology in universal human experience,[21] and Gordon Kaufman of the tendency to ground it in western culture.[22] The inadequacies of these viewpoints have already been explored (see pp. 66–88).

So what has liberalism to offer? Many liberal writers have emphasized the importance of relating Christianity to its intellectual environment, suggesting that this is a distinctive contribution which this movement can still make to contemporary Christianity. Yet it must be noted that a concern for the intellectual climate in which Christianity finds itself at any moment is not a unique, or indeed even a *defining*, feature of liberalism. Thomas Aquinas took seriously the Aristotelianism of the thirteenth-century University of Paris in writing both his *Summa contra Gentiles* and *Summa Theologia*. I have yet to find Aquinas described as a liberal for that reason. In fact, this approach is typical of reflective and intellectually responsible Christianity down the ages. Such an outlook is characteristic of thoughtful Christian reflection over two thousand years of its history, not the exclusive or defining trait of liberalism.

A more modern example will make this point unequivocally clear. One of the most significant contributions to the modern philosophy of religion comes from a group of American writers, including Alvin Plantinga and Nicholas Wolterstorff. Their discussion of the theme of 'faith and rationality' has become a landmark in recent debates centring on this theme.[23] Yet the group has no inclination whatsoever towards liberalism, representing instead what one might call the 'classic Reformed approach', drawing its inspiration from the writings of John Calvin. In short: there is nothing distinctively liberal about being academically serious and culturally informed.

The need to be sensitive and responsive to developments within society is beyond dispute. Nevertheless, to its critics, liberalism appears to have been possessed of a willingness to allow its agenda and the resources which it brings to bear upon that agenda to be shaped by transient, non-universal cultural trends. The French sociologist Jacques Ellul (1912–94) identifies this trend, which appears to have reached its zenith in the late 1960s and early 1970s, and puts his finger on one of the most worrying aspects of liberalism during the 1960s: its tendency to fashion theologies in order to justify decisions that have been made on other grounds.

> What troubles me is not that the opinions of Christians change, nor that their opinions are shaped by the problems of the times; on the contrary, that is good. What troubles me is that Christians conform to the trend of the moment without introducing into it *anything* specifically Christian. Their convictions are determined by their social milieu, not by faith

in revelation; they lack the uniqueness which ought to be the expression of that faith. Thus theologies become mechanical exercises that justify the positions adopted, and justify them on grounds that are absolutely not Christian.[24]

Radical new theologies – 'radical' being a word which then ensured the cultural credibility of the ideas attached to it – were fashioned, generally with minimal or highly selective reference to the Christian tradition, which provided *post hoc* rationalizations of attitudes and ideas, whose ultimate origin lay firmly in the social milieu. To many, it seemed that liberal theology was little more than a transient agglomerate of ideas and values, deriving primarily from the social milieu in which liberal writers were based – usually universities, detached from the pastoral and social concerns of ordinary lay Christians, and increasingly dominated by a secular outlook which theology was expected to share, if it were to maintain any 'academic credibility'. Liberalism slipped easily from being the addresser to being the addressee of a secular culture.

The outcome of this trend is inevitable. In their *American Mainline Religion: Its Changing Shape and Future*, sociologists Wade Clark Roof and William McKinney provide an important study of the steady numerical decline in mainline churches.[25] The importance of the book, however, does not lie merely in its documentation of trends, confirmed by survey after survey, and noted in an earlier chapter of this book. Roof and McKinney look ahead to the future, and ask what the outcome of these developments will be. Their conclusion? In the 1990s, the challenge to mainline Christianity will not be from 'the conservatives it has spurned, but from the secularists it has spawned'.[26]

Yet a more worrying question remains. Where is liberalism going? What has it to offer? Perhaps the most devastating criticism of political liberalism is due to Michael Oakeshott, who defined it as a purposeless civil association structured by adverbial rules.[27] It does not really have any purpose. Thus Ronald Dworkin argues that the virtue of liberalism does not lie in its active promotion of any concept of morality or the purpose of life, but in its refusal to promote *any* way of life.[28] It is neutral. The same agenda has passed across into theological liberalism, which has become decidedly reticent to speak of evangelism on account of its alleged claims to privilege. Unless liberalism regains a firm commitment to the gospel of Jesus Christ, it is difficult to see what can keep it going. It will be ignored by the church and by society at large. And this haunting fear of being condemned to irrelevance underlies one of the most interesting recent developments within an increasingly beleaguered liberalism – the quest for a 'public theology', to which we may now turn.

Liberalism and the quest for a 'public theology'

A repetitive theme of the contemporary cultural scene is the recognition that the Enlightenment is over. The rise of postmodernism in the culture at large, of the New Age in the realm of personal spirituality,[29] and postliberalism in the field of Christian theology, all point to the collapse of belief in the Enlightenment worldview, especially its rationalism and quest for universal foundational principles. Yet news of the lingering death of the Enlightenment seems to have been remarkably slow to travel to some quarters. It is almost as if some thinkers cannot bear the thought. A recent article in the *Christian Century* illustrates this point. In this article, two liberal Christian ethicists – Max L. Stackhouse and Dennis P. McCann – emphasize the need for a revival of 'a public theology'.[30] In the light of the new situation following the collapse of socialism as a credible worldview, they argue, there is a need to move away from 'confessional particularities, exclusive histories and privileged realms of discourse'. 'This agenda for Christian thought requires a public theology, a way of speaking about the reality of God and God's will for the world that is intellectually valid in the marketplace of ideas and morally effective in the marketplace of goods and services.'

There is much to commend this proposal. It insists that Christian theology address the widest of publics, demanding a hearing in even the most secular of contexts. Unless Christians are merely to 'preach to their choirs', they must find some 'intellectually valid' way of engaging the secular world at large. Yet on closer inspection, the proposal advanced with such earnestness by these writers turns out to be fatally flawed. It rests upon the assumption that, while the language and values of Christian theology are shaped by history, the values and language of secular culture are unconditioned by such influences. At the heart of the argument lies an appeal to the 'context-transcending principles of truth, justice and love'. In other words, these three abstract notions are universally valid, and determine the framework which a public gospel must address.

There are three major flaws with this approach. In the first place, these three notions are barren abstractions, which can come to life only when they are given substance. They must be particularized, located in real-life situations. This point has been appreciated by most Christian preachers and pastors, concerned to deal with the issues of real life, rather than the dulling abstractions of general principles. We all need to learn the lessons that Reinhold Niebuhr learned in downtown Detroit during the 1920s. In his *Leaves from the Notebook of a Tamed Cynic* (1929), Niebuhr wrote:

> If a minister wants to be a man among men he need only stop creating a devotion to abstract ideals which everyone accepts in theory and denies in practice, and to agonize about their validity and practicability in the social issues which he and others face in our present civilization. That immediately gives his ministry a touch of reality and potency.[31]

Yet Niebuhr is an excellent example of a theologian who pursued a theological critique of prevailing liberal economic, social and political notions; the kind of 'public theology' offered to us by Stackhouse seems to do theology with the idea of *defending* the liberal vision of culture. The cultural vision comes first; the theological framework appears to be a disposable afterthought.

For, in the second place, this approach actually tends to be little more than a capitulation to secular culture. Stackhouse and McCann speak of 'going public'; in reality, they have gone secular.

The driving force behind their enterprise is to prove the public relevance of theology; it still has things to say which are worth listening to. Yet the intended audience for these pronouncements is one which has little interest in Christian thought; its sole question is likely to be the intensely pragmatic 'Can you give us additional justifications for what we are already doing, and what we already know to be right?' 'Public theology' has shown that it is entirely willing to give even better reasons for the liberal democratic ethos of modern America than modern liberal democrats can. Mesmerized by the spectre of being 'relegated to irrelevance' within western culture, they have thrown aside the distinctive resources of the Christian tradition – which they refer to condescendingly as 'confessional particularities, exclusive histories and privileged realms of discourse' – in their headlong rush to mimic the world. As a result, the 'truth' of the Christian gospel is transformed into a pale echo of some form or other of late-twentieth-century liberal democratic thought.

The result of this approach is quite simple: it silences Christians, forbidding them to have any distinctive insights which need to get a public hearing. Christians must become secular liberals before they are allowed a public hearing. 'To demand neutral discourse in public life . . . should now be recognized as a way of coercing people to speak publicly in someone else's language and thus never to be true to their own' (Os Guinness).[32] Lesslie Newbigin comments on the inevitable outcome of this stance:

> We are like the Christian congregations under the *milet* systems of the Persian and Muslim empires: we use the mother tongue of the Church on Sundays, but for the rest of our lives we use the language imposed upon us by the occupying power. But if we are true to the language of the Church and the Bible, we know that this is not good enough.[33]

There is, however, a third, and more serious, problem. Stackhouse and McCann appear to have overlooked the fact that the Enlightenment has ended. The belief that the language and values of secular culture are universally valid is no longer taken seriously. Stackhouse and McCann retain a faith in the idea of some universal way of speaking and thinking, which transcends the irritating particularities of being a Christian (or Jew, or socialist, or whatever). They believe in some kind of moral and religious Esperanto, which offers to break down divisive particularities, and allow all to speak the same language, and live happily ever after. The 'Esperanto' in question turns out to be an artificial language, an invention. Yet the language of morals must make sense to whole communities, before we can get anywhere. The rise of postmodernism is a telling indicator of the general collapse of confidence in the foundational belief of the Enlightenment in 'universal morality'. How, one wonders, can a Christian theology hope to maintain intellectual credibility in a postmodern world, if one were to adopt the outdated and discredited approach of Stackhouse and McCann, who seem to hanker after the good old days of the (now defunct) Enlightenment?

The task of constructing a public theology is too serious to be based upon outdated fairy-tale notions of 'universal cultural values'. 'Truth, justice and love' all require to be defined – and they are defined in different manners by different people. Far from being 'context-transcending', they are radically dependent upon their context for their meaning. Stackhouse and McCann appear to believe that secular culture is unconditioned by the contingencies of history, in contrast to what they clearly regard as the irritating and petty distinctive characteristics of Christianity. It is perhaps no cause for wonder that liberal Christianity is losing its voice, both within church and society. Liberalism has spent its fuel.

For this reason, we may now turn to consider postliberalism in more detail.

The postliberal critique for liberal foundationalism

The emergence of postliberalism may be regarded as a telling indication that the intellectual and cultural credibility of liberalism has been decisively challenged. The notion of 'common human experience' is now regarded as little more than an experiential fiction, in much the same way that 'universal rationality' is now seen as little more than the idle daydream of reason. The belief in cultural or experiential metanarratives (to borrow from the conceptualities of postmodernism) is acknowledged to be at best flawed, and at worst an invitation to oppression. Ideas such as 'religion' and 'culture', which an earlier generation of liberal writers happily appealed to as constituting universal foundations of non-particularist forms of Christianity, are now seen to be fictitious constructs, generally reflecting a specifically western set of presuppositions. Most significantly of all, it is no longer regarded as 'arrogant' or 'imperialist' to suggest that Christian theology concerns the quest for justifiable particularity.

Liberal critics of postliberalism have argued that it represents a lapse into a 'ghetto ethic' or some form of 'fideism' or 'tribalism', on account of its retreat from universal norms of value and rationality. Yet these same liberal critics seem unable to accept that the Enlightenment is over, and that any notion of a 'universal language' or 'common human experience' is simply a fiction, like – to use Gadamer's famous analogy – Robinson Crusoe's imaginary island. 'Foundationalism' of any kind – whether philosophical or religious – is widely regarded as discredited.[34] Postliberalism has comes to terms with the death of the Enlightenment, where liberalism stumbles pathetically and randomly across the intellectual terrain, looking desperately for an absolutely firm foundation in a world which no longer accepts its existence. The birth of postmodernity seems to have been overlooked by liberalism, which appears to prefer living in the past rather than confronting the harsh new world of today. It is to the credit of postliberal writers that they have faced up to the cultural abandonment of universal norms and values, even if the movement's liberal critics prefer the cosy nostalgia of the myth of a 'universal language' or 'public discourse'.

As Mary Midgley once commented, the 'sad little joke' of 'universal languages' is that nobody seems to speak them.[35] To criticize postliberalism for its abandonment of 'universal discourse' is like abusing a child who no longer believes in Santa Claus. It may be a reassuring, cosy and useful illusion — but it is an illusion. And, as postmodernism has emphasized, the illusion of universal norms can all too easily become profoundly oppressive, forcing observation to conform to the theory, and repressing distinctiveness on the part of, for example, a religion on account of the prior dogmatic conviction that all are saying the same thing. The reassertion of the distinctiveness of Christianity both reflects this reaction against the illusion of universality, and a growing awareness of the genuinely singular character of Christian faith. We shall explore this latter point in the following section; our concern now focuses on the critique of liberal foundationalism which undergirds the postliberal enterprise.

The basic argument is that liberal theology feels itself to be under some kind of obligation to ground itself in something in the public arena – such as philosophical concepts or 'common human experience'.[36] Lindbeck states this liberal concern in terms of a 'commitment to the foundational enterprise of uncovering universal principles or structures', whether these turn out to be metaphysical, existential or otherwise.[37] The impulse, which is fundamentally apologetic in intent, is to find a common base for Christian theology and public discourse by a prior analysis of human knowledge, culture or experience. The merit of this critique is probably most evident in the case of Paul Tillich, whose apologetic theology is widely regarded as dictated by extrabiblical and non-Christian concerns, and inadequately grounded in the particularities of the Christian tradition.

This attempt to liberate Christian theology from extrabiblical presuppositions will be welcomed by evangelicals.[38] This certainly indicates that evangelicals can ally themselves, at least to some extent, with postliberalism's emphasis upon Scripture as the sole normative source of Christian theology and living. Evangelicals and postliberals thus seem to share the kind of concerns so frequently expressed by Karl Barth concerning the potential enslavement or debasement of Christian thought through the intrusion of alien assumptions resulting from a deficient theological method, through which ideas originating from outside the church are allowed to assume a controlling influence within it. We have explored the vulnerability of liberalism at this point (pp. 60–61); indeed, it is necessary even to concede that evangelicalism itself has been unduly influenced by Enlightenment presuppositions, particularly in the case of the Old Princeton School (pp. 166–174).

Nevertheless, this does not exclude the apologetic procedure of attempting to identify commonalities between the gospel and human experience, reason or culture as possible 'points of contact' for evangelism.[39] Nor would it involve the rejection of using extrabiblical terminologies and conceptualities in an attempt to explicate or render more intelligible the distinctive character of Christianity to a secular audience. Liberalism ended up making secularism credible to Christianity rather than the other way round. Postliberalism avoids this apologetic disaster.

Whereas the older and now discredited liberal strategy involved the search for foundational universal principles, thence – in effect rather than by intention – reducing Christianity to such principles, postliberalism offers a mediating position by which Christianity may be explicated and commended using mediating terminologies and conceptualities *without* allowing them to be systematically prior to the gospel, or to control our understanding of the gospel itself.[40] Apologetics is thus understood to be grounded in and controlled by systematic theology, with each and every apologetic strategy being regarded as provisional and heuristic, responding to the particular situation being addressed.[41]

Rediscovering the distinctiveness of Christianity

There is a growing acceptance within academic theology, not simply that Christianity *is* distinct, but that any worldview which refuses to acknowledge such distinctiveness must be rejected as seriously at variance with the observable facts. After all, Jesus Christ was not crucified just for reinforcing what everyone already knew. With the end of the Enlightenment and its intellectual satellites – including liberalism and pluralism – the embargo on distinctiveness has been lifted. No longer is the claim to be saying something *different* seen as equivalent to being irrational. Jews are special; they have a special story, and a different set of values. In the same way, Christians are special; they have a special story, and a different set of values.[42] Postliberalism embodies a willingness to respect – indeed, to celebrate – the distinctiveness of the Christian tradition, and sees Christian theology as concerned with the articulation of the distinctive grammar of the Christian faith.

This view is perhaps seen at its clearest in the writings of Paul Holmer, most notably his *Grammar of Faith* (1978). For Holmer, Christianity possesses a central grammar which regulates the structure and shape of Christian 'language games'.[43] This language is not invented or imposed by theology; it is already inherent within the biblical paradigms upon which theology is ultimately dependent. The task of theology is thus to discern these intrabiblical rules (such as the manner in which God is worshipped and spoken about), not to impose extrabiblical rules. For Holmer, one of liberalism's most fundamental flaws was its attempts to 'reinterpret' or 'restate' biblical concepts, which inevitably degenerated into the harmonization of Scripture with the spirit of the age. 'Continuous redoing of the Scripture to fit the age is only a sophisticated and probably invisible bondage to the age rather than the desire to win the age for God.'[44] Theology is grounded on the intrabiblical paradigm, which it is obliged to describe and apply as best it can. To affirm that theology has a *regulatory* authority is not to imply that *it* can regulate Scripture, but to acknowledge that a distinctive pattern of regulation already exists within the biblical material, which theology is to uncover and articulate.

The critical question which arises from this approach, to which we shall return later in this chapter, is whether theology is simply about the grammar of faith – that is to say, regulation of Christian discourse. To what does this discourse relate? Is there some reality or set of realities outside the biblical text to which the biblical narrative relates? Do theological assertions simply articulate biblical grammar, or do they relate to some objective order, irrespective of whether we recognize this relation or not? As we shall see, one central evangelical anxiety concerning the postliberal approach is that it appears to represent a purely intratextual affair, with little concern for its possible relation to an external objective reality.

The most significant statement of this approach is provided in the writings of George Lindbeck, especially his *Nature of Doctrine*. One of the many merits of this book is the debate which it has initiated over this unjustly neglected aspect of Christian theology, which has assumed new importance recently on account of the impact of the ecumenical movement.[45] It is therefore only proper that this attempt to explore the relation between evangelicalism and postliberalism should begin by outlining and – however provisionally – responding to Lindbeck's analysis.

One of the most tantalizing aspects of Lindbeck's *Nature of Doctrine* is that he clearly intends it to be a *pre-theological* text, rather than an exercise in systematic theology. The work outlines a research programme, rather than articulating its outcome. Lindbeck regards the volume as providing a framework for the exploration of theological questions and issues, rather than as addressing those issues directly. This makes the text somewhat difficult for an evangelical with a specific interest in the outcome of the application of a method, in that evangelicalism judges the reliability of a theological method partly in terms of its consequences. It may reasonably be pointed out that the *Nature of Doctrine* was published in 1984, allowing ample time for the subsequent application of its approach; however, Lindbeck himself has not yet produced a substantial work which indicates evidence of a transition from pre-theological enquiry to theological statement.

In what follows, my analysis is therefore necessarily limited to the *Nature of Doctrine* itself, linking analysis of its approach with an attempt to explore what the consequences of its application might be. However, in that part of Lindbeck's pre-theological programme includes evaluation of existing approaches, it is particularly appropriate to set out and critique his evaluation of rival approaches. We therefore turn to consider Lindbeck's exposition of 'cognitive-propositional' approaches to doctrine.

Lindbeck's critique of evangelicalism

In his analysis of the nature of doctrine, Lindbeck identifies three 'theories' or understandings of the nature of doctrine. We have already endorsed and expanded Lindbeck's analysis of the approach to doctrine which is characteristic of theological liberalism, particularly in North America, which Lindbeck refers to as the 'experiential-expressive' approach (see pp. 73–75). Although Lindbeck does not explicitly indicate that he intends to engage with evangelicalism, one of the approaches he critiques would clearly be associated with the movement.

This is the view, designated by Lindbeck as 'propositionalist' or 'cognitive', which treats doctrines as 'informative propositions or truth claims about objective realities'.[46] This style of approach has a long association with evangelicalism, and became of especial importance in the evangelical renaissance of the 1960s, when evangelicals such as Carl Henry reacted against the approaches to revelation associated with neo-orthodoxy by stressing the informative content of divine revelation, which was to be articulated in propositional form. While I have argued that this approach to Christian doctrine is inadequate, in that it fails to do justice to the full complexity of the biblical notions of revelation, it remains axiomatic for evangelicals that both revelation and doctrine have cognitive or informational aspects. Lindbeck's explicit critique of such approaches thus clearly impact on evangelicalism, even if Lindbeck himself does not explicitly make such connections.

Lindbeck argues that this approach is to be rejected as voluntarist, intellectualist and literalist, even making the suggestion that those who 'perceive or experience religion in cognitivist fashion' are those who 'combine unusual insecurity with naïveté'.[47] A first hesitation about this criticism concerns its reliability: it appears to be based upon a questionable understanding of the 'cognitive-propositional' position, apparently grounded upon the belief that those inclined towards this position hold that it is possible to state the objective truth about God definitively, exhaustively and timelessly in propositional form.

This cannot be considered to be an adequate representation of this position, in either its classical or its post-critical form. It fails to register the historical and linguistic sophistication of cognitive approaches to doctrine.[48] For example, Lindbeck's suggestion that the 'cognitive-propositional' approach to doctrine treats any given doctrine as 'eternally true'[49] fails to take account of the evident ability of proponents of this approach to reformulate, amplify or supplement a doctrine with changing historical circumstances.[50] Lindbeck attributes an unmerited inflexibility to cognitive approaches to doctrine through playing down the notion of 'relative adequacy' of doctrinal statements, where 'adequacy' can be assessed in terms of both the original historical context of a doctrinal formulation and whatever referent it is alleged to represent.

Most theologians of the medieval period understood dogma as a dynamic concept, a 'perception of divine truth, tending towards this truth' (*perceptio divinae veritatis tendens in ipsam*).[51] It is true that certain medieval writings do indeed suggest that doctrine may be treated as Euclidean theorems: Alan of Lille's *Regulae theologiae* and Nicholas of Amien's *De arte catholicae fidei* are excellent examples of this genre dating from the twelfth century,[52] later found in such writings as Morzillus' *De naturae philosophiae* (1560) and Morinus' *Astrologia gallica* (1661). Nevertheless, a considerably more nuanced approach to the nature of theological statements is much more characteristic of Christian theology in the patristic and medieval periods.[53] Theology is recognized to be concerned in the first place with the clarification of the manner in which affirmations about God are derived, and in the second place, with how they relate to analogous affirmations drawn from the more familiar world of the senses. It is an attempt to achieve conceptual clarity, to avoid confusion through subjecting statements concerning God to close scrutiny. What does the word 'God' stand for? How does the question, 'Does God exist?', relate to the apparently analogous question, 'Does Socrates exist?'? What reasons might be adduced for suggesting that 'God is righteous'? And how does this statement relate to the apparently analogous statement 'Socrates is righteous'? Thus Alan of Lille (to note one of the more propositionalist of medieval theologians) is concerned with identifying the ways in which we might be misled by theological affirmations – for example, by treating them as descriptions of physical objects, or assuming that terms and conceptualities relating to God possess the same meanings as in everyday discourse.[54] Underlying such attempts to achieve clarity of concepts and modes of discourse is the recognition that doctrinal affirmations are to be recognized as perceptions, not total descriptions, pointing beyond themselves towards the greater mystery of God himself.

For such theologians, doctrines are reliable, yet incomplete, descriptions of reality. Their power lies in what they represent, rather than what they are in themselves. The point at which interrogation is appropriate concerns whether such doctrines are adequate (to the strictly limited degree that this is possible) representations of the independent reality to which they allegedly relate. Given that they cannot hope to represent it in its totality, and given the inevitable limitations attending any attempt to express in words something which ultimately lies beyond them, is the particular form of words employed the most reliable conceivable? The Nicene controversy is an obvious example of a struggle to articulate insights in this manner. If an experience is to be articulated in words, in order to communicate or to attempt a communal envisioning of this experience, some form of a 'cognitive-propositionalist' dimension is inevitable. Yet this is not to reduce the experience to words, but simply to attempt to convey it through words.[55]

This point concerning the verbalizing of experience is valid, irrespective of whether the words used are thought to convey an ontological truth or not. For example, consider Longfellow's lines from the *Saga of King Olaf*:

> I heard a voice that cried,
> Balder the beautiful
> Is dead, is dead.

These words would not be thought of as ontologically true. To use Lindbeck's terms, they are intrasystemically true, in that they are consistent within the context of the Nordic Valhalla myth.[56] This statement implies nothing concerning ontological truth or falsity, unless the myth is read as history. Yet C. S. Lewis wrote thus of his reaction to reading Longfellow's lines: 'I knew nothing about Balder; but instantly I was uplifted into huge regions of northern sky, I desired with almost sickening intensity something never to be described (except that it is cold, spacious, severe, pale and remote) and then . . . found myself at the very same moment already falling out of that desire and wishing I were back in it.'[57]

It would be absurd to suggest that words can adequately capture experience; Ludwig Wittgenstein, who lamented the inability of words to describe or convey the aroma of coffee, has ensured that we are fully aware of this point. Yet is this such a significant matter? Words may not be able to provide a totally comprehensive description of the aroma of coffee; nevertheless, words are good enough to let me know where to find coffee, how to ensure that what I have found is indeed coffee, and then to experience its aroma. Cognitive theories of doctrine recognize that words are on the borderlands of experience, intimating and signposting the reality which they cannot capture. To apply pejorative epithets such as 'intellectualist' or 'literalist' to the cognitive-propositionalist approach to doctrine is to fail to appreciate the power of words to evoke experience, to point beyond themselves to something inexpressible, to an experience which their author wishes to share with his or her readers. It is also, of course, to fail to do justice to the many levels at which cognitive or propositional statements operate.

Theological statements simply do not operate at the same level as mathematical equations. The charge of 'literalism' is vulnerable to the extent that it risks overlooking the richness of non-literal language, such as metaphor, as a means of articulation, and the importance of analogy or 'models' as a heuristic stimulus to theological reflection. It is simply a theological truism that no human language can be applied to God univocally; indeed, it is from the recognition, rather than the denial, of this point that cognitive approaches to doctrine begin. On occasion, Lindbeck's unsympathetic and somewhat dismissive approach to cognitive theories of doctrine suggests he understands their proponents to adopt a crudely realist approach to theological statements, such as that criticized by the English writer John Robinson in *Honest to God* (1963) – for example, the idea that God really is an elderly man located at an unspecified point in the stratosphere.

The vague charge of 'literalism' levelled against 'cognitive' theories of doctrine appears to lack the discriminatory apparatus necessary to distinguish, for example, the radically different interpretations of the statement 'This is my body' (Mt. 26:26) found with Luther (it is literally true), Zwingli (it is a form of metaphor) and Calvin (it is metonymical). Cognitive theories presuppose use of the non-literal 'four master tropes' of thought and discourse (metaphor, metonymy, synecdoche and irony) in the process of conceptual thinking, rather than reducing them to a crudely literal conception of representation, as Lindbeck seems to suggest.[58] Calvin and Zwingli are two sixteenth-century figures who make extensive use of rhetorical analysis and non-literal modes of discourse, both in their analysis of texts (such as Scripture) and in their positive theological affirmations.[59] Such rhetorical analyses of experience offer a means by which a cognitive account may be given of experience without in any sense reducing experience to propositional form or degenerating into 'literalism' in the vague but ultimately pejorative sense of the term employed by Lindbeck. The impatience of many modern theological writers with 'cognitive' theories of doctrine seems at times to represent little more than impatience with the vexatious nature of human language, and a reluctance to engage with its ambivalence and polysemy.

It is also important to stress that the science of cognitive psychology has important insights to contribute to this model of doctrine, in that it is able to address the mental processes by which experience is interpreted and expressed in words.[60] For example, there appear to be significant parallels between the cognitive processes implicated in aesthetic and in religious reflection, so that aesthetic cognition may be regarded as a relatively good analogue of religious cognition. The attempt to symbolize personal experience (which also underlies important affinities between doctrinal formulations and psychotherapeutic insights) suggests that both the difficulties and positive insights of defensible 'cognitive' approaches to Christian doctrine are paralleled at other points of major importance in the intellectual spectrum relating to human attempts to express experience in words. Although the study of these parallels is only now beginning, it is to be expected that cognitive models of doctrine may be better understood and appreciated in their light. Inevitably, this has implications for Lindbeck's criticism of 'cognitive' theories of doctrine.

I concede that Lindbeck's criticism has considerable force when directed against neo-scholastic understandings of revelation, such as the approach associated with Hermann Dieckmann, to the effect that supernatural revelation merely transmits conceptual knowledge by means of propositions. This is clearly open to serious criticism along the lines suggested by Lindbeck. In this respect, Lindbeck has provided a valuable corrective to deficient cognitive models of doctrine. Nevertheless, not all cognitive theories of doctrine are vulnerable in this respect. It is necessary to make a clear distinction between the view that an exhaustive and unambiguous account of God is transmitted conceptually by propositions on the one hand, and the view that there is a genuinely cognitive dimension, component or element to doctrinal statements on the other. Doctrinal statements need not be and should not be treated as *purely* cognitive statements.

The fundamental insight here is that human words cannot adequately define experience, but may nevertheless point towards it, as signposts. Although emphasis upon the experiential aspects of doctrine is especially associated with the later Renaissance and the rise of experientially orientated theologies in the Romantic period, hints of such insights are evident in the writings of Augustine of Hippo and his medieval interpreters. Christian doctrine attempts to give shape to the Christian life by laying the foundations for the generation and subsequent interpretation of Christian experience.

Underlying the profundity of human experience and encounter lies an unresolved tension – the tension between the wish to express an experience in words, and the inability of words to capture that experience in its fullness. Everything in human experience which is precious and significant is threatened with extinction, in that it is in some sense beyond words, and yet requires to be stated in words for it to become human knowledge. It is threatened with the spectre of solipsism, in that unless an experience can be communicated to another, it remains trapped within the private experiential world of an individual. Words can point to an experience, they can begin to sketch its outlines – but the total description of that experience remains beyond words. Words point beyond themselves, to something greater which eludes their grasp. Human words, and the categories which they express, are stretched to their limits as they attempt to encapsulate, to communicate, something which tantalizingly refuses to be reduced to words. It is the sheer elusiveness of human experience, its obstinate refusal to be imprisoned within a verbal matrix, which points to the need for poetry, symbolism and doctrine alike. An impatience with precisely this elusiveness appears to underlie the rejection of any cognitive component to doctrinal statements.

The intimation of something further, beyond and signposted by experience, is characteristic of human experience. We live on the borderlands of something more – something intimated, something ultimately lying beyond the horizons of our comprehension, yet on occasion intruding into our consciousness. Experience and language point beyond themselves, testifying that something lies beyond their borderlands, yet into which we tantalizingly cannot enter. Everyday language founders as it attempts to grasp beyond the threshold of the empirical and observable, to capture what it knows lies beyond. As Wordsworth suggests, human beings are 'borderers', firmly based in the real world of human experience, yet reaching out in aspiration beyond its limits.[61]

This sense of reaching after something unattainable, intimated yet not delivered by experience, has strongly religious overtones and important religious consequences. It is, however, not in any way confined to what we might reasonably designate 'religious' experience or 'religious' situations. The observation is often made that humans entertain lofty ideals, which they repeatedly – and often tragically – fail to meet. There is a tension at the moral level between the faulty and finite creatures which we are, and the high destiny to which we feel ourselves called.

A similar tension, captured by C. S. Lewis, exists at the aesthetic level, in the quest for beauty.[62] The same sense of bittersweet longing, of *Sehnsucht*,[63] of the inability both of experience to deliver what it promises, and of human words to capture that experience and the aspirations it engenders, permeates the writings of Evelyn Waugh, perhaps most powerfully in the exquisite poignancy of *Brideshead Revisited*, as memories of the past invade, illuminate and transform the present.

> Perhaps all our loves are merely hints and symbols; vagabond-language scrawled on gate-posts and paving stones along the weary road that others have tramped before us; perhaps you and I are types and this sadness which sometimes falls between us springs from disappointment in our search, each straining through and beyond the other, snatching a glimpse now and then of the shadow which turns the corner always a pace or two ahead of us.[64]

The language of Christian theology functions under constraints similar to those affecting poetry: it is obliged to express in words things which by their very nature defy reduction to these words; nevertheless, there is a fundamental resonance between words and experience. Keats's experience on reading Chapman's Homer; Wordsworth's experience on seeing a vast expanse of Cumbrian daffodils; both demanded expression and communication through words, a medium perhaps fundamentally unsuited for their purpose, but which remained the only vehicle at their disposal. Schleiermacher suggests that the function of Christian doctrine is to effect a decisive transition within the language of the Christian community from the poetic and rhetorical to the 'descriptive-didactic':[65] poetic and doctrinal language are thus distinct, but related, levels of discourse available to the community of faith. Precisely because the primary language of the Christian community is poetic and rhetorical, doctrine is essential for the sake of responsible preaching to the community in its primary language.[66]

This insight can be developed, to take account of the apologetic and evangelistic aspects of doctrine. Preaching may be directed towards those outside the community of faith, not merely those within, with a view towards evoking understanding and a response on their part (see pp. 47–50).

To caricature Christian doctrine, then, as mere word-play or as an attempt to reduce the mystery of God to propositions is to fail to appreciate the manner in which words serve us. In order for my experience to be expressed, communicated to or aroused in another, it demands statement in cognitive forms. That these cognitive forms fail to capture such an experience in its totality is self-evident, and hardly a matter for rhetorical exaggeration: it is one of the inevitable consequences of living in history and being obliged to communicate in historical forms. Schleiermacher recognized that doctrine expressed an experience constituted by the language of the Christian community, thus pointing to the delicate interplay of cognitive and experiential elements in doctrinal formulations.

'Experience' and 'meaning' are thus two sides of the same coin, forbidding us to reduce Christianity to bare propositions on the one hand, or to inchoate experience on the other. Every experience includes, and is modified by, interpretative elements.[67] As modern theories of scientific observation have made clear, experience is not pre-theoretical data, but is actually theory-laden, accompanied by interpretative elements.[68] The brute empiricism which treats experience purely as raw data which require interpretation is inadequate: experience is actually 'given' within an interpretative framework, however provisional. Theory plays a much more determinative role in our approach to experience than pure empiricism suggests: theory itself determines, at least to some extent, the experience which that theory is supposed to explain or interpret. As Husserl's phenomenology stresses, prior knowledge and beliefs play a constitutive role in determining what we observe and experience. It is for this reason that Lindbeck's treatment of 'cognitive' and 'experiential' models of doctrine as antithetical is so profoundly unsatisfactory. The cognitive dimension of Christian doctrine is the framework upon which Christian experience is supported, the channel through which it is conveyed. It is a skeleton which gives strength and shape to the flesh of experience.

Doctrine also provides a conceptual apparatus by which experience may be interpreted and criticized. The preliminary judgments of experience are interpreted within a conceptual framework, ultimately based upon the scriptural narrative and its doctrinal intimations, expressed by doctrine, in order that it may be viewed in a new light. This point has been stressed by Gerhard Ebeling, who notes the need to be able to approach experience itself in such a way that it may be experienced in a new manner.[69] By being viewed in a particular light, experience is correlated with the scriptural narrative and the conceptual framework it engenders, and allowed to assume a new significance. Doctrine thus opens the way to a new 'experience with experience'.[70]

We have already noted (pp. 71–88) how experience itself is an inadequate foundation for theological affirmation; nevertheless, on being interpreted, experience affords central insights into the existential dimension of the Christian faith. The new relevance of the 'theology of the cross', as expounded by Jürgen Moltmann and Eberhard Jüngel, points to the need for theology to interpret experience, without being reduced to its categories or bound by its preliminary intimations. Cognitive approaches to theology, such as those affirmed by evangelicalism, retain this vital function of doctrine, seeing it as a net cast over experience, in order that it may be more adequately grasped and understood.

Lindbeck's cultural-linguistic approach

As noted earlier, Lindbeck draws on the writings of the cultural anthropologist Clifford Geertz[71] and Ludwig Wittgenstein[72] in setting up his distinctive approach to the nature of theology. Lindbeck suggests – and the parallel with Wittgenstein here will be clear – that religions may be compared to languages, with religious doctrines functioning as grammatical rules. Religions are cultural frameworks or mediums which engender a vocabulary and precede inner experience.

> A religion can be viewed as a kind of cultural and/or linguistic framework or medium that shapes the entirety of life and thought . . . It is not primarily an array of beliefs about the true and the good (although it may involve these), or a symbolism expressive of basic attitudes, feelings or sentiments (though these will be generated). Rather, it is similar to an idiom that makes possible the description of realities, the formulation of beliefs, and the experiencing of inner attitudes,

feelings and sentiments. Like a culture or language, it is a communal phenomenon that shapes the subjectivities of individuals rather than being primarily a manifestation of those subjectivities. It comprises a vocabulary of discursive and nondiscursive symbols together with a distinctive logic or grammar in terms of which this vocabulary can be meaningfully deployed.[73]

Just as a language is correlated with a form of life (as Wittgenstein pointed out in relation to 'language games'), so a religious tradition is correlated with the form of life it engenders and reflects.

A fundamental element in this understanding of doctrine, and its attending theory of truth, is the concept of *intrasystemic consistency*. In part, this understanding concerns rational coherence of systems: doctrines regulate religions, in much the same way that grammar regulates language. The ideational content of a doctrinal statement is effectively set to one side, in order that its formal function may be emphasized. Lindbeck illustrates this point with reference to Shakespeare's *Hamlet*: the statement 'Denmark is the land where Hamlet lived' makes no claim to ontological truth or falsity, but is simply a statement concerning the internal ordering of the elements of Shakespeare's narrative.[74] Narrative in itself is neither fact nor fiction: it is a vehicle for either or both. Fact-like narratives are not necessarily factual.[75] Only if the narrative is taken as *history* are any claims being made concerning the ontological truth or falsity of this statement. Thus the Bible may, Lindbeck suggests, be read as a 'vast, loosely-structured non-fictional novel', the canonical narrative of which offers an identity description of God. Developing this point, Lindbeck suggests – citing the parable of the prodigal son as an example – that the 'rendering of God's character' is not necessarily dependent upon the facticity of the scriptural story.

Meaning is constituted by the uses of a specific language, rather than being distinguishable from it. Thus the proper way to determine what 'God' signifies, for example, is by examining how the word operates within a religion and thereby shapes reality and experience rather than by first establishing its propositional or experiential meaning and reinterpreting or reformulating its uses accordingly. It is in this sense that theological description in the cultural-linguistic sense is intrasemiotic or intratextual.[76]

The chief difficulty raised by this approach concerns the origin of the cultural-linguistic tradition regulated by doctrines. Lindbeck seems to assume it is simply 'given'. It is an axiomatic point of departure. The 'language' is just there. Lindbeck notes that languages originate from outside, thus raising the obvious question concerning the origins of the Christian tradition of speaking about God, or articulating human aspirations, in its particular manner, or range of manners. How does the Christian idiom come into being? Throughout his analysis, there seems to be a studied evasion of the central question of revelation – in other words, whether the Christian idiom, articulated in Scripture and hence in the Christian tradition, originates from accumulated human insight, or from the self-disclosure of God in the Christ-event.

Yet Lindbeck's insistence upon the primacy of 'the objectivities of religion, its language, doctrine, liturgies and modes of action' raises the unanswered question of how these primary data may be accounted for. Where do Christian doctrines come from? How can they be evaluated? To what is the Christian language a response? What extra-linguistic reality is it attempting to describe or depict? Evangelicals find themselves in the position of being able to agree in broad terms with Lindbeck as far as he goes, yet wish that he went much further. For this reason, the most fundamental evangelical critique of postliberalism concerns the inadequacy of its commitment to extralinguistic and extrasystemic realities. We shall explore this point in what follows.

An evangelical critique of postliberalism

On the basis of our analysis so far, we can begin to mount an evangelical critique of postliberalism. Any such critique must be prefaced by a commendation of its virtues, including the following.

1. Its emphasis on the distinctiveness of Christianity, and its studied and principled refusal to follow liberalism's headlong rush into the identification of the truth of the gospel with late-twentieth-century liberal American cultural norms.

2. Its insistence upon Scripture as the supreme source of Christian ideas and values.

3. Its reassertion of the centrality of the figure of Jesus Christ within the life and thought of the Christian church.

Indeed, evangelicalism can learn from postliberalism, not least in respect of the latter's strong sense of community, which shows up evangelicalism's tendency towards social atomism. Yet having said this, three fundamental criticisms must be made, which I shall formulate as questions addressed to three leading postliberal thinkers: Lindbeck, Hauerwas and Frei.

1. What is truth?

To what do theological statements refer? In his *Grammar of Faith*, Paul Holmer sets out a regulative theory of theology which has clearly had some influence on Lindbeck's approach. Theology is essentially concerned with describing the intrabiblical rules for speaking about God, Christ, and so forth. These rules are not established by theology; they are already given in the biblical material itself.[77] In this sense, theology introduces nothing new to the biblical material, but simply sets out the structures which are already present, in much the same way as grammar sets out the rules governing the use of that language.[78] The grammar is descriptive; it does not establish rules, but simply reports back on the rules that are already operational.

Lindbeck believes that theology is concerned with the articulation and exploration of the intrasystemic aspects of Christian faith. Lindbeck here follows the tradition associated with Schleiermacher in adopting an essentially descriptive conception of doctrine. For Schleiermacher, dogmatic theology is 'the knowledge of doctrine now current in the church'.[79] In essence, theology is an enquiry concerning the adequacy of doctrines to articulate the faith which they express. The theologian is required to consider the 'ecclesiastical value' and the 'scientific value' of doctrines – in other words, their adequacy as expressions of religious feeling, and their consistency within the context of the theological vocabulary as a whole. Doctrine is descriptive, concerned primarily with intrasystemic cohesion.

Lindbeck thus appears to suggest that the cultural-linguistic approach to doctrine may dispense with the question of whether the Christian idiom has any external referent. Language *functions* within a cultural and linguistic world; it does not necessarily, however, *refer* to anything. Doctrine is concerned with the internal regulation of the Christian idiom, ensuring its consistency. The question of how that idiom relates to the external world is considered to be improper. Lindbeck offers by way of illustration a comparison between an Aristotelian and non-Aristotelian grammarian. Both would be in agreement that proper sentences have certain components, such as a subject and an object. The Aristotelian would then argue that this sentence somehow 'mirrors' reality, whereas the non-Aristotelian would hold that this grammatical affirmation has no necessary ontological implications. In a similar way, Lindbeck argues, the Christian theologian may remain 'grammatically orthodox' without making any metaphysical claims, by contenting herself with following the rules, rather than accepting their ontological implications.[80]

For Lindbeck, doctrine is the language of the Christian community, a self-perpetuating idiolect. Indeed, at points he seems to suggest that conceiving theology as the grammar of the Christian language entails the abandonment of any talk about God as an independent reality and any suggestion that it is possible to make truth claims (in an ontological, rather than intrasystemic, sense) concerning him.[81] Lindbeck thus argues that theology is a 'second-order' activity which does not make truth claims, this function being reserved for 'first-order' assertions.

> Just as grammar by itself affirms nothing either true or false regarding the world in which language is used, but only about language, so theology and doctrine, to the extent that they are second-order activities, assert nothing either true or false about God and his relation to creatures, but only speak about such assertions.[82]

'Truth' is thus equated with – virtually to the point of being reduced to – internal consistency. Yet Lindbeck himself seems to blur the crucial distinction which he introduces between 'first-order' and 'second-order' assertions. As Bruce Marshall, one of Lindbeck's former students, has pointed out, there are strong parallels between the approaches to truth associated with Thomas Aquinas and with Lindbeck.[83] An implicit commitment to views of truth with which evangelicals would find little to disagree underlies Lindbeck's analysis, even through he himself may not explicitly articulate this himself.

Thus, on the basis of the citation just noted, it would be concluded that theology regulates the way in which Christians speak about God, but does not comment on the truth claims of such statements. 'Religion' is thus the language; theology is just the regulating grammar. It makes little sense to ask whether the Greek, Latin or English language is *true*; it does make sense, however, to uncover the rules which govern their operation, in order that they may be understood. Yet it is a simple matter of fact – which Lindbeck seems to concede implicitly, even if he does not draw attention to it – that religions do make truth claims, rendering the direct comparison of 'religion' and 'language' deficient in at least this respect. If language is to be adopted as a model for religion, it must be recognized to have its limitations, specifically in this regard.

This apparent evasion of truth claims can be seen in Lindbeck's discussion of the *homoousion*. While illustrating his understanding of the regulative function of doctrines within theology, Lindbeck suggests that the Nicene creed 'does not make first-order truth claims'.[84] In other words, the *homoousion* makes no ontological reference, but merely regulates language concerning both Christ and God.[85] This case study is important, in that it provides one of the few historical, worked examples of Lindbeck's thesis, thus allowing both his historical and theological competence to be judged, in however provisional a manner. Lindbeck asserts that Athanasius understands the term *homoousios* to mean 'whatever is said of the Father is said of the Son, except that the Son is not the Father', thus demonstrating that Athanasius 'thought of it, not as a first-order proposition with ontological reference, but as a second-order rule of speech'.[86] Only in the medieval period, Lindbeck suggests, were metaphysical concepts read into this essentially grammatical approach to the *homoousion*. In the patristic period, he argues, the term was understood as a rule of discourse, quite independent of any reference to extralinguistic reality.

Yet Lindbeck appears to overlook the fact that Athanasius bases the regulative function of the *homoousion* on its substantive content. In other words, *given* the ontological relation of Father and Son, the grammatical regulation of language concerning them follows as a matter of course. For Athanasius, it would seem that 'the *homoousion*, regulatively construed, rules out ontological *innovation*, not ontological reference'.[87] This is not, it must be stressed, to say that the patristic Christological debates failed to recognize the referential or regulative function of Christian doctrine. Nevertheless, it would seem that Lindbeck has perhaps attributed to the *homoousion* regulative functions which, strictly speaking, were associated with the *communicatio idiomatum*. The grammatical or regulative functions of the *communicatio idiomatum* would seem to be grounded upon the ontological affirmations of the *homoousion*.

With this point in mind, let us return to 'Denmark'. But which Denmark? Are we talking about the 'Denmark' in Shakespeare's *Hamlet*, or the modern nation state of that name? They are not necessarily the same. It may indeed be proper to ensure, in a Lindbeckian manner, that the term 'Denmark' is consistently employed within the matrix of Shakespeare's drama *Hamlet*. Yet the question inevitably and properly arises: how does this 'Denmark' relate to the definite identifiable geographical and political reality called 'Denmark', located in the world of human experience?

How can we ascertain whether *Hamlet* is fact or fiction? The significance of this question can hardly be denied. How does Shakespeare's Denmark relate to the Denmark of the real world? And how, we must ask as theologians, does the 'Jesus' of the Christian idiom relate to Jesus of Nazareth? Has it any identifiable connection with him? Does it *refer* to him, or to something else? Can it be shown to originate from him – or is it an independent construction of the human mind?

Lindbeck here appears to illustrate neatly what Rowan Williams identifies as one of the most serious weaknesses of modern theology – the perennial tendency 'to be seduced by the prospect of bypassing the question of how it *learns* its own language'.[88] The possibility – which Lindbeck seems unwilling and unable to consider – is that the discourse which he identifies Christian doctrine as regulating may be based upon an historical misunderstanding; that it may signify nothing other than the accidental forms of historical 'givenness', giving it a socio-historical rootedness which vitiates its wider validity; that it may represent a serious misrepresentation, or even a deliberate falsification, of historical events; that it may represent a completely spurious interpretation of the significance of Jesus of Nazareth. The Christian idiom cannot simply be taken as 'given': it must be interrogated concerning its historical and theological credentials.

Lindbeck's approach to the Christian idiom appears, at least superficially, to be uncomfortably similar to Rudolf Bultmann's approach to the *kerygma*: both are assumed just to be there, given, lying beyond challenge or justification. The interrogation to which the 'new quest of the historical Jesus' subjected Bultmann's kerygmatic Christology must be extended to Lindbeck's understanding of the nature of doctrine. Doctrine, like the *kerygma*, is not something that is just there, demanding that we take it or leave it: it is something which purports to represent adequately and accurately the significance of an historical event, and is open to challenge concerning its adequacy as an interpretation of that event.[89] The Reformation and the Enlightenment are obvious historical instances of received doctrines being challenged concerning their historical credentials. Lindbeck, by accident or design, is perhaps somewhat equivocal over whether his cultural-linguistic approach to doctrine involves the affirmation or setting aside of epistemological realism and a correspondence theory of truth; nevertheless, the overall impression gained is that he considers that consistency is more important than correspondence, raising precisely the questions I have just noted.[90] It is at this point that evangelicalism directs one of its most serious criticisms against postliberalism. For evangelicals, postliberalism reduces the concept of 'truth' to 'internal consistency'. There can be no doubt that intrasystemic consistency is a quality which is to be admired. However, it is perfectly possible to have an entirely coherent system which has no meaningful relation to the real world. Christianity is not simply about interpreting the narrated identity of Jesus, or giving a coherent account of the grammar of faith. It is about recognizing the truth of Jesus Christ as Saviour and Lord. It is about the recognition of the truth of the gospel, and thereby the recognition of the need for Christian theology to give as reliable an account as possible of his identity and significance.

For evangelicalism, theology is grounded upon, and evaluated on the basis of, the self-revelation of God. This is the ultimate foundation and criterion of Christian theology. The sixteenth-century Reformation frequently figures prominently in evangelical self-reflection on account of the principle of constantly examining the life and thought of the church in the light of Scripture, and undertaking a process of correction as and where appropriate.[91] The Christian language, which is prone to historical development, needs to be periodically corrected in the light of an external criterion. For Luther and Calvin, this criterion was provided by Scripture, read and interpreted within the living community of the Christian church.

While acknowledging postliberalism's hesitations over potentially naïve approaches to the issue of truth, evangelicalism nevertheless insists that theology must be concerned with the question of telling the truth about God. That truth may take the form of a narrative ('telling the truth') or a doctrinal framework (in which a narrative has been transposed into conceptual forms), or a simple affirmation of the truthfulness and trustworthiness of God. However the concept of truth may be stated, it is firmly understood to be located *outside* the language of Christianity, as well as within it. Christianity aims to provide a systematic, regulated and coherent account of who God is and what God is like – that is to say, that there is an extrasystemic referent which functions as both foundation and criterion of the Christian language game.[92] Or, to put it another way, evangelicalism is insistent that Christian 'truth' must designate both a reality outside the language game, and the adequacy of that language game to represent it. That is to say, Christian theology must accurately and consistently render the truth of the identity and purposes of God.

For evangelicalism, this theological enterprise is to be undertaken on the basis of Scripture. Postliberalism echoes this emphasis, and thus provides us with our cue to move on to explore a second area of the complex interaction between evangelicalism and postliberalism.

2. Why the Bible?

In his highly stimulating work *Community of Character*, Stanley Hauerwas stresses the importance of Scripture in shaping the beliefs and values of the Christian community. The Bible makes normative claims on the Christian community, which that community has been happy to accept and reaffirm down the ages.[93] The Christian church has affirmed and submitted itself to Scripture down the ages; consequently, the proper sphere of interpretation of Scripture must be the Christian community itself.[94] The church may therefore expect to find its ideas and values existing in tension with those of secular society, which does not orientate itself around the scriptural narrative, but recognizes other narratives as authoritative.

Hauerwas presents an important and persuasive account of the manner in which Scripture is used within the church, which is particularly welcome on account of the close connection he establishes between the Bible and the church. Yet the critical reader is left with a question: why does the Bible possess such authority? Why is it the narrative of Jesus Christ which exercises this controlling authority? Is the authority of Scripture something which has been imposed upon the text by a community which is willing to submit itself to this authority – but, in principle, would have been prepared to acknowledge additional or alternative authorities? Or is there something inherent to the text itself which establishes such authority, prior to the recognition of this by the community? To ask such questions is to raise the issue of the role of revelation within postliberal theories of theology.[95]

The specific criticism which evangelicalism directs against postliberalism at this point is the following: the prioritization of Scripture is not adequately grounded at the theological level. In effect, the priority of Scripture is defended on grounds which appear to be cultural, historical or contractual. The role of the Qur'an within Islam could be justified on similar grounds. The normative role of Scripture within the Christian community is unquestionably Christian (just as the normative role of the Qur'an within Islam is Islamic); but is it *right*? For the evangelical, truth claims cannot be evaded at this juncture. Scripture has authority, not because of what the Christian community has chosen to make of it, but because of what it *is*, and what it conveys.

This point can also be seen clearly in Carl Henry's important critique of David Kelsey's *Uses of Scripture in Recent Theology* (1975).[96] Henry notes Kelsey's positive attitude towards Scripture, yet confesses himself puzzled by Kelsey's curt dismissal of any attempt to speak of the 'authority of Scripture', save in purely functionalist and intrasystemic terms. As Henry points out, the notion of theology as a human response to an objective external norm is precluded by Kelsey's approach, which ultimately leaves the whole idea of 'doing theology' caught up in a matrix of an irresolvable epistemological relativism.

Evangelicals have long insisted that the prioritization of Scripture rests in its inspiration, regardless of whether a given community or individual acknowledges it as such.[97] It is not my intention to defend this general evangelical consensus, or to articulate any of its specific formulations. My concern here is to note a clear tension between this evangelical consensus and the general thrust of the postliberal position, which reflects a deeper and more fundamental tension over the entire doctrine of revelation.

Furthermore, at least in the writings of Holmer and Lindbeck, the postliberal emphasis on Scripture runs the risk of suggesting that Christianity focuses on a text, rather than a person. The maxim of Roland Barthes comes to mind: *il-n'y-a pas de hors-text* (there is nothing outside the text). For evangelicals, there is something real which lies beyond the text of Scripture, which is nonetheless rendered and mediated by that text[98] – that is, the Christian experience of being redeemed in Christ. The emphasis on intratextuality tends to obscure the fact that the person of Jesus Christ stands at the centre of the Christian faith – and did so before the texts of the New Testament were ever written down. The historical and theological priority of the person of Jesus Christ over his textual embodiment and interpretation must be acknowledged. Yet postliberalism, at least in the forms associated with Holmer and Lindbeck, risks obscuring this point; its emphasis on Christianity as a language with associated grammatical rules threatens to sever its vital connection with the person of Christ.

Yet 'threatens' implies a possibility, rather than an actuality. Perhaps postliberalism is wiser in its intuitions than in its ostensive statements. Certainly the writings of Hans Frei demonstrate a genuine commitment to a focus on the person of Jesus Christ. However, as will become clear in what follows, evangelicals will want to express reservations about the particular mode of this approach.

3. Why Jesus Christ?

A further question focuses on the role played by Jesus Christ within a postliberal theological scheme. It is clear that, for both Hauerwas and Frei, the narrative of Jesus Christ is of central importance to the legitimation of Scripture as a norm for Christian life and thought. However, the question of why this narrative possesses such an authority cannot be ignored. Frei and Hauerwas, like Lindbeck, perhaps allow us to gain the impression that this is just the way things are. The narrative is 'given' and prior to the community, with the result that the historical identity of the community is linked with its founder. In what follows, I shall concentrate on the writings of Hans Frei, and attempt to explore the particular role which Jesus Christ plays in his hermeneutical scheme. (I use the term 'attempt' deliberately, in that I must confess myself to have been verbally defeated by Frei's prose, which is the most opaque I have ever been obliged to wrestle with.)

Frei's position on the relation of 'meaning' and 'truth' in the gospel narratives is notoriously difficult to untangle.[99] In a highly sympathetic analysis, George Hunsinger argues that Frei has succeeded in showing that believers' 'knowledge of Christ as present to faith is grounded in their prior knowledge of his identity as depicted in the gospel narratives'.[100] A more critical interpreter of Frei would argue that he goes some way towards demonstrating the internal consistency of the gospel narrative of Jesus Christ, and the connection between this narrative and the community of faith – but that the grounding of this narrative is neither adequately addressed nor explicated. For example, Frei treats the resurrection of Christ as an intrasystemic affirmation of the identity of the self-manifestation of Jesus with the self-manifestation of God, and explicitly excludes reference to an extrasystemic occurrence.[101] Without in any way wishing to minimize the importance of Frei's analysis, it would seem to me that Wolfhart Pannenberg's essay on Christological method shows the kind of possibilities which exist for the exploration of the relation of the narrative of Jesus Christ with history.[102]

The problem is that Frei's approach seems to rest on the prioritization of the narrative of Jesus on grounds similar to those set out by Albrecht Ritschl in 1874. For Ritschl, the priority of Jesus within the community of faith is to be grounded primarily at the historical level; Jesus is prior to the community, which bases its ideas and values upon him. Although Ritschl is innocent of Frei's interest in the specific narrative form and literary character of the synoptic gospels, the same themes emerge as significant. The Christian ethos is to be understood as the spatio-temporal extension of the ideas and principles represented in the person of Jesus within the community of faith – in other words, the 'tradition of Christ propagated in the church' (*die in der Kirche fortgepflanzten Überlieferung von Christus*). This 'tradition' is essentially empirical and historical, referring to a general ethical and religious principle or idea first embodied in the historical Jesus. This idea was then taken up and propagated by the community of faith, and made available to this day. 'Christ comes to act upon the individual believer on the one hand through the historical recollection of him which is possible in the church.'[103]

As a consequence, Christ occupies a unique position towards all those within the community of faith, expressed in a religious judgment concerning his status. Those who 'believe in Christ' (in Ritschl's sense of the phrase) participate in the kingdom of God, and are therefore reconciled to God, participating in the same qualitative relationship to God as the founder of their religion. Although Ritschl is severely critical of the Christologies of the Enlightenment, it is very difficult to avoid the conclusion that he regards Christ as an archetypally significant and unsurpassable individual, whose significance is primarily to be articulated in terms of his being the founder of the Christian community, thus possessing temporal priority over those who followed after. Ritschl argues that, although it is conceivable that another individual could arise, equal in his religious and ethical status to Christ, 'he would stand in historical dependence upon Christ, and would therefore be distinguishable from him'.[104] The concession is significant, in that it indicates that Christ's uniqueness is understood historically rather than ontologically, a first among equals whose primacy arises through the historical accident of his being the unique founder of the Christian church.

This approach to the significance of Jesus Christ was severely criticized by Emil Brunner.[105] The unique position of Jesus Christ within the community of faith, he argued, was thereby understood to rest upon little more than historical precedence. And this is the concern that even the most sympathetic of evangelical critics would wish to express concerning Hans Frei's approach. Frei allows us to explicate the significance of the narrative of Christ as 'reflection within faith' for the Christian community;[106] it does not, however, allow us to understand the basis of this claim to significance, either in its original historical context, or in the present situation. While the approach does indeed allow us to identify a *Christian* approach to the identity and significance of Jesus Christ, it leaves us with the acutely difficult question of whether this approach is itself justified.

Thus Frei declares that 'the New Testament story deals simply and exclusively with the story of Jesus of Nazareth, whether it is fictional or real'.[107] While immediately conceding the positive dimensions of this point, not least its focus on Jesus, the central difficulty becomes clear at once. *Is* the 'story' fictional or real? How could one tell that it is not simply 'a piece of hyperfiction claiming to be self-warranting fact'?[108] While this question may be dismissed as naïve by some theologians, it remains of foundational importance. The central anxiety which eventually led to the crumbling of the Bultmannian approach to Christology focused on the minimalist Christological foundation of the *kērygma* – '*das Dass*'. But what if the *kērygma* got Jesus wrong? The Christological implications of this were momentous, and demanded exploration, as the development of the 'new quest' got under way. As the writings of Ernst Käsemann, Joachim Jeremias and Günther Bornkamm demonstrate,[109] the relation between faith and history, dismissed by Bultmann as an irrelevance, became a central issue of New Testament scholarship and Christological reflection.[110] Yet Frei seems to take us back down a discredited Bultmannian route, without any due regard for its perceived weaknesses and subsequent developments.

In view of the importance of this point, we may explore the differences between Bultmann and Gerhard Ebeling on this point.[111] The differences between Bultmann and Ebeling relate directly to their assessment of the theological significance of the historical figure of Jesus of Nazareth. For Bultmann, all that could be, and could be required to be, known about the historical Jesus was the fact that (*das Dass*) he existed. For Ebeling, the person of the historical Jesus is the fundamental basis (*das Grunddatum*) of Christology, and if it could be shown that Christology was a misinterpretation of the significance of the historical Jesus, Christology would be brought to an end. In this, Ebeling may be seen as expressing the concerns which underlie the 'new quest of the historical Jesus'. Ebeling here points to a fundamental deficiency in Bultmann's Christology: its total lack of openness to investigation (perhaps 'verification' is too strong a term) in the light of historical scholarship. Might not Christology rest upon a mistake? How can we know that there is a justifiable transition from the preaching *of* Jesus to the preaching *about* Jesus? Ebeling develops criticisms which parallel those made elsewhere by Ernst Käsemann,[112] but with a theological, rather than a purely historical, focus. Most importantly for our purposes, Ebeling stresses that even Bultmann's minimal *das Dass* actually requires justification in terms of *das Was* or *das Wie* – that is, in terms of the implicit content of the *kērygma*. This same issue seems to emerge as significant in relation to Frei's attitude to history.

Evangelicalism has difficulty with any approach, whether originating from Bultmann or from Frei, which apparently sits so lightly to history. It is no accident that evangelicalism places a high emphasis on the importance of New Testament scholarship. It is not merely the internal logic of the New Testament which is regarded as important; it is the demonstration that this logic can be shown to have arisen in response to genuine pressures as a consequence of what is known about the history of Jesus of Nazareth. This does not in any sense make Christology dependent upon an 'unknown' historical figure. Rather, it attempts to uncover and explore the correlation between history and theology in the New Testament.[113]

Conclusion

So what is the future relation between evangelicalism and postliberalism? It is clear that the dialogue is still at an early stage. In particular, it should be noted that postliberalism is still perhaps best seen at present as a research programme, rather than a definite set of doctrines.[114] However, as Jeffrey Stout once remarked, a preoccupation with method alone is like clearing your throat before a public lecture: you can only do it for a while before your audience loses interest. And sooner or later, postliberalism will have to address a series of doctrinal issues of major importance to evangelicalism. It will be at this juncture that the future relation of the two movements will become clearer. Nevertheless, the identity of at least some of the questions which evangelicalism will wish to address to postliberalism is clear; several of them have already been dealt with in the present chapter. The dialogue is clearly going to be both critical and positive, and may well be of considerable importance to both the academy and the church.

Our attention now shifts to the enormously complex and convoluted agenda thrown up for evangelicalism by the rise and fall of 'modernity'.

4

Evangelicalism and postmodernism

The term 'postmodernism' came into its own in the mid-1970s. Although it had been used before then, it gained increasing acceptance and credibility from that point onwards, and especially with the publication of Jean-François Lyotard's *La condition postmoderne* in French in 1979, and in English five years later. The term has now gained wide acceptance, even if there is continuing debate over precisely what it means, and whether it can be said to offer an accurate assessment of the contemporary cultural mood. In the present chapter, our concern is to explore the contours of this movement, and assess the implications for evangelicalism in such a context. We begin by exploring the Enlightenment, to which postmodernism may be regarded as a reaction.

Defining the Enlightenment

At some point around 1750, a major shift began to take place in western Europe and North America. The period in question is known as the 'Enlightenment', which was destined to have a major impact upon Christianity in those regions.[1] The primary feature of the movement may be seen as its assertion of the omnicompetence of human reason. Reason, it was argued, was capable of telling us everything we needed to know about God and morality. The idea of some kind of supernatural revelation was dismissed as an irrelevance. Jesus Christ was just one of many religious teachers, who told us things that anyone with a degree of common sense could have told us anyway. Reason reigned supreme.

The regions of the world in which the Enlightenment gained its greatest influence (western Europe and north America) were those in which Christianity was the dominant religion. As a result, it is Christianity, of all the world's religions, which was subjected to the most devastating and penetrating criticisms at the hands of this aggressive rationalism. The criticisms directed against Christianity could equally have been directed against, for example, Judaism or Islam; with rare exceptions, they were not. The result of this frontal assault was to create something approaching a siege mentality within sections of Christianity.

Some welcomed this development, regarding it as a permanent change in human culture. The contributors to an influential work of English liberal theology, *The Myth of God Incarnate* (1977), seem to have regarded the Enlightenment as something that was given and fixed for all time. It was here to stay, and theology was obliged to submit to its hegemony. Thus one contributor, Leslie Houlden, argued that we have no option but to accept the rationalist outlook of the Enlightenment, and restructure our Christian thinking accordingly. 'We must accept our lot, bequeathed to us by the Enlightenment, and make the most of it.'[2] Yet even as Houlden was writing, the Enlightenment worldview was dying.

The rise of the movement which is now generally known as 'postmodernism' throughout the western world is a direct result of the collapse of this confidence in reason, and a more general disillusionment with the so-called 'modern' world.[3] Postmodernism is the intellectual movement which proclaims, in the first place, that the Enlightenment rested on fraudulent intellectual foundations (such as the belief in the omnicompetence of human reason), and in the second, that it ushered in some of the most horrific events in human history – such as the Stalinist purges and the Nazi extermination camps.[4] The new cultural mood which developed in the 1980s rebelled against the Enlightenment. Who wanted anything to do with an intellectually dubious movement, which had given rise to the Nazi holocaust and the Stalinist purges? In the 1880s, Nietzsche declared, somewhat prematurely as it turned out, that

'God is dead!' More recently, it is the death of the Enlightenment which is being proclaimed. It remains far from clear what will replace it. But what is clear is that the claustrophobic and restrictive straitjacket placed upon western Christianity by rationalism has gone.

The interplay between 'the Enlightenment' and 'modernity' is notoriously complex, paralleling, at least in some respects, the relation between 'the Renaissance' and 'humanism'.[5] For some commentators, one can be thought of as a cultural movement; the other, its ideational or intellectual core. For others, the relationship is far more nuanced, with there being at least substantial areas of overlap, if not a total identity, thus making the continued use of the two terms equivalent to a distinction without a difference.

The fundamental concern of the Enlightenment enterprise can be said to be to strip human beings of their 'particularities', and thus to lay bare the core of human nature – an 'independent, autonomous, and thus essentially non-social moral being.'[6] For the Enlightenment, 'particularity' was scandalous, in that it compromised the central axiom of the universal constancies of humanity. Human nature and rationality remained the same, independent of its specific historical, social, cultural or chronological location. The entire 'Enlightenment project' can therefore be understood as a sustained effort on the part of its thinkers to develop objective science, universal morality and law, and autonomous art according to their inner logic.[7] Behind the historical contingencies of religion, therefore, a universal and rational principle was to be discerned, which transcended each of its specific manifestations or representations.

The general characteristics of this approach can be seen from the 1787 essay by G. W. F. Hegel dealing with the history of Greek and Roman religion.[8] The particularizations of classical religion were, he argued, due to the political and cultural specifics of a system in which religious, family and tribal leaders maintained authority over their subjects through various forms of manipulation. However, an intellectual élite emerged, capable of discerning the universal truths which lay behind these particularities, and thus to emancipate people from oppressive religious superstitions. Hegel argued that the same pattern could be discerned in modern Germany. On the one hand, there was a pure, universal and ethical religion of reason. On the other were the particularities of Christianity, to which many ordinary people were deeply attached. The only way in which progress could be made was to maintain a commitment of some sort to Christianity, while simultaneously undermining its claims to uniqueness or universality. For this reason, Hegel argued that Christianity was to be interpreted as one of several particular embodiments of a universal religion of reason. In this early work, we can see a fundamental impulse of modernism: the desire to subsume everything under a centralizing narrative – in this case, the supremacy and sufficiency of unaided human reason.

Yet it soon became clear that this was little more than a dream. What Enlightenment writers had assumed to be 'universal' turned out to be ethnocentric. The emphasis upon individual thought turned out to be little more than a failure to realize the extent to which allegedly 'free' thinkers were, in fact, conditioned by their own history and culture. Kant, perhaps the most vigorous advocate of Enlightenment, was severely mauled by the German philosopher Johann Georg Hamann (1730–88), who had little difficulty in showing that Kant's 'knowing subject' was fundamentally shaped by unacknowledged social forces[9] – forces which would eventually render the entire Enlightenment undertaking spurious.

Our attention now turns to the remarkable inroads which the Enlightenment made within evangelicalism.

The influence of the Enlightenment on evangelicalism

The Enlightenment is increasingly a voice from the past, with a diminishing significance for evangelical apologetics and theological reflection. It no longer possesses the influence, positive or negative, it once had; all the indications are that its influence will diminish still further in the future. With the slow death of the Enlightenment has come the general discrediting of rationalism. Reason is no longer regarded as having the potential to deliver unaided the theological insights upon which the church must depend. Yet this does not mean that reason has ceased to be of importance theologically. It simply means that the way is clear to recover the proper role of reason in theology, now that the distortions and illusions of rationalism are behind us. To reject the supremacy of reason in theology is in no way to reject the real and valid role of reason in this context.[10] Rationalism is one thing; a rational faith is quite different. Reason will always have a role to play within evangelicalism. As Theodore Beza pointed out in his oration at the inauguration of the Genevan Academy on 5 June 1559, 'since God has endowed us, as members of the human race, with intelligence, we are under an obligation to use this gift.'[11] But there is all the difference in the world between seeing reason as the sole means for gaining knowledge, and the evangelical recognition of the proper yet limited role of reason within the scheme of God's self-revelation. Curiously, however, evangelicalism has been deeply influenced by the rationalism of the Enlightenment. In what follows, we shall explore the reasons for, and extent of, this influence.

It might be thought that evangelicalism would spurn the harsh rationalism of the Enlighenment. In fact, however, evangelicalism has showed itself to be more open to such ideas and methods than many within the movement might care to admit. The origins of the close relationship between the Enlightenment and evangelicalism is a matter of historical debate; there are at least some grounds for suggesting that trends within Protestantism itself were responsible for the origins of the Enlightenment.[12] Whatever the explanation may be, it is a matter of historical fact that the Enlightenment worldview, in various local forms, came to be dominant in those areas in which evangelicalism expanded as a consequence of the revivals and renewals of the eighteenth century, and in which it had to defend itself in the nineteenth.[13] Thus the Enlightenment had little impact in such countries as Spain, Greece and Italy,[14] in which evangelicalism had virtually no presence, but was dominant in Germany, England, Scotland and America.[15] As a result, a number of foundational Enlightenment assumptions appear to have been absorbed uncritically into the movement at these formative stages.

An excellent example is provided by the 'philosophy of common sense', a style of philosophy with a recognizably Reformed pedigree, yet strongly influenced by Enlightenment ideas, which emerged at the universities of Glasgow and Edinburgh in the late eighteenth century, and was associated with thinkers such as Francis Hutcheson, Thomas Reid, Adam Smith, Adam Ferguson, Hugh Blair and William Robertson.[16] This philosophy, particularly in the forms associated with Reid and Hutcheson, was introduced to what would become Princeton University (then still known as the 'College of New Jersey') by John Witherspoon, who migrated from Scotland to be president of the college in 1768.[17] Yet, paradoxically, this philosophy is to be seen as a 'liberal vanguard' rather than as 'conservatives bringing reason to the service of a decadent orthodoxy'.[18]

The development of the Enlightenment in America thus witnessed an alliance emerging between what Henry F. May has described as 'the Moderate Enlightenment' and forms of Reformed theology at the height of the 'Great Awakening' in American Christianity.[19] The overall result of this confluence was that the evangelical fervour of the 'Great Awakening' was tempered by forms of Enlightenment moralism and rationalism, especially at Princeton. The results were soon obvious. Harvard, which adopted the same philosophy, was unitarian by 1810. The theological outlook at Princeton was initially dominated by Archibald Alexander, with a ferocious reputation for the orthodoxy of his Reformed views. Yet the philosophical foundation upon which those views were built, and on the basis of which they were developed, are those of the Scottish Enlightenment. As Ahlstrom points out, if one were to read Alexander's *Outline of Moral Science*, ignorant of the identity of its author, one would conclude simply that it was the work of 'some mild English latitudinarian bent on mediating the views of Butler, Reid and Price'.[20] In effect, a destabilizing tension exists between the theological substance of the Princeton school, and the philosophy used in its justification, defence and exposition. And Princeton was to be the crucible in which the great nineteenth-century evangelical theories of biblical inspiration and authority were forged. The result? The theories of writers such as Charles Hodge (1797–1858) are deeply influenced by Enlightenment preconceptions. As George Marsden has pointed out, Princeton theology was dominated by the assumption that 'any sane and unbiased person of common sense could and must perceive the same things' and that 'basic truths are much the same for all person in all times and places'.[21]

The strongly rationalist tone of this philosophy is particularly evident from the works of Benjamin B. Warfield,[22] but is clearly evident in the earlier works of Charles Hodge. In his perceptive analysis of the deductivist theory of biblical inspiration associated with Hodge, Kern Robert Trembath demonstrates the remarkable extent to which his theology was dependent upon the 'Scottish philosophy of common sense'. For example, Hodge tends to evade the critical question of the extent to which human reason may be flawed or misguided as a consequence of sin, leading to a questionably high estimation of the role of human reason in theology. 'Hodge failed to notice how far his uncritical acceptance of commonsense philosophy deviated from the traditional Augustinian and Calvinist concepts of the totality of the effects of original sin.'[23]

Perhaps more significantly, the philosophy of language associated with the 'commonsense' school had a dramatic impact on Hodge's understanding of the significance of biblical language. Words can be known directly and immediately by the human mind, without the need for any intermediaries. To know the words of Scripture is thus to know immediately the realities to which they relate.[24] This theory of language is of foundational importance, as it undergirds Hodge's belief that today's reader of Scripture can be 'assured of encountering the very words, thoughts, and intentions of God Himself'.[25] Yet this metaphysical idea has been borrowed, along with others of equally questionable theological parentage, from the Enlightenment. Hodge's analysis of the authority of Scripture is ultimately grounded in an unacknowledged and implicit theory of the nature of language, deriving from and reflecting the Enlightenment agenda.

Such was the influence of the Old Princeton School that its rationalism passed into modern American Reformed evangelicalism.

Evangelicals, unaware of the complex provenance of the Princeton approach, were content to absorb its results, without troubling themselves to ask where they came from. Donald G. Bloesch has argued that a strongly rationalist spirit can even be discerned within the writings of such modern American evangelicals as Carl F. H. Henry, John Warwick Montgomery, Francis Schaeffer and Norman Geisler.[26] Thus even Carl Henry can offer such hostages to fortune as his affirmation of belief in a 'logically consistent divine revelation'.[27] In the end, Henry risks making an implicit appeal to a more fundamental epistemological foundation in his affirmation of the authority of Scripture, leading to the conclusion that the authority of Scripture itself is derived from this more fundamental authority. Thus for Henry, 'without non-contradiction and logical consistency, no knowledge whatever is possible'.[28]

The uncritical use of the phrase 'logically consistent' reinforces Bloesch's fundamental criticism that this tradition, emanating from Protestant scholasticism and the Old Princeton School, places a questionably high 'confidence in the capacity of reason to judge the truth of revelation.' What logic is to be allowed this central role? Whose rationality provides the basis of scriptural authority?

The danger of this approach will be obvious. Not only does it reduce Scripture to 'a code book of theological ordinances';[29] it opens the way to making the truth of divine revelation dependent on the judgments of fallen human reason. Evangelicals, of all people, cannot allow revelation to be imprisoned within the flawed limits of sinful human reason. Whatever the extent to which the human mind is noetically compromised by sin, it is imperative that those finite and fallen human minds should not be permitted to be the judges of what is and what is not divine revelation. How can theology so willingly allow itself to be imprisoned by logicians? Modern evangelicalism has no desire to follow the path of 'evangelical rationalism', which arose in the second half of the sixteenth century as evangelical writers sought to achieve cultural acceptability and credibility by allowing extra-biblical norms to validate or judge the scriptural witness. Yet this is the effect (although not, I am convinced, the intention) of the strategy proposed by Henry.

The serious consequences of such a development have long been recognized within Christian theology. Writing in the third century, Tertullian pointed out the danger of grounding or judging the gospel in what passed for human wisdom.[30] An excellent case study, illustrating the grave consequences of talking loosely about the 'logical nature' of divine revelation is provided by the doctrine of the two natures of Christ – in other words, the definitive Christian teaching that Christ is both divine and human. This foundational Christian doctrine, to which evangelicalism is fiercely committed, has regularly been criticized as 'illogical' by secular philosophers. Even in the patristic period, such philosophers were quick to point out this alleged logical flaw in the doctrine.

Those criticisms were intensified at the time of the Enlightenment, with many critics of traditional Christianity following Spinoza in declaring that talk of Jesus as being both God and man made about as much logical sense as talking about a square circle. Henry renders evangelicalism intensely – and needlessly – vulnerable at this point. Indeed, some evangelicals have even developed 'one-nature' Christologies in response to the rationalist pressure, here endorsed by Henry, to conform to 'logic', despite the seriously unorthodox consequences of this move.[31] Yet why should evangelicals feel under any such pressure to conform to the highly questionable dictates of the limits of fallen human reason? And how often has it been pointed out, even by secular philosophers, that 'logic is the enemy of truth'?

If divine revelation appears to be logically inconsistent on occasion (as it undoubtedly does: witness the doctrine of the two natures of Christ), this cannot be taken to mean that the doctrine in question is wrong, or that the doctrine is not divine revelation on account of its 'illogical' character. Rather, this merely illustrates the fact that fallen human reason cannot fully comprehend the majesty of God. This point was made regularly by Christian writers as diverse as Thomas Aquinas and John Calvin.

Evangelicalism, if it were to follow Henry's lead at this juncture, would set itself on the road that inevitably allows fallen human reason to judge God's revelation, or become its ultimate foundation. This is a road which evangelicalism cannot allow itself to take, even if it did once offer a short-term apologetic advantage within a culture which accepted the Enlightenment worldview. But that was yesterday. Today, evangelicalism is free to avoid the false lure of foundationalism, and to maintain the integrity of divine revelation on its own terms and in its own categories. Let Scripture be Scripture!

The theological style adopted by Henry also gives the impression of preferring to deal with general principles or 'objective facts' (a characteristic Enlightenment notion) rather than with the historical narrative of revelation.[32] Henry insists, in true Enlightenment fashion, that each and every aspect of the Bible may be reduced to first principles or logical axioms. 'Regardless of the parables, allegories, emotive phrases and rhetorical questions used by these [biblical] writers, their literary devices have a logical point which can be propositionally formulated and is objectively true or false.'[33] Henry adopts an approach which Hans Frei discerned as characteristic of rationalism: the extraction of logical propositional statements from an essentially narrative piece of writing.

It is, then, clear that a cluster of significant evangelical writers have, implicitly or explicitly, drawn on assumptions associated with the Enlightenment, rather than the Christian tradition. There is an obvious and important parallel here with the development of Christian theology during the patristic period, in which a confident and growing church expanded from its original Palestinian context into a more intellectually sophisticated context, dominated by the ideas of secular Greek philosophy. It must be stressed that the extent to which this happened and its precise implications for Christian theology remain disputed.[34] Nevertheless, there is widespread agreement that early Christian theology stole some of the clothes of Greek philosophy in order to ensure that it received a hearing in the Hellenistic world.[35] While the initial concerns may have been apologetic – that is, to gain a hearing for the gospel from a secular audience – it seems that the 'dialogue' ended up with Christianity being decisively influenced by the ideas and worldviews of those it sought to address.

It is tempting to argue that this represents a capitulation on the part of Christian theology to Greek philosophy, provoking

Tertullian's celebrated outburst: 'What is there in common between Athens and Jerusalem? between the Academy and the church?'[36] However, a more sensitive reading of the sources suggests a more significant – and potentially more worrying – explanation of developments. Christian theologians of the patristic period seem to have assumed that certain ideas and methods were self-evidently correct, and did not require justification. It was therefore entirely natural and proper to incorporate these 'neutral' insights into theology. More than that; as they were shared by all thinking people, they could act initially as the basis of an apologetic strategy, and subsequently as the foundation of a coherent Christian theology. On the basis of the perceived 'neutrality' and 'universality' of Greek philosophical ideas, Christian theology thus became increasingly enmeshed in a series of intellectual adventures which brought it further and further away from the gospel of the New Testament.

Evangelicalism has been affected in much the same way by the Enlightenment. Certain central Enlightenment ideas appear to have been uncritically taken on board by some evangelicals, with the result that part of the movement runs the risk of becoming a secret prisoner of a secular outlook which is now dying before our eyes. Evangelicals are under an absolute obligation to ensure that their central ideas are Scripture-based, not the result of the influence of the Enlightenment. To fail to do so is to allow ideas and values originating from outside the Christian faith to exercise a controlling influence within in – and thus inevitably to increase the degree to which theology is culturally conditioned.

In what ways does this continuing influence of the Enlightenment show itself? Four areas may be identified, as follows.

1. The nature of Scripture

There is a tendency within evangelicalism to treat Scripture as simply a sourcebook of Christian doctrines, and to overlook, suppress or deny its narrative character. We have already discussed the work of Hans Frei (see pp. 105–106), who argues that one of the most distinctive features of biblical hermeneutics during the period of the Enlightenment has been to deny its narrative character, or to treat it as something of an embarrassment which is best dealt with by extracting whatever conceptual information may be had.[37] In particular, Frei traces the development of this trend to reduce the meaning of Scripture to 'a grammatically and logically sound propositional statement' to the continuing influence of the philosophy of John Locke during the eighteenth century.[38] The general tendency to treat Scripture as a source-book of purely propositional truths may be argued to rest particularly on the Old Princeton School, especially the writings of Charles Hodge and Benjamin B. Warfield, in which the influence of Enlightenment presuppositions is particularly noticeable.

Happily, evangelicalism is now gradually beginning to purge itself of this dubious vestige of the Enlightenment,[39] and moving towards a position which is much more sensitive to the nature of Scripture itself. For example, there is increased sensitively to the role of narratives, particularly in the Old Testament, in which the biblical narratives can be seen to build up to give a cumulative account of the nature and character of God.[40] Instead of forcing Scripture into a mould dictated by the concerns of the Enlightenment, evangelicalism can dedicate itself to allowing Scripture to be *Scripture*.

2. Spirituality

There is a tendency to regard spirituality in terms of understanding the biblical text – that is, to reading it, making sense of its words and ideas, and understanding its historical background and its meaning for today. The emphasis continues to be on reason. Yet we need to reach behind the Enlightenment, and recover older and more authentic evangelical approaches to spirituality, such as those found in writers such as Jonathan Edwards, or John and Charles Wesley. The strongly rationalist ethos of the Enlightenment was often reflected in what might be styled as a spiritual embargo on any kind of emotional involvement with Scripture, or any use of the human faculty of imagination – two approaches to the reading of Scripture which earlier evangelicalism had treasured.

It is widely accepted that Protestantism, in all its forms, was influenced by the rationalism of the Enlightenment to a far greater extent than, for example, Roman Catholicism or Eastern Orthodoxy. This has had a devastating impact on evangelical spirituality, and placed it at a serious disadvantage in relation to the spirituality of both Roman Catholicism and Eastern Orthodoxy. The Enlightenment forced evangelicalism into adopting approaches to spirituality which have resulted in rather cool, detached, and rational approaches to Scripture. The traditional 'Quiet Time' has been deeply influenced by this outlook.[41]

Yet the Enlightenment is over. We need to purge rationalism from within evangelicalism. And that means recovering the relational, emotional and imaginative aspects of biblical spirituality, which the Enlightenment declared to be improper. As Martin Luther constantly insisted, Christianity is concerned with *totus homo*, the 'entire human person', not just the human mind. In this, Luther was doing nothing more than stressing the importance of maintaining a biblical understanding of human nature in every aspect of Christian living.

The Australian writer Robert Banks points out the implications for spirituality of this biblical view of human nature when he notes that spirituality concerns 'not only our spirit – also our minds, wills, imaginations, feelings and bodies'. This insight was familiar to the evangelical tradition before the Enlightenment. It is high time we rediscovered it. For Banks, spirituality is about 'the character and quality of our life with God, among fellow-Christians and in the world'. Banks deliberately avoids two inadequate approaches to spirituality, the first of which is purely intellectual or cerebral, engaging the mind and nothing else, and the second of which is purely interiorized, bearing no relation to the realities of everyday life or to the truths of Scripture. We have a lot of lost ground to make up here. But it can be done. We can reclaim our own heritage again, by retrieving evangelical approaches to spirituality which were suppressed by the Enlightenment, but which are of vital importance today.

3. Apologetics

In relation to apologetics, evangelicalism has shown itself to be willing to operate within the Enlightenment paradigm of a universal human rationality, such as that which influenced John Locke's classic text of rationalist apologetics, *The Reasonableness of Christianity* (1695). On the basis of the highly questionable assumption that 'everyone agrees what is reasonable,' the rational credentials of the Christian faith are set forth. This approach, however, has shown itself to be deeply flawed in two respects. First, it assumes that the appeal of Christianity is purely rational; second, it rests upon a network of universalizing assumptions which fail to relate to the strongly particularizing environments in which the gospel must be proclaimed at the global level. As evangelicalism has expanded far beyond its traditional English-speaking western homelands, these difficulties are becoming especially evident. And even in its traditional homelands, the Enlightenment has largely given way to postmodern outlooks.

This has had significant implications for evangelical apologetics in the postmodern context (which no longer accepts the fundamental Enlightenment assumption of a universal human rationality), and in non-western contexts (where the 'universal' reason in question turns out to be uncompromisingly western). As a result, much evangelical apologetics is unable to function effectively in these two significant contexts. In the case of postmodernism, evangelicalism finds that its foundational assumption of universal categories of evidence and rationality is rejected from the outset, thereby preventing an effective presentation of the gospel in such a context. In the case of non-western contexts, the evangelical is obliged to convert an audience to western modes of thinking before the credibility of the gospel can be articulated. Yet where in the New Testament is the *credibility* or the *communicability* of the gospel made dependent on non-Christian beliefs in such a way? Evangelicalism needs to allow its approach to evangelism to be reshaped and fashioned by the New Testament, rather than the outmoded presuppositions of a now defunct Enlightenment. There is a serious danger that evangelicalism may simply prolong the influence of the Enlightenment by a continuing uncritical endorsement of some of its leading presuppositions and values, of which at least some are potentially hostile to the evangelical ethos.

4. Evangelism

Finally, in relation to evangelism, evangelicalism has shown itself to be vulnerable to a form of rationalism. Evangelism, on the basis of an Enlightenment worldview, is about persuading people of the *truth* of the gospel – with that crucial word 'truth' being understood in a strongly rational manner as 'propositional correctness'. Evangelism thus concerns the proclamation of the cognitive truth of the gospel, with a demand for its acceptance. There are a number of difficulties in this approach, most significantly in relation to the concept of 'truth' itself. A non-biblical concept of 'truth', defined by Cartesian rather than Christian considerations, comes to exercise a controlling function.[42] When the New Testament affirms that Jesus Christ is the 'truth' (Jn. 14:6), it does not intend us to understand merely that Christ is propositionally correct. 'Truth' in this context clearly has personal as well as cognitive aspects.

Evangelicalism needs to rediscover the richness and distinctiveness of the biblical concept of truth.[43] The fundamental association of the Hebrew root normally translated as 'truth' or 'true' (as in 'the true God') is 'something which can be relied upon', or 'someone who can be trusted'.[44] There are clear parallels here with the biblical notion of 'righteousness', which has little to do with Enlightenment notions of personal morality, but relates essentially to covenant faithfulness.[45] The notion of personal trustworthiness, so magnificently articulated in Martin Luther's distinctive concept of faith as *fiducia* ('confidence'), must be regarded as foundational to any authentically biblical concept of truth. Evangelism is the proclamation and commendation of the trustworthiness of God and the gospel. It is a travesty of the biblical idea of 'truth' to equate it with the Enlightenment notion of conceptual or propositional correspondence, or the derived view of evangelism as the proclamation of the propositional correctness of Christian doctrine.

This deficient concept of evangelism opens the way to the types of rationalism and formalism which have destroyed the vitality of Christian faith in the past. Faith comes to mean little more than intellectual assent to propositions, losing the vital and dynamic connection with the person of Jesus Christ, who, for Christians, alone *is* the truth. The statements of John's gospel must be taken with the utmost seriousness: Jesus does not merely show us the truth, or tell us the truth; *he is the truth* – and any concept of 'truth' which is unable to comprehend the fact that truth is personal is to be treated with intense suspicion by evangelicals.

'Truth', in the New Testament sense of the term, is not abstract or purely objective; it is personal, and involves the transformation of the entire existence of those who apprehend it and are themselves apprehended by it. It is necessary here to rediscover the full richness of the biblical concept of truth, and to rescue evangelism from this truncated and secularized notion of truth. In particular, the *covenantal* dimensions of the biblical concept of truth should be appreciated. The Danish philosopher Søren Kierkegaard went some considerable way towards recovering the biblical associations of truth, not least in his insistence that to know the truth is to be known by the truth. 'Truth' is something which affects our inner being, as we become involved in 'an appropriation process of the most passionate inwardness'.[46] This is in no sense to deny or to de-emphasize the cognitive aspects of Christian theology. It is merely to observe that there is more to theology than cerebralized information. A theology which touches the mind, leaving the heart unaffected, is no true Christian theology.

To treat evangelism simply as the proclamation of an 'objectively true' gospel is to do serious violence to the New Testament concept of the proclamation of Christ – not propositions about Christ, but the full person and work of Christ himself. The concept of the 'love of God', so central to the New Testament, reminds us that evangelism is about the proclamation of an objective truth with the expectation that this will give rise to a subjective response – that is to say, a response which involves the heart, mind and total being of those who hear it. The Enlightenment notions of 'truth' and 'knowledge', as critics such as Kierkegaard pointed out with such vigour, fail to engage with human nature in all its fullness, and focus instead on a purely cerebral 'faith', devoid of emotion and transformation.

The concept of knowledge found in the writings of John Calvin represents a far more reliable guide to modern evangelicalism. John Mackay, a leading North American exponent of the significance of John Calvin, wrote as follows of his achievement:

> A system of religious thought and a form of church organization, which were created by a man whose heart was set on fire, cannot be true to their nature unless the reality of a life inflamed with a passion for God and accustomed to communion with God is given a central place. For deep in the heart of Calvinism, and in Presbyterianism in its truest and most classical form, resides a profound piety, that is, a personal experience of God linked to a passionate devotion to God.[47]

All these elements must find their way into a responsible evangelical approach to evangelism. The Johannine affirmation that Jesus Christ *is* the truth is a reminder that a purely propositional approach to Scripture or evangelism is seriously impoverished and inadequate. Evangelism is discourse concerned to present the person of Jesus Christ, in all his fullness, to his world, in order that it may be refashioned and renewed after his likeness.

In the light of this analysis, it will be evident that evangelicalism is under an obligation to ensure that it does not remain a secret prisoner to rationalism. Appeals to 'common sense' all too often amount to the naïve acceptance of a rationalist worldview, in which values and rationalities from outside the Christian faith come to exercise a normative role within it.

The death of modernity

Postmodernity is a vague and ill-defined notion, which perhaps could be described at one level as the general intellectual outlook arising after the collapse of modernity.[48] Although there are those who maintain that modernity is still alive and active, this attitude is becoming increasingly rare. Modernity believed in a world which, in principle, could be understood and mastered. Postmodernity not merely tends to regard the world as ultimately being beyond either comprehension or mastery; it regards such comprehension and mastery as being, in any case, immoral. And so, in the telling phrase of Alan Wilde, 'a world in need for mending is superseded by one beyond repair'.[49] Postmodernism is characterized by its fundamental disillusionment with the great themes of modernity, which it tellingly places within an insulating sceptical battery of quotation marks. Even at the level of their orthography, postmodern writings on 'truth', 'reason', 'justice' or 'reality' make it clear that what were once regarded as universals are now treated as outmoded and questionable. As cultural analyst Os Guinness remarks:

> Where modernism was a manifesto of human self-confidence and self-congratulation, postmodernism is a confession of modesty, if not despair. There is no truth; only truths. There is no grand reason; only reasons. There is no privileged civilization (or culture, belief, norm and style); only a multiplicity of cultures, beliefs, norms and styles. There is no universal justice; only interests and the competition of interest groups. There is no grand narrative of human progress; only countless stories of where people and their cultures are now. There is no simple reality or any grand objectivity of universal, detached knowledge; only a ceaseless representation of everything in terms of everything else.[50]

The trauma of the Holocaust is now generally seen as a powerful and shocking indictment of the pretensions and delusions of modernity.[51] There has been a general collapse of confidence in the Enlightenment trust in the power of reason to provide foundations for a universally valid knowledge of the world, including God. Reason fails to deliver a morality suited to the real world in which we live. And with this collapse in confidence in universal and necessary criteria of truth, relativism and pluralism have flourished. As Jean-François Lyotard declared, postmodernism 'refines our sensitivity to differences and reinforces our ability to tolerate the incommensurable'.[52] The implication is clear: postmodernism eliminates the urge to universalize by creating an environment in which incompatible differences can be tolerated. On a postmodern reading of the world, the Jew and the Nazi can coexist, without each feeling the need to generate an ideology which demands the elimination of the other.

The modernist tendency towards universalization and uniformity can be seen particularly well in the field of architecture. The ideology of design associated with modernism is based, at least in part, on the International School, founded in the 1920s and 1930s by Walter Gropius and others.[53] The movement was committed to development on a technically rational scale with emphasis on the functionally efficient elements of buildings, and a particular use of the rectangle and straight line.[54] To those who conceived it in the 1920s, this style would be liberating; in reality, it proved to be deeply oppressive. The utter tedium of Stalinist city planning demoralized those who lived in such modern cities. As Leon Krier remarked, 'modernism has fathered a meaningless uniformity and uniform meaninglessness . . . Auschwitz, Birkenau and Milton Keynes are children of the same parents'.[55] The design of Nazi concentration camps, such as Auschwitz and Birkenau, showed the modernist concern for functional efficiency and its prioritization of rectangles and straight lines at its worst. The neatly arranged rows of rectangular huts symbolized the oppression of both Nazism and the architectural style it favoured. As Frederick Jameson has argued in his major analysis of postmodern culture, architecture thus provided a visible and tangible way in which dissatisfaction could be expressed with the relentless drive towards uniformity associated with modernity.[56]

To understand why the agenda of modernism is now seen so negatively, we may focus on two images: a landscape, and an angel. In the year 1720, the German philosopher Christian Wolff published a work with a title which could be translated as *Rational Thoughts about God, the World, the Human Soul, and Everything Else*. The title makes immediate claims to universality and rationality, thus summarizing its general theme of the liberation and emancipation which will come about through the sovereignty of human reason. The frontispiece to this work consists of a remarkable illustration. It portrays a landscape, embracing mountains, forests and towns, enveloped in dark clouds. Yet the rays of a smiling sun of reason are breaking through the clouds, enlightening the hitherto darkened landscape. The message is clear: reason enlightens, dispelling the clouds of life.

At its height, the Enlightenment and its allies seemed to offer hope for the future, whether this hope was understood in the quasi-messianic terms of the coming of a socio-economic revolution which would usher in an era of peace and justice, or in terms of the vision of a world which could be universally understood by human reason, and hence controlled by that same reason. The threat to human existence caused by the unpredictability and chaos of the natural order and the irrationality of human affairs would thus be eliminated, giving way to paradise – an ordered and structured world in which humanity could dwell without worry. As Jean-François Lyotard has pointed out, modernity has continually been forced to seek its legitimacy in the future.[57] This can be seen in the ethics of Lévinas, for example, which often turns on a 'utopian moment' in which there is a recognition of 'something which cannot be realized but which, ultimately, guides all moral action'. For Lévinas, there can therefore be no moral life without utopianism.[58]

But this was not the way it proved to be. Such theories found themselves in increasing tension with human experience of life. Paradise was postponed to the point where it became increasingly clear that it was little more than a visionary utopia. Instead of admitting its own failure to deliver what it promised, modernity kept deferring and delaying the arrival of its utopia. Paradise was always round the next corner. The vision may remain living for some; nevertheless, it stands in the midst of a landscape scarred by the debris of its failures. Perhaps the most visionary critique of modernism is due to the German Marxist writer Walter Benjamin (1892–1940), who saw the rise of Nazism in the later 1930s as a telling sign of the futility of modernism. Benjamin saw the Nazi-Soviet Pact of 1939 as a devastating indicator of the failure of Marxism, and, unable to live with the despair of this realization, committed suicide shortly afterwards.

Benjamin's 'Theses on the Concept of History' are of

fundamental importance to an understanding of the failure of the modernism of the Enlightenment.[59] A pivotal passage takes the form of a meditation on a drawing of an angel by the German artist Paul Klee. Benjamin interpreted this angel (styled *Angelus Novus* by Klee) as the 'angel of history', reduced to total impotence and despair at the uncontrollable storm which rages around him. The angel looks

> . . . as though he is about to move away from something he is fixedly contemplating. His eyes are staring, his mouth is open, his wings are spread. This is how one pictures the angel of history. His face is turned toward the past. Where we perceive a chain of events, he sees one single catastrophe which keeps piling wreckage and hurls it in front of his feet. The angel would like to stay, awaken the dead, and make whole what has been smashed. But a storm is blowing from Paradise, it has got caught in his wings with such violence that the angel can no longer close them. This storm irresistibly propels him into the future to which his back is turned, while the pile of debris before him grows skyward. This storm is what we call progress.[60]

Benjamin here reflects the sense of disillusionment with the modernism of the Enlightenment, which has done so much to lead to the emergence of postmodernism in recent years. Modernity led simply to the social, political, economic and technological means to exterminate humanity – or a large section of it.[61]

The Enlightenment break with tradition may initially have seemed to be liberating. However, as Benjamin so clearly saw, it turned out to be profoundly oppressive. What Czeslaw Milosz has termed the 'refusal to remember'[62] is an integral element of the Nietzschean 'will to power' – in this case, a determination not to be fettered by the past. However, as the rise of Nazism and Stalinism in the 1930s made clear, to break with tradition could easily amount to breaking with civilization and all its inbuilt safeguards against totalitarianism.

What has been said thus far might convey the impression that there is a fundamental divergence between postmodernism and modernism. While there is unquestionably some truth in this impression, the picture is somewhat more complex than this analysis suggests. For example, it is possible that, in the longer term, postmodernism may be seen to relate to modernism in much the same way as Romanticism related to Enlightenment rationalism – a corrective reaction to the movement, which nevertheless failed to bring about its decisive reversal or redirection.[63] Is postmodernism a movement within modernism – or its future replacement? It is too early to say. But another point must be noted: for all their divergences, both movements are directly or indirectly concerned with the fostering of human freedom. The postmodern emphasis on the absolute freedom of individual self-definition merely extends trends which were always implicit within modernism. But this is to anticipate what follows; we must now attempt to give a more thorough definition of what postmodernism actually is.

Defining postmodernism

Postmodernism is generally taken to be something of a cultural sensibility without absolutes, fixed certainties or foundations, which takes delight in pluralism and divergence, and which aims to think through the radical 'situatedness' of all human thought. In each of these matters, it may be regarded as a conscious and deliberate reaction against the totalization of the Enlightenment. To give a full definition of postmodernism is virtually impossible.[64] In part, this is because there is substantially less than total agreement on the nature of the 'modernity' which it displaces and supersedes. In fact, the word 'postmodernism' itself might be argued to imply that 'modernity' is sufficiently well defined and understood that – whatever it is – it may be said to have ended and been superseded. The problem is particularly acute in the case of literature, where 'modernism' has always been a contested notion. Does the term refer to the genre of writing associated with Mallarmé and Joyce (as favoured by formalists), or that found in Joseph Conrad's 'Preface' to *The Nigger and the Narcissus* or Virginia Woolf's essay 'Modern Fiction' (as favoured by the subjectivists)?[65] Nevertheless, it is possible to identify its leading general feature, which is the deliberate and systematic abandonment of centralizing narratives. The general differences between modernity and postmodernity have been summarized in terms of a series of stylistic contrasts, including the following:[66]

Modernism	Postmodernism
Purpose	Play
Design	Chance
Hierarchy	Anarchy
Centring	Dispersal
Selection	Combination

Note how the terms gathered together under the 'modernism' category have strong overtones of the ability of the thinking subject to analyse, order, control and master. Those gathered together under the 'postmodernism' category possess equally strong overtones of the inability of the thinking subject to master or control, with the result that things need to be left as they are, in all their glorious and playful diversity. This applies just as much to the religions as to everything else.

It will thus be clear that there is an inbuilt precommitment to relativism or pluralism within postmodernism in relation to questions of truth. To use the jargon of the movement, one could say that postmodernism represents a situation in which the signifier has replaced the signified as the focus of orientation and value. In terms of the structural linguistics developed initially by Ferdinand de Saussure, and subsequently by Roman Jakobson and others, the recognition of the *arbitrariness* of the linguistic sign and its interdependence with other signs marks the end of the possibility of fixed, absolute meanings. According to de Saussure, a 'sign' consists of three things: the *signifier* (the acoustic image of the spoken words as heard by the intended recipient of the message), the *signified* (the meaning which is evoked in the mind of this recipient through the stimulus of the signifier), and the *unity of these two*. For de Saussure, the unity of the signifier with the signified is a cultural convention. There is no universal or transcendent foundation which relates signifier and signified: it is arbitrary, reflecting the contingencies of cultural conditioning.[67]

Developing such insights, writers such as Jacques Derrida, Michel Foucault and Jean Baudrillard argued that language was ultimately whimsical and capricious, and did not reflect any overarching absolute linguistic laws. It was arbitrary, incapable of disclosing meaning. Thus Baudrillard argued that modern society was trapped in an endless network of artificial sign systems, which *meant* nothing, and merely perpetuated the belief systems of those who created them.[68]

One aspect of postmodernism which illustrates this trend particularly well, while also indicating its obsession with texts and language, is *deconstruction* – the critical method which virtually declares that the identity and intentions of the author of a text are an irrelevance to the interpretation of the text, prior to insisting that, in any case, no fixed meaning can be found in it. This movement arose primarily as a result of Jacques Derrida's reading of the works of Martin Heidegger in the late 1960s.[69] Two general principles can be seen as underlying this approach to the reading of texts.

1. Anything that is written will convey meanings which its author did not intend and could not have intended.

2. The author cannot adequately put into words what he or she means in the first place.

All interpretations are thus equally valid, or equally meaningless (depending upon your point of view).[70] As Paul de Man, one of the leading American proponents of this approach, declared, the very idea of 'meaning' smacked of Fascism. This approach, which blossomed in post-Vietnam America, was given intellectual respectability by academics such as de Man, Geoffrey Hartman, Harold Bloom, and J. Hillis Miller.[71] 'Metanarratives' – that is, generalizing narratives which claimed to provide universal frameworks for the discernment of meaning – were to be rejected as authoritarian. Far from *discerning* meaning, such narratives *imposed* their own meanings in a fascist manner.

Developing this approach in an article published early in 1986, Lyotard argued that all universal narratives, such as Marxism, were totalitarian in their outlook, and hence potentially capable of generating mindsets which were conducive to 'crimes against humanity'.[72] If people are convinced of the rightness of their own position, there is inevitably a temptation to control or destroy those who disagree with them.[73] A similar approach was taken the following year by Oxford literary critic Terry Eagleton, who argued that notions such as 'truth' or 'meaning' were intensely repressive, and were to be rejected as a form of academic terrorism:

> Post-modernism signals the end of such 'metanarratives' whose secretly terroristic function was to ground and legitimate the illusion of a 'universal' human history. We are now in the process of awakening from the nightmare of modernity, with its manipulative reason and fetish of the totality, into the laid-back pluralism of the post-modern, that heterogeneous range of life-styles and language games which has renounced the nostalgic urge to totalize and legitimate itself . . . Science and philosophy must jettison their grandiose metaphysical claims and view themselves more modestly as just another set of narratives.[74]

Note in particular the adjectives used to refer to modernism and postmodernism: the former is 'terroristic' and 'manipulative', whereas the latter is 'laid back' and 'modest'. There is here a significant, if implicit, appeal being made to the cultural norms of a section of modern western society which values being 'laid back'. But this, as we shall see, is to raise the awkward question of where those values come from. And if those values are not universally accepted, can postmodernism ever have a universal appeal? By virtue of its very modesty, postmodernism seems to be the worldview of those who like it.

The implications of the kind of position outlined above became publicly apparent with the sensational publication in 1989 of some wartime articles of Paul de Man, by then established as a leading figure in the postmodern movement. On 1 December of that year.

the *New York Times* reported the discovery of anti-Semitic and pro-Nazi articles, written by de Man for the Belgian Nazi newspaper, *Le Soir*. A scandal resulted. Was de Man's deconstructionalism an attempt to deny his own past? Was de Man himself really a former Fascist, trying to escape from his own guilt? And, given the axiomatic status of the 'fallacy of authorial intention' within postmodernism, nobody could argue that de Man had actually meant something different from the impression created by those articles; after all, the author's views were, according to deconstruction, an irrelevance. No attempt could be made to excuse le Man by an appeal to his historical circumstances; for le Man himself had written that 'considerations of the actual and historical existence of writers are a waste of time from a critical viewpoint'. Deconstruction thus seemed to sink into the mire of internal inconsistency.

The area of Christian theology which is most sensitive to this development is apologetics, traditionally regarded as an attempt to defend and commend the truth claims of Christianity to the world.[75] Apologetically, the question which arises in the postmodern context is the following. How can Christianity's claims to truth be taken seriously, when there are so many rival alternatives, and when 'truth' itself has become a devalued notion? No-one can lay claim to possession of the truth. It is all a question of perspective. The conclusion of this line of thought is as simple as it is devastating: 'the truth is that there is no truth'.[76]

All claims to truth are thus equally valid; there is no universal or privileged vantage-point which allows anyone to decide what is right and what is wrong. This situation has both significant advantages and drawbacks for the Christian apologist. On the one hand, apologetics no longer labours under the tedious limitations of the intensely restrictive Enlightenment worldview, fettered by the illusions and pretensions of pure reason. Christianity can no longer be dismissed as a degenerate form of rational religion. The severe limitations of the modern mentality are intellectually *passé*, and need no longer be a serious difficulty for the apologist. The Princeton theologian Diogenes Allen summarizes this development well:

In a postmodern world, Christianity is intellectually relevant. It is relevant to the fundamental questions, Why does the world exist? and Why does it have its present order, rather than another? It is relevant to the discussion of the foundations of morality and society, especially on the significance of human beings. The recognition that Christianity is relevant to our entire society, and relevant not only to the heart but to the mind as well, is a major change in our cultural situation.[77]

But with that advance has come a retreat. Postmodernism declares that all belief-systems are to be regarded as equally plausible. Something is true if it is true for me. Christianity has become acceptable, because it is believed to be true by some – not because it *is* true. How can Christianity commend itself in such a context, when the truth question is virtually dismissed out of hand in advance? This has important implications in the area of college evangelistic work. The Christian campus apologist will wish to stress that Christianity believes itself, on excellent grounds, to possess insights which are both true and relevant. How can Christianity commend itself on campus, when the merits of truth are not conceded?

The vulnerability of postmodernism: Foucault and Lyotard

Postmodernism has an endemic aversion to questions of truth, believing that the notion of 'truth' is at best illusory and at worst oppressive. But the need to have the truth question on the agenda is relatively easily argued. Postmodernism insists that it is not possible to act coherently in respect to the world, for the fundamental reason that the world is a collection of perpetually shifting fragments rather than a unified, stable and coherent whole. To think or act in a coherent manner is therefore either *repressive* (in that it forces order upon something which is intrinsically disordered) or *illusory* (in that it ignores the way the world actually is). Political correctness suggests that the idea of 'truth' can approach intellectual Fascism, on account of its authoritarian overtones. Allan Bloom summarizes this outlook in *The Closing of the American Mind*:

> The danger . . . is not error but intolerance. Relativism is necessary to openness; and this is the virtue, the only virtue, which all primary education for more than fifty years has dedicated itself to inculcating. Openness – and the relativism that makes it the only plausible stance in the face of various claims to truth and the various ways of life and kinds of human beings – is the great insight of our times. The true believer is the real danger. The study of history and of culture teaches that all the world was mad in the past; men always thought they were right, and that led to wars, persecutions, slavery, xenophobia, racism and chauvinism. The point is not to correct the mistakes and really be right; rather it is not to think that you are right at all.[78]

Yet beneath all the rhetoric about 'openness' and 'toleration' lies a profoundly disturbing possibility – that people may base their lives upon an illusion, upon a blatant lie, or that present patterns of oppression may continue, and be justified, upon the basis of beliefs or outlooks which are false. Even the most tolerant pluralist has difficulties with that aspect of Hinduism which justifies the inequalities of Indian society by its insistence upon a fixed social order, or forcibly burning alive a widow on her late husband's funeral pyre.

Furthermore, the attractiveness of a belief is all too often inversely proportional to its truth. In the sixteenth century, the radical writer and preacher Thomas Müntzer led a revolt of German peasants against their political masters. On the morning of the decisive encounter between the peasants and the armies of the German princes, Müntzer promised that those who followed him would be unscathed by the weapons of their enemies. Encouraged by this attractive and meaningful belief, the peasants went into battle, filled with hope.

The outcome was a catastrophe. Six thousand of their number

were slaughtered in the ensuing battle, and six hundred captured. Barely a handful escaped. Their belief in invulnerability was relevant. It was attractive. It was meaningful. It was also a crude and cruel lie, without any foundation in truth. The last hours of that pathetic group of trusting men rested on an utter illusion. It was only when the first salvoes cut some of their number to ribbons that they realized that they had been deceived.

To allow criteria such as 'tolerance' and 'openness' to be given greater weight than 'truth' is, quite simply, a mark of intellectual shallowness and moral irresponsibility. The first, and most fundamental, of all questions must be: is it true? Is this worthy of belief and trust? Truth is certainly no guarantee of relevance – but no-one can build his or her personal life around a lie. A belief system, however consoling and reassuring, may prove to be false in itself, or rest upon utterly spurious foundations.

If I were to insist that the American Declaration of Independence took place in 1789, despite all the evidence which unequivocally points to the year 1776, I could expect no commendations for maintaining my intellectual freedom or personal integrity; nor could I expect to receive tolerance from my fellow historians. The much-vaunted virtue of academic 'openness' would be rendered ridiculous were it to allow me to be taken seriously. I would simply be obstinately and stubbornly *wrong*, incapable of responding to evidence which demanded a truthful decision. An obedient response to truth is a mark of intellectual integrity. It marks a willingness to hear what purports to be the truth, to judge it, and, if it is found to be true, to accept it willingly. Truth demands to be accepted, because it inherently deserves to be accepted – and acted upon. Academic integrity and political responsibility alike demand a passionate commitment to discovering, telling and acting upon the truth. It is important to insist, not just that truth matters, but that Christianity is true.

Stanley Hauerwas once wrote that 'the only reason for being a Christian . . . is because Christian convictions are true'.[79] Princeton philosopher Diogenes Allen tells the story of the person who asked him why he should go to church when he had no religious needs. 'Because Christianity's true', was Allen's riposte.[80] Gordon Lewis's book *Testing Christianity's Truth Claims*[81] is important, not simply on account of its documentation of recent developments in apologetics, but because it firmly declares that truth claims are being made, that they are capable of being tested, and that, as a matter of principle, they *ought* to be tested. And if pluralism is resistant to having *its* truth claims tested, it can hardly expect to be taken seriously, save by those who – for the culturally conditioned moment – share its prejudices. It will be a sad day when a claim to be telling the truth is met with the reply that there is no truth to tell, or that telling the truth is tantamount to oppression.

To postmodern suggestions that 'truth is fascist', or that all worldviews are equally valid, or that something can be 'true for me' but not 'true', the following questions might be raised. Is Fascism as equally true (or perhaps we should say 'valid') as democratic libertarianism? Consider the person who believes, passionately and sincerely, that it is an excellent thing to burn widows alive on Hindu funeral pyres.[82] Or the person who argues that it was entirely proper to gas millions of Jews during the Nazi period. Such beliefs may certainly be 'true for them'. But can they be allowed to pass unchallenged? Are they as valid as beliefs such as that one ought to live in peace and tolerance with one's neighbours, including Jews? The moral seriousness of such questions often acts as the intellectual equivalent of a battering-ram, bringing out the fact that certain views just cannot be allowed to be true. There must be some criteria, some standards of judgment, which allow one to exclude certain viewpoints as unacceptable. Otherwise, postmodernism will be seen to be uncritical and naïve, a breeding-ground of the political and moral complacency which allowed the rise of the Third Reich back in the 1930s. Even postmodernism has difficulties in allowing that Nazism is a good thing. Yet precisely that danger lies there, as evidenced by the celebrated remark of Sartre: 'Tomorrow, after my death, certain people may decide to establish Fascism, and the others may be cowardly or miserable enough to let them get away with it. At that moment, Fascism will be the truth of man.'

This is an important point, perhaps the point at which postmodernism is at its most vulnerable. To lend extra weight to it, we may consider the consequences of the ethical views of Michel Foucault and Jean-François Lyotard, generally regarded as two of the intellectual pillars of postmodern thought.

Foucault argues passionately, in a series of highly original and creative works, that the very idea of 'truth' grows out of the interests of the powerful. Lying behind this can be discerned a direct engagement with the Nietzschean notion of 'will to power', with its implications for the concept of 'truth'.[83] For Foucault, there is a direct line of connection between truth and power. 'Truth' can support systems of repression, by identifying standards to which people can be forced to conform.[84] Thus what is 'mad' or 'criminal' does not depend upon some objective criterion, but upon the standards and interests of those in authority. Each society has its 'general politics of truth', which serves its vested interests.

'Truth' thus serves the interests of society, by perpetuating its ideology, and providing a rational justification for the imprisonment or elimination of those who happen to contradict its general outlook. And philosophy can too easily become an accomplice in this repression, by providing the oppressors with rational arguments to justify their practices. *Knowledge* is inextricably linked with *power*. Philosophers have allowed society to believe that it was persecuting its marginal elements on the basis of 'truth' or 'morality' – universal and objective standards of morality, of what is right and wrong – rather than on the basis of its own vested interests. The basic Enlightenment belief in the *goodness* of knowledge is thus called into question. Knowledge can enslave as much as it can liberate. The task of philosophy is therefore to criticize, in order that emancipation may result.

> Philosophy is precisely the challenging of all phenomena of domination at whatever level or under whatever form they present themselves – political, economic, sexual, institutional, and so on. This critical function of philosophy, up to a certain point, emerges right from the Socratic imperative: 'Be concerned with yourself', i.e., ground yourself in liberty, through the mastery of self.[85]

For such reasons, Foucault believes that the very idea of objective truth or morality must be challenged. Ideas – such as 'truth' – which legitimate or perpetuate repression are to be spurned. This belief has passed into the structure of much of postmodernism. But is it right? Is not the truth that Foucault's criticism actually rests upon a set of quite definite beliefs about what is right and what is wrong? To give an illustration: throughout Foucault's writings, we find a passionate belief that repression is wrong. Foucault himself is thus committed to an objective moral value – that freedom is to be preferred to repression. Foucault's critique of morality actually presupposes certain moral values. Beneath his critique of conventional ethics lies a hidden set of moral values, and an unacknowledged commitment to them. Foucault's critique of the moral values of society seems to leave him without any moral values of his own – yet his critique of social values rests upon his own intuitively accepted (rather than explicitly acknowledged and theoretically justified) moral values, which he clearly expects his readers to share.

Yet *why* is struggle preferable to submission? Why is freedom to be chosen, rather than repression? And what moral frameworks or criteria are proposed, by which this implicit assumption may be defended? These normative questions demand answers, if Foucault's position can be justified – yet Foucault has vigorously rejected an appeal to general normative principles as an integral part of his method. In effect, he makes an appeal to sentimentality rather than to reason, to pathos rather than to principles.[86] That many shared his intuitive dislike of repression ensured he was well received – but the fundamental question remains unanswered. Why is repression wrong? And that same question awaits a convincing answer from postmodernism, which is vulnerable precisely where Foucault is vulnerable. As Ben Meyer so devastatingly commented:

> The followers of Nietzsche and Foucault are passionately persuaded that truth is a mere rhetorical device employed in the service of oppresion, and say so at length. What, then, is the status of their saying so? We should give them their choice. Is it false? Or in the service of oppression?[87]

Postmodernism thus denies in fact what it affirms in theory. Even the casual question 'Is postmodernism true?' innocently raises fundamental criteriological questions which postmodernism finds embarrassingly difficult to handle.

It is now widely accepted that there is an inner contradiction at this point, similar to that pointed out by Francis Schaeffer in the case of the ethical nihilism of Jean-Paul Sartre. Sartre's fundamental point was that ethics was something of an irrelevance. If there was any ethical component to an action, it lay in the exercise of choice, not the moral decision reached. This famous attitude attracted considerable attention. Then Sartre signed the Algerian Manifesto – a protest against the continuing French occupation of Algeria. Events in the real world called into question his ethical views.

> [Sartre] took up a deliberately moral attitude and said it was an unjust and dirty war. His left-wing political position which he took up is another illustration of the same inconsistency. As far as many secular existentialists have been concerned, from the moment Sartre signed the Algerian Manifesto he was regarded as an apostate from his own position, and toppled from his place of leadership of the avant-garde.[88]

This illustrates Schaeffer's point that Sartre and other nihilists 'could not live with the conclusions of their system' – and so points to the need for the evangelical apologist to explore what those conclusions might be. 'The more logical a man who holds a non-Christian position is to his own presuppositions, the further he is from the real world; and the nearer he is to the real world, the more illogical he is to his own presuppositions.'[89] Foucault's anti-oppressional ethics would seem to be a case in point, in that they illustrate the need for foundational principles which Foucault has declared in advance to be oppressive themselves. Yet it is not as simple as this.

Foucault seems to assume that the use of force is associated only with injustice. But is this really the case? In a recent essay on the nature of cruelty, Hélé Béji notes that 'the one thing which justice shares with injustice is that they both need to be exercised with the authority of force'.[90] The essential point at issue is that people need to be persuaded that 'justice' is in their own interest before they will serve it. For evangelicalism, one central aspect of the doctrine of original sin is that humanity is radically self-centred, having no place for altruism unless its own specific interests are thereby served. One of the central merits of the political philosophy of Thomas Hobbes and Jeremy Bentham is that it explicitly recognizes that human beings are 'deficient in altruism and therefore require the threat of coercion to encourage them to seek majority interests rather than their own'.[91] Foucault seems either to define justice in terms purely of individual fulfilment and self-gratification, or else to remain innocent of the harsher realities of human behaviour.

As noted above, Foucault is unable to offer any normative standard by which one might be able to distinguish acceptable social régimes (such as the liberal-democratic) from unacceptable totalitarian régimes. This point was noted and developed in Michael Walzer's essay 'The Politics of Michel Foucault',[92] which remains one of the most penetrating analyses of Foucault's moral and social thought to have appeared to date. Walzer argues that, in the end, Foucault must be recognized as a 'moral as well as a political anarchist'. It is, of course, possible to argue that this may amount to a misrepresentation of Foucault. However, this objection raises the whole question of 'authorial intent'. Foucault's career could easily be seen as representing a sustained effort to destroy the idea that the reading of a text involves issues of truth or falsehood in respect of its interpretation. For Foucault, what the author intended to mean in a given text is of no importance; texts – including Foucault's own texts – can be read in a variety of ways, all of which are equally valid.

However, Walzer's point seems impossible to discredit. Ethics are the free creation of individuals, and do not have universal validity and force.[93] They are something created by individuals, which need not and cannot be justified or criticized by an appeal to any universal concept of justice or ethical criterion. To do so is either an act of delusion or attempted oppression. Foucault's ethics are a radical self-creation. As Richard Rorty, perhaps the most distinguished American philosopher to develop Foucault's dislike of general principles and normative standards, remarks, a consequence of this approach must be the recognition that

> There is nothing deep down inside us except what we have put there ourselves, no criterion that we have not created in the course of creating a practice, no standard of rationality that is not an appeal to such a criterion, no rigorous argumentation that is not obedience to our own conventions.[94]

But if this approach is right, what justification could be given for opposing Nazism? Or Stalinism? Rorty cannot give a justification for the moral or political rejection of totalitarianism, as he himself concedes. If he is right, Rorty admits, then he has to acknowledge that

> When the secret police come, when the torturers violate the innocent, there is nothing to be said to them of the form 'There is something within you which you are betraying. Though you embody the practices of a totalitarian society, which will endure forever, there is something beyond those practices which condemns you.'[95]

It is difficult to avoid the conclusion that, for Rorty, the truth of moral values depends simply upon their existence. And it is at this point that many postmodernists feel deeply uneasy. Something seems to be wrong here. And this sense of unease is an important point of entry for the Christian insistence that, in the first place, truth *matters*, and in the second, that it is *accessible*. This point will be reinforced by considering the position of Lyotard on this point.

Lyotard argues that one immediate result of the inherent diversity of the postmodern world must be the abandonment of any notion of a moral or intellectual 'consensus'.[96] Yet Lyotard is reluctant to draw the conclusion that 'justice' ceases to be a universal notion. Although he ruthlessly dismisses the idea of 'consensus' as 'an outmoded and suspect value', he explicitly excludes justice from this judgment. Yet how can justice be a universal value, given the presuppositions of postmodernity?

Lyotard is silent in this respect, probably aware that pursuit of this question would do little to advance his theoretical cause.

This commitment to relativism can also be seen in Lyotard's attitude to the natural sciences. For Lyotard, the natural sciences depend upon 'paralogy' – that is, faulty or even contradictory reasoning, which abandons any claim to be in possession of or governed by centralizing narratives.

> Postmodern science – by concerning itself with such things as undecidables, the limits of precise control, conflicts characterized by incomplete information, *'fracta'*, catastrophes and pragmatic paradoxes – is theorizing its own evolution as discontinuous, catastrophic, non-rectifiable, and paradoxical. It is changing the meaning of the word *knowledge*, while expressing how such a change can take place. It is producing not the known, but the unknown.[97]

This account of the methods, goals and achievements of the natural sciences simply cannot be taken seriously. As Steven Connor points out, there is a serious disjunction between Lyotard's approach and the realities of the empirical sciences.

> Lyotard paints a picture of the dissolution of the sciences into a frenzy of relativism in which the only aim is to bound gleefully out of the confinement of musty old paradigms and to trample operational procedures underfoot in the quest for exotic forms of illogic. But this is simply not the case. If some forms of the pure sciences, mathematics and theoretical physics again being the obvious examples, are concerned with the exploration of different structures of thought for understanding reality, then this still remains bound, by and large, to models of rationality, consensus and correspondence to demonstrable truths.[98]

Arguments such as these will probably cut little ice with a postmodern audience, who may feel inclined to dismiss such appeals to 'values' or 'truth' as an irrelevance, given their presuppositions.

But the considerations I have noted above are not necessarily aimed at a committed postmodern constituency. I have two specific audiences in mind.

1. An *evangelical* constituency, which needs to have its confidence in its own arguments and rationalities bolstered. These arguments will reinforce and encourage evangelicals in their convictions, confirming the plausibility and integrity of their beliefs in the face of postmodern criticism.

2. A *wider public*, overhearing this conversation between evangelicalism and postmodernism. Such an audience is likely to be dismayed by the practical implications of the postmodern dismissal of truth, even if postmoderns themselves can live with them. The considerations noted above serve to undermine the public plausibility of postmodernism, by demonstrating the incongruity of postmodernism at a series of vital junctures. If the evangelical cannot persuade the postmodern of the importance of the truth question, he or she can show that postmodernism stands defenceless in the public arena, charged with lending covert support to beliefs and practices which are regarded with intense distaste by the population as a whole.

Conclusion

The present chapter has surveyed the complex network of issues relating to the rise of both modernism and postmodernism, and their impact upon evangelicalism. It will be clear that my fundamental belief is that evangelicalism demonstrates a high degree of resilience and coherence in the face of the very different challenges posed by each of these worldviews, one of which seeks to justify totalization, and the other fragmentation.

In the past, evangelicalism was confronted with the challenge of modernity. It chose, for reasons which it regarded as convincing, to meet this challenge using the methods and assumptions of its rival. Evangelicalism, perhaps having gained the impression during the nineteenth century that modernity was here to stay, allowed itself to incorporate several critical aspects of the modern worldview into its apologetic strategy, and gives at least some indication of having allowed them also to exert a degree of covert influence upon its theological methods. The time has come for evangelicalism to purge itself of the remaining foundational influences of the Enlightenment, not simply because the Enlightenment is over, but because of the danger of allowing ideas whose origins and legitimation lie outside the Christian gospel to exercise a decisive influence on that gospel. Evangelicalism has yet to complete the apologetic and theological adjustment to the decline of modernity; this task remains a priority for the movement.[99]

Yet the slow if inexorable demise of moderity does not mean that evangelicalism need take on board the postmodern agenda. Indeed, evangelicalism provides a significant vantage-point from which to critique aspects of the postmodern worldview, not least its apparent over-reaction to the Enlightenment emphasis on truth. Truth remains a matter which is of passionate importance to evangelicalism, even if there is considerable cultural pressure in western society to conform to its prevailing 'my view is as good as yours' outlook. That pressure is perhaps most intensely focused and experienced in relation to the issues raised by religious pluralism, to which we now turn.

5

Evangelicalism and religious pluralism

Evangelicalism is adamant that the Christian gospel is unique, and cannot be confused or identified with any other religion or philosophy of life. This vigorous defence of the distinctiveness of the gospel, which is rigorously grounded in a set of coherent Christological affirmations concerning the uniqueness of the person and work of Jesus Christ, is regarded with hostility by many, on account of its negative implications for the liberal attempt to treat all religions as essentially identical (despite their superficial differences) and equally valid outlooks on life.

It is often suggested that the issue of religious pluralism is something new, which introduced hitherto unimagined difficulties in the path of Christian claims, particularly those concerning the uniqueness and finality of Jesus Christ. It needs to be pointed out, however, that religious pluralism was as much a fact of life in the context in which Paul first preached the gospel in Europe as it is today. The rise of pluralism poses no fundamental objection to the theory or practice of Christian evangelism; indeed, if anything, it brings us closer to the world of the New Testament itself. Commenting on the situation confronted by the early church, as described in the Acts of the Apostles, leading evangelist Michael Green remarks:

> I find it ironic that people object to the proclamation of the Christian gospel these days because so many other faiths jostle on the doorstep of our global village. What's new? The variety

201

of faiths in antiquity was even greater than it is today. And the early Christians, making as they did ultimate claims for Jesus, met the problem of other faiths head-on from the very outset. Their approach was interesting . . . They did not denounce other faiths. They simply proclaimed Jesus with all the power and persuasiveness at their disposal.[1]

Religious pluralism has become an issue of substantially greater importance today for a number of reasons, including the rise of a strongly rights-orientated western culture, especially in the United States, linked with a political polity which does not wish to disadvantage anyone on account of his or her religious beliefs. It is important to appreciate that a cultural issue is often linked in with this debate: to defend Christianity is to be seen to belittle non-Christian religions, which is unacceptable in a multicultural society. This point is brought out clearly by the Roman Catholic writer Joseph A. Di Noia, OP, who described his experience as one of five panelists at a recent meeting of theologians convened to discuss the question 'Is Jesus Christ the unique mediator of salvation?' Di Noia was the only panelist to offer an unequivocally positive answer to this question; the other four were reluctant to do so, on account of their belief that such an affirmation would be offensive to other religions.[2]

Especially to those of liberal political convictions, the multicultural agenda demands that religions should not be permitted to make truth claims, in order to avoid triumphalism or imperialism. Indeed, there seems to be a widespread perception that the rejection of religious pluralism entails intolerance, or unacceptable claims to exclusivity. In effect, the liberal political agenda dictates that all religions should be treated on an equal footing. It is, however, a small step from this essentially *political* judgment concerning toleration to the *theological* declaration that all religions are the same. Indeed, those who are totally committed to a pluralist worldview seem to think that it is vital to the future of human civilization to treat 'the great religious traditions as different ways of conceiving and experiencing the one ultimate divine reality'.[3] But is there any reason for progressing from the entirely laudable and acceptable demand that we should respect religions other than our own, to the more radical demand that we regard them all as the same, or as equally valid manifestations of some 'ultimate divine reality', or as equally valid routes to a common salvation?

The nature of pluralism

The rise of an ideology of religious pluralism – which is best seen as a subcategory of intellectual and cultural pluralism in its own right, rather than as a specific entity – is the consequence not so much of any perception of a weakness on the part of Christianity, but as of the collapse of the Enlightenment idea of universal knowledge. It is true that attention is sometimes diverted from the collapse of the Enlightenment vision by implying that religious pluralism represents a new and unanswerable challenge to Christianity itself. The Princeton theologian Diogenes Allen rightly dismisses this as a spurious claim:

> Many have been driven to relativism by the collapse of the Enlightenment's confidence in the power of reason to provide foundations for our truth-claims and to achieve finality in our search for truth in the various disciplines. Much of the distress concerning pluralism and relativism which is voiced today springs from a crisis in the secular mentality of modern western culture, not from a crisis in Christianity itself.[4]

Yet these relativistic assumptions have become deeply ingrained within secular society, particularly within postmodernism, often with the specific assumption that they are to the detriment of Christian faith.

Commenting on the theme of 'the gospel in a pluralist society', Lesslie Newbigin remarks:

> It has become a commonplace to say that we live in a pluralist society – not merely a society which is in fact plural in the

variety of cultures, religions and lifestyles which it embraces, but pluralist in the sense that this plurality is celebrated as a thing to be approved and cherished.[5]

Newbigin here makes a distinction between pluralism as a fact of life, and pluralism as an ideology – that is, the belief that pluralism is to be encouraged and desired, and that normative claims to truth are to be censured as imperialist and divisive. The former is uncontentious; typically, however, prescriptive pluralists tend to use the obviousness of the former to smuggle in the latter. In what follows, I shall refer to the former as 'descriptive pluralism' and the latter as 'prescriptive pluralism'. Pluralism, in the descriptive sense of the term, has been explicitly recognized by Christian theology in its formative periods. The early Christian proclamation took place in a pluralist world, in competition with rival religious and intellectual convictions, whether we consider the emergence of the gospel within the matrix of Judaism or the later expansion of the gospel in a Hellenistic milieu.[6] The proclamation and consolidation of the gospel within a religiously pluralist context subsequently continued, as can be seen from the expansion of the church in pagan Rome, the establishment of the *Mar Thoma* church in southern India, or the uneasy co-existence of Christianity and Islam during the period of the Islamic Caliphate. All of these are examples of situations in which Christian apologists and theologians, not to mention ordinary Christian believers, have been aware that there are religious alternatives to Christianity on offer.[7]

It is quite possible that this insight may have been lost to at least some popular British or American religious writers of the late nineteenth or early twentieth centuries. For such writers, pluralism might have meant little more than a variety of forms of Protestantism, while 'different religions' would probably have been understood to refer simply to the age-old tension between Protestantism and Roman Catholicism. Pluralism was situated and contained within a Christian context. In part, this reflects a general trend within European culture, particularly during the eighteenth century, which tended to generalize about 'Asian' or 'eastern' peoples, without any real understanding of their religious or cultural heritages.[8] Islam, for example, was generally regarded with both ignorance and distaste.[9] Montesquieu spoke of its spread in Asia, Europe and Africa as 'the eclipse of half of the world'. In his *Natural History of Religion*, David Hume treated 'Mahometanism' as an oppressive and intolerant religion. Serious consideration of non-western religions was thus significantly impeded by a more general western ignorance of foreign cultures. Western theology was simply not in any position to reflect on the relation of the religions, partly on account of a lack of any real knowledge of their contents, and partly through an absence of any social pressure to consider the issues. Apart from a few desultory attempts on the part of some Enlightenment writers to argue that all positive religions represent the corruption of an original 'religion of nature', the issue remained unexamined.

The new social conditions that emerged in many western cities during the second half of the twentieth century as a result of immigration from Africa, south-east Asia, and the Indian subcontinent has led to a radical change in settled western attitudes towards other religions.[10] In England, Hinduism and Islam have become foci of identity for ethnic minorities. France has been shaken by the new presence of Islam through immigration from its former North African colonies. The great cities of Australia and the western seaboard of North America have become home to large numbers of peoples from south-east Asia, so that 'eastern religions' (to use an ethnocentric term typical of the western tendency to stereotype) are a familiar presence in these regions. As a result, western theologians (who still seem to dominate global discussion of such issues) have at long last become aware of and begun to address matters which are routine facts of everyday life for Christians in many parts of the world, and have been so for centuries.

Yet often, as we shall see, this belated awakening to religious pluralism is often formulated and discussed on the basis of a set of western liberal, rather than Christian, assumptions. Furthermore, the theological approaches to other religions developed within non-western Christian communities with long histories of existence in a religiously pluralist culture have not had any impact on western theology. The approaches adopted are based on western assumptions, either explicitly stated on the part of western theologians, or somewhat passively accepted by those from such regions of the world who have been educated in an allegedly more advanced western context. We shall explore this presently by looking at that elusive word 'religion' in a little more depth.

The basic phenomenon of pluralism, then, is nothing new. What is new is the intellectual response to this phenomenon: the suggestion that plurality of beliefs is not merely a matter of observable fact, but is theoretically justified – in intellectual and cultural life in general, and in particularly in relation to the religions. Claims by any one group or individual to have any exclusive hold on 'truth' are thus treated as the intellectual equivalent of Fascism. This form of pluralism is strongly prescriptive, seeking to lay down what may be believed, rather than merely describe what is believed. Significantly, as we shall see, the first casualty of the prescriptive pluralist agenda is truth.

My basic concern is to show that such forms of prescriptive pluralism are fatally flawed and riddled with internal contradictions, and that they fail to correspond with the world as it really is. In other words, they are compromised by a series of fatal intra-paradigmatic and extra-paradigmatic inconsistencies, which cumulate to render them implausible, save to those who are totally precommitted to them for cultural reasons. My approach involves bringing to the level of conscious articulation some of the central presuppositions and methods of a pluralist ideology, in order to subject them to the critical scrutiny which is so long overdue. My anxiety, shared by many other Christians, is that some mainline churches are rushing into commitment to some kind of pluralist outlook, without giving the issue the full care and attention which it so obviously demands.

Sadly – indeed, ironically – my conclusion is not merely that prescriptive pluralism is intellectually vacuous at certain critical junctures; it also seems guilty of precisely the dogmatism and imperialism of which orthodox Christians are so freely (and uncritically) accused. The idea of a dogmatic liberalism may seem a contradiction in terms. Nevertheless, under serious threat from a spiritually and intellectually renewed evangelicalism, liberalism seems, to many observers, to have retreated into defensive positions, which it is prepared to maintain with all the vigour of an Athanasius defending the divinity of Christ against the world. A pluralist ideology has become an integral part, perhaps even a cornerstone, of that defensive strategy. For this reason, it is important to probe the foundations of that ideology.

What is religion?

An example of excessive reliance upon western categories can be seen in relation to the term 'religion' itself. The word 'religion' needs further examination. In his classic, but highly problematic, work *The Golden Bough* (1890), Sir James Frazer made the fundamental point that 'there is probably no subject in the world about which opinions differ so much as the nature of religion, and to frame a definition of it which would satisfy everyone must obviously be impossible'. Yet there has recently been a determined effort within liberalism to reduce all religions to the same basic global phenomenon.

Earlier, we noted the attempts of various liberal writers to treat 'culture' and 'experience' as universals, capable of avoiding the particularism which they felt to be such an unacceptable feature of traditional Christian thought. In much the same way, 'religion' – or, occasionally, the hybrid category of 'religious experience' – is introduced as a third potential universal, in an attempt to avoid particularity. Each of these three, however, is simply a pseudo-universal notion, deriving what little credibility it possesses from the totalizing agenda of their proponents. This is now especially clear in the case of the category of 'religion', which is widely conceded to be a false category, incapable of bearing the theological strain of the more adventurous and ambitious pluralist theologies erected upon its spurious foundation.

There is clearly a question of intellectual power here, raising the agenda noted by Michel Foucault. Who makes the rules which establish what is a religion, and what is not? The rules of this game determine the outcome: so who decides on them? The answer to this question is quite simple: the rules have been drawn up and 'policed' – to use Foucault's term, with all the authoritarian overtones it rightly implies – by liberal western academics, on the basis of a set of politically correct assumptions which bear little relation to the empirical realities of the religions.

Yet many liberal writers are anxious about the violation of the integrity of the different religions which this homogenizing approach entails. David Tracy is an example of a liberal theologian who is profoundly sceptical of such an approach, pointing out that, as a matter of simple observation, there 'is no single essence, no one content of enlightenment or revelation, no one way of emancipation or liberation' to be discerned within the religions of the world.[11] Underlying much recent western liberal discussion of 'the religions' is the assumption that 'religion' is universally a genus, an agreed category. In fact, it is nothing of the sort. In an important recent study, the Cambridge theologian John Milbank makes the point that the 'assumption about a religious genus' is central to

> . . . the more recent mode of encounter as dialogue, but it would be a mistake to imagine that it arose simultaneously among all the participants as the recognition of an evident truth. On the contrary, it is clear that the other religions were taken by Christian thinkers to be species of the genus 'religion', because these thinkers systematically subsumed alien cultural phenomena under categories which comprise western notions of what constitutes religious thought and practice. These false categorizations have often been accepted by western-educated representatives of the other religions themselves, who are unable to resist the politically imbued rhetorical force of western discourse.[12]

Ninian Smart has also made the point that much of the loose talk about 'classical religion' actually means *western* classical, and is therefore a reflection of western culture, rather than a universal category.[13]

We must therefore be intensely suspicious of the naïve assumption, common to western students of religion (and ultimately reflecting their culturally conditioned outlook), that 'religion' is a well-defined category, which can be sharply and surgically distinguished from 'culture' as a whole. The fact that classical Greek mythology, Confucianism, Taoism, the various and diverse religions of India which have been misleadingly brought together under the generic term 'Hinduism', Christianity, totemism and animism can all be called 'religions' points to this being an alarmingly broad and diffuse category, without any real distinguishing features. Again, John B. Cobb, Jr, a pioneer of Christian–Buddhist dialogue, comments:

> I see no a priori reason to assume that religion has an essence or that the great religious traditions are well understood as religions, that is, as traditions for which being religious is the central goal. I certainly see no empirical evidence in favor of this view. I see only scholarly habit and the power of language to mislead.[14]

The first step in addressing religious pluralism is to eliminate notions of religion which reflect western cultural bias. There is no place in global theology for an ethnocentric notion of 'religion', so clearly reflecting western assumptions and misunderstandings of non-western cultural phenomena. Western theology has singularly failed to do this. Sociology has been much more open to respecting the astonishing variety of beliefs within the religions. As Anthony Giddens, professor of sociology at the University of Cambridge, points out, 'religion' cannot be defined in western terms:

> First, religion should not be identified with monotheism . . . Most religions involve several deities . . . In certain religions there are no gods at all. Second, religion should not be identified with moral prescriptions controlling the behaviour of believers . . . Third, religion is not necessarily concerned with explaining how the world came to be as it is . . . Fourth, religion cannot be identified with the supernatural, as

209

intrinsically involving belief in a universe 'beyond the realm of the senses'.[15]

In short, there is a need to respect the individuality of what we still insist on referring to as 'religions', instead of constructing artificial and reductionist definitions of what 'religion' is. This is simply cultural imperialism, in which western liberal – not *Christian* – understandings of 'religion' have been imposed globally. It amounts to what Michel Foucault referred to as 'policing' – that is to say, a repressive enforcement of a predetermined notion of what something or someone should be, rather than a willingness to accept them for what they actually are. This is a classic example of the 'fetish of totalization', so characteristic of modernity, and so vigorously contested by postmodern writers (see pp. 179–196). This point seems to have been appreciated in more recent discussions, even if its full implications for a pluralist perspective have yet to be explored. Paul Knitter has noted how, in his own thinking, he has been guilty of 'implicitly, unconsciously, but still imperialistically imposing our notions of Deity or the Ultimate on other believers who, like many Buddhists, may not even wish to speak about God or who experience the Ultimate as *Sunyata*, which has nothing or little to do with what Christians experience and call God'.[16]

Generalizations may be helpful in allowing us to understand religions; yet such generalizations are only descriptions and can never be permitted to become instead prescriptions of what religion can and cannot be. The whole issue of religious pluralism has been fatally flawed by a mentality which demands that all shall be reduced to the same mould. Perhaps most arrogant of all is the (happily increasingly rare) use of the term 'higher religions' to refer to those religions which are regarded as superior to others, on the basis of western sensibilities. The use of such terms is insulting and degrading to the religions of sub-saharan Africa in particular, and ought to be abandoned. At best, they are meaningless, and have value only to those with reductionist agendas; at worst, they are imperialist and offensive.

Any discussion about the place of Christianity among the world religions must be conducted on the basis of mutual respect, both on the part of Christians for those who are not Christians, and on the part of those who are not Christians for those who are. This respect can be expressed in dialogue, which is to be understood as an attempt on the part of people with different beliefs to gain a better understanding of each other. But this dialogue cannot be conducted on the basis of the deeply patronizing assumption that 'everyone is saying the same thing'. Dialogue implies respect, but does not presuppose agreement. Yet that word 'dialogue' needs further exploration.

Dialogue and mutual respect

Every now and then, one gains the impression that a word has become overworked, and is increasingly incapable of bearing the strain that has been placed upon it. The word 'dialogue' has had the misfortune to be treated in this way in recent years. The literature of pluralism is saturated with this word, almost to the point of inducing an intellectual torpor on the part of its unfortunate readers. This fixation is understandable, given the presuppositions of pluralism, especially the unjustified (and, in any case, unjustifiable) foundational belief that 'religion' constitutes a genus. If the pluralist assumption that the various religions, as members of a common genus, must be understood to complement one another is correct, it follows that truth does not lie in an 'either-or' but in a 'both-and' approach.

This naturally leads to the idea that dialogue between religions can lead to an enhancement of truth, in that the limited perspectives of one religion can be complemented by the differing perspectives of another. As all religions are held to relate to the same reality, dialogue thus constitutes a privileged mode of access to truth.

Yet the time has surely come to emancipate 'dialogue' from the bonds of such assumptions. It is perfectly possible for the Christian to engage in dialogue with non-Christians, whether of a religious persuasion or not, without in any way being committed to the intellectually shallow and paternalist view that 'we're all saying the same thing'.[17] As Paul Griffiths and Delmas Lewis put it in an aptly entitled article, 'it is both logically and practically possible for us, as Christians, to respect and revere worthy representatives of other traditions while still believing – on rational grounds – that some aspects of their world-view are simply mistaken'.[18] Contrary to John Hick's homogenizing approach, John V. Taylor remarked that dialogue is 'a sustained conversation between parties who are not saying the same thing and who recognize and respect the differences, the contradictions, and the mutual exclusions between their various ways of thinking'.[19] Dialogue thus implies respect, not agreement, between parties. It has become an essential aspect of the ethos of civility characteristic of western culture.

The distinctive emphasis placed upon 'dialogue' within pluralism seems to rest upon a Socratic model of dialogue.[20] Such an approach assumes that the participants in the dialogue are all speaking of substantially the same entity, which they happen to see from different perspectives. Dialogue thus provides a style of approach which allows these perspectives to be pooled, leading to the generation of a cumulative perception which transcends the particularities of each, and thus allows each participant to go away enriched and informed. In the context of inter-religious dialogue, the approach is often compared to a king and his courtiers, who amuse themselves by arranging for blind people to feel different parts of an elephant. Their very different reports on what they felt, though superficially irreconcilable, can easily be harmonized as different perspectives on the same greater reality. As John Hick puts it – using, it must be noted, strongly ethnocentric Kantian categories which adherents of non-western religions find totally inappropriate – the religions could be understood as 'different phenomenal experiences of the one divine noumenon; or in another language different experiential transformations of the same transcendent informational input'.[21] Each perspective is genuine and valid; on its own, it is, however, inadequate to describe the greater reality of which it is but part.

But how appropriate is this mode of discourse in general, and this analogy in particular, to an understanding of the relation between the religions of the world? Lesslie Newbigin makes a vitally important observation which needs to be weighed carefully, in relation to an often-cited analogy for the relation of the religions.

> In the famous story of the blind men and the elephant . . . the real point of the story is constantly overlooked. The story is told from the point of view of the king and his courtiers, who are not blind but can see that the blind men are unable to grasp the full reality of the elephant and are only able to get hold of part of it. The story is constantly told in order to neutralize the affirmations of the great religions, to suggest that they learn humility and recognize that none of them can have more than one aspect of the truth. But, of course, the real point of the story is exactly the opposite. If the king were also blind, there would be no story. The story is told by the king, and it is the immensely arrogant claim of one who sees the full truth, which all the world's religions are only groping after. It embodies the claim to know the full reality which relativizes all the claims of the religions.[22]

Newbigin brings out the potential arrogance of any claim to be able to see all the religions from the standpoint of one who sees the *full* truth. For someone to assert that she or he sees the big picture, while Christians and others see only part, amounts to imperialism, unless it can be shown to be universally available, a public knowledge which is open to general scrutiny and critical evaluation.

The claim to privileged access to a total and comprehensive knowledge of reality is generally treated with intense scepticism, not least on account of its clear lack of empirical foundations, and its resistance to verification or falsification. There is general agreement that there is no privileged position from which the 'big picture' can be seen. Writers such as John Hick have insisted that the obvious differences between the world 'religions' are due to their different perceptions of 'the Real'. Yet no empirical evidence of any substance has been offered for this assertion. It makes just as much sense to say that the religions are different, and should be respected for that – or, for that matter, that some are simply wrong. Ninian Smart, who is committed to documenting the observable phenomena of religion rather than forcing it into preconceived moulds, stresses that the 'judgement as to whether there is a basic common core of religious experience must be based on the facts, and not determined *a priori* by theology'. On adopting this phenomenological approach, he argues that it is quite unreasonable to think that 'there is sufficient conceptual resemblance between God and nirvana (as conceived in Theravada Buddhism) to aver that the Theravadin and Christian are worshipping the same God (for one thing, the Theravadin is not basically *worshipping*)'.[23] Similarly, Buddhist writers themselves are intensely resistant to the suggestion that Taoism, Confucianism and Buddhism are just different roads up the same mountain.[24]

Lesslie Newbigin, commenting on the related views of Wilfrid Cantwell Smith, makes much the same point:

> It is clear that in Smith's view 'The Transcendent' is a purely formal category. He, she, or it may be conceived in any way that the worshipper may choose. There can therefore be no such thing as false or misdirected worship, since the reality to which it is directed is unknowable. Smith quotes as 'one of the theologically most discerning remarks that I know' the words of the *Yogavasistha*: 'Thou art formless. Thy only form is our knowledge of Thee'. Any claim for uniqueness made for one concept of the Transcendent, for instance the Christian claim that the Transcendent is present in fullness in Jesus (Colossians 1:19), is to be regarded as wholly unacceptable. There are no criteria by which different concepts of the Transcendent may be tested. We are shut up to a total subjectivity: the Transcendent is unknowable.[25]

Until and unless the 'full reality which relativizes all the claims of the religions' is made publicly available and subjected to intense empirical analysis, the claim that all the religions somehow instantiate its various aspects is little more than an unverified claim without any legitimate basis. Indeed, it represents both an unverifiable and unfalsifiable claim, an intrusion into the world of speculation rather than solid empirical research. How does John

Hick *know* that the religions are just 'different phenomenal experiences of the one divine noumenon; or in another language different experiential transformations of the same transcendent informational input'? How could he demonstrate this to an unbiased audience?

Discussions about religious pluralism have been seriously hindered by a well-meaning but ultimately spurious mindset which is locked into the 'we're all saying the same thing really' worldview, which suppresses or evades the differences between faiths in order to construct some artificial theory which accounts for commonalities. The deliberate suppression or evasion of differences is academically unacceptable, and cannot be tolerated by any concerned to do justice to the religions of the world as they are viewed by their own adherents, rather than in the artificially reconstructed versions of these faiths which emerge from the homogenizing tendencies of scholars of religion.

In an important recent study, Yale theologian Kathryn Tanner argues that liberal pluralist theology has succumbed to 'colonialist discourse',[26] by attempting to reduce the religions to manifestations of the same transcendental impulses, or to minimize their differences for the sake of theoretical neatness:

> Pluralist generalizations about what all religions have in common conflict with genuine dialogue, in that they prejudge its results. Commonalities, which should be established in and through a process of dialogue, are constructed ahead of time by pluralists to serve as presuppositions of dialogue. Pluralists therefore close themselves to what people of other religions might have to say about their account of these commonalities. Moreover . . . a pluralist focus on commonalities slights differences among the religions of the world. The pluralists' insistence on commonalities as a condition of dialogue shows an unwillingness to recognize the depth and degree of diversity among religions, or the positive importance of them.[27]

In addition, Tanner makes the point that pluralists conceal the 'particularities of their own perspectives by claiming to form generalizations about the religions of the world'. Apart from being untrue, Tanner remarks, this approach 'brings pluralist theorists of religion close to the kind of absolutism that it is part of their own project to avoid.[28]

It is perfectly obvious that differences exist among the religions of the world, whether one looks at matters of historical interpretation or of doctrinal exposition. The New Testament is emphatic: Jesus died on a cross. The Qur'an is equally emphatic: he did not. There are two major views on this matter within Islam. The orthodox view is that Jesus was neither killed by the Jews, nor crucified 'although it seemed so to them' (*shubbiha la-hum*), but that he was translated to heaven, with some other unnamed person taking his place on the cross.[29] The phrase 'it seemed so to them' would thus bear the sense of either 'the Jews thought that Jesus died on the cross' or 'the Jews thought that the person on the cross was Jesus'.

The second view, found in the translation of this sura in the version of the Qur'an associated with the Ahmadiyya movement, both Lahori and Qadiyani, does not exclude the placing of Jesus on the cross, but explicitly denies that he *died* on the cross.[30] The Ahmadis (who are regarded as heretical by mainstream Sunnis) argue that Jesus recovered from his wounds in the tomb, before eventually making his way to Kashmir, where he finally died.[31]

The fundamental importance of this point is totally beyond dispute. It matters decisively whether Jesus Christ died upon the cross, both as history and as theology. The historical aspect of the question is crucial: both the New Testament and the Qur'an cannot be right. If one is correct on this historical issue, the other is incorrect. For the purposes of stating this point, it does not matter *which* is correct; the simple fact is that both cannot be true.[32] The theological aspects of the matter are also beyond dispute. If Jesus did not die on the cross, an entire series of distinctively and authentically Christian beliefs is called into question. As the Ahmadi writer Muhammad Zafrulla Khan (1893–1985) commented, 'Once it is established that Jesus did not die on the cross, there was no accursed death, no bearing of the sins of mankind, no resurrection, no ascension and no atonement. The entire structure of church theology is thereby demolished.'[33] Even allowing for the generally anti-Christian tone of Ahmadi writings, the point being made is significant: if Jesus Christ did not die on the cross, there is no Christian gospel.

Here, then, is a simple case of disagreement on a matter – an *important matter* – of history. This is brought out clearly by Hans Küng, in many ways one of the most liberal of recent Roman Catholic writers. Yet Küng refuses to allow his liberal precommitment to influence the undeniable fact that Christianity is different from other faiths. For Küng, a vitally important distinctive element is the cross of Jesus Christ.[34]

We now need to bring out more clearly a decisive point for determining what is specifically Christian, which hitherto has caused difficulties not only for Jews and Muslims and the adherents of other religions, but also for many Christians: the significance of the cross as a distinguishing mark of Christians. Already at this juncture it becomes abundantly clear that the popular verdict that all religions and their 'founders' are the same is an untenable prejudice. If one merely compares the deaths of the founders, the differences are unmistakable: Moses, Buddha and Kung-Fu-Tse all died at a good old age, after rich success, among their disciples and followers, 'full of life' like the patriarchs of Israel; Muhammed even in the arms of his favourite wife after enjoying a good life in his harem. And Jesus of Nazareth? He died as a young man after an amazingly brief period of at best three years, perhaps only a few months; betrayed and denied by his disciples and followers; mocked and scorned by his opponents; abandoned by God and his fellow human beings in the most abominable and thorough rite of dying, which according to Roman jurisprudence could not be afflicted on criminals who were Roman citizens, but only on slaves and political rebels: the cross.

To deny that Christianity and Islam are in disagreement over some such fundamental issue would appear to amount to replacing reasoned argumentation with special pleading and petulant assertion.[35] Honest disagreement is no sin. Furthermore, a willingness to recognize differences removes the most basic criticism directed against inter-faith dialogue: that it is not prepared to acknowledge genuine differences. Only someone of highly questionable intellectual integrity would argue that it is true both that 'Jesus did die on the cross' and that 'Jesus did not die on the cross'. Differences *must* be acknowledged, and their implications explored.

Consider the dialogue between Jews and Christians, with which I have been involved personally. In an important recent study, the distinguished Jewish writer Jacob Neusner has argued that, as a matter of fact, there has been *no* Jewish-Christian dialogue, in that the central belief of each faith – the doctrine of the incarnation in the case of Christianity, and the divine vocation of Israel in the case of Judaism – has been evaded by those engaged in such discussions.[36] Can this be real dialogue, he asks, if there has been a failure to face up to such clear and overt differences? Why is it that such interfaith discussions seek to establish points of agreement, and pass over such major differences?

In part, the answer to his question is simple: the purpose of such dialogue is usually to establish commonalities, in order to enhance mutual understanding and respect in a highly polarized modern world, in which religious differences are of substantial political importance – a point stressed by Gilles Kepel, of the Institute of Political Studies in Paris.[37] Yet this entirely praiseworthy goal has its more negative side. It can all too easily lead to the deliberate suppression of differences, in the interests of harmony. It is entirely proper that the religions of the world should be recognized as disagreeing with each other in matters of their beliefs. Christianity regards God's final self-revelation as having taken place in Jesus Christ; Islam regards it as having taken place through Muhammed. Although agreed on the idea of a final revelation of God, the two religions happen to differ fundamentally and irreconcilably, both on the specific mode of revelation and on its content. Christians insist Jesus was crucified; Moslems insist he was not. If the religious believer actually believes *something*, then disagreement is inevitable – and proper. As the distinguished American philosopher Richard Rorty remarked, nobody 'except the occasional cooperative freshman' really believes that 'two incompatible opinions on an important topic are equally good'.[38]

It is no crime to disagree with someone. It is, however, improper to suppress or evade such differences on account of an *a priori* belief that no such differences can exist. George Lindbeck has written of the liberal tendency to 'homogenize' everything; the approach adopted here is to honour and respect genuine differences, and seek to explore their implications. There is no place for an intellectual dishonesty which refuses to acknowledge, for example, that Christians worship and adore Jesus Christ as Lord and Saviour, whereas Muslims regard the Qur'an as the authoritative word of God and Muhammed as his prophet. Both religions are committed to evangelism and conversion (to use two Christian terms which have no exact parallels within Islam),[39] in the belief that they are correct; neither regards their mutual differences as a threat to their distinctiveness. For Islam, Christianity is different – and wrong.

One of the most serious difficulties which arises from John Hick's model is that it is not individual religions which have access to truth; it is the western liberal pluralist, who insists that each religion must be seen in the context of others, before it can be evaluated. As many have pointed out, this means that the western liberal doctrine of religious pluralism is defined as the only valid standpoint for evaluating individual religions. Hick has set at the centre of his system of religions a vague and undefined idea of 'the Eternal One', which seems to be little more than a vague liberal idea of divinity, carefully defined – or, more accurately, deliberately *not* defined, to avoid the damage that precision entails – to include at least something from all of the major world religions Hick feels it is worth including.

Yet is not this approach shockingly imperialist? Hick's implication is that it is only the educated western liberal academic who can *really* understand all the religions. Their adherents may naïvely believe that they have access to the truth; in fact, only the western liberal academic has such privileged access, which is denied to those who belong to and practise such religion. Despite not being a Buddhist, Hick is able to tell the Buddhist what he or she really believes (as opposed to what they think they believe). Perhaps one of the most astonishing claims made by liberals in this respect can be found in *The Myth of Christian Uniqueness*, in which a number of contributors – such as Paul Knitter, Langdon Gilkey, Rosemary Radford Ruether and Tom Driver – assert that all the religious traditions can share a common outlook on justice and liberation. This arrogant imposition of political correctness upon the world religions glosses over the patently obvious fact that the world religions have differed – and continue to differ – significantly over social and political matters, as much as over *religious* ideas.

An evangelical approach to religions and salvation

If a naïve pluralism has gained the upper hand in the academic world, it is partly because evangelicals have allowed it to do so, by failing to articulate a credible, coherent and convincing and *Christian* interpretation of the place of the world religions,[40] and to ensure that this is heard and noticed in the public arena. Earlier, I stressed the importance of developing a framework to make sense of, and evaluate, the place and ideas of other religions. Carl E. Braaten makes this point as follows:

> For Christian theology, the religions cannot establish their meaning in a final way apart from the light that falls on them from the gospel: that is, we know what we know about what God is doing in them in the light of Christ; otherwise, we would not know what sense to make of them. Some definite perspective needs to guide our interpretations and appropriations.[41]

Evangelicalism can offer such a 'definite perspective', which is rigorously grounded in the Christian doctrines of creation and redemption. The first insight encountered by the reader of Scripture is that God created the world. Is it therefore surprising that this creation should bear witness to him? Or that the height of his creation, human nature, should carry a recognizable imprint of his nature?[42] And that this imprint might have considerable value as a starting-point for understanding the religious impulse of the human race? Through the grace of God, the creation is able to point to its

220

creator. Through the generosity of God, we have been left with a latent memory of him, capable of stirring us to recollect him in his fullness. Although there is a fracture, a disjuncture, between the ideal and the empirical, between the realms of fallen and redeemed creation, the memory of that connection lives on, along with the intimation of its restoration through redemption.

Yet the Christian doctrine of redemption affirms that human nature, as we now see and know it, is not human nature as God intended it to be. It forces us to draw a sharp dividing-line between pristine and fallen human nature – between the ideal and the real, the prototype and the actual. The image of God in us is marred, but not destroyed. We continue to be the creatures of God, even if we are nonetheless the *fallen* creatures of God. We have been created for the presence of God; yet, on account of our sin, that presence is but a dream. What should have been filled with the knowledge, glory and presence of God instead lies empty.

There is thus a fractured relationship with God and an unfulfilled receptivity towards God within us. Creation establishes a potentiality, which sin frustrates – yet the hurt and pain of that frustration live on in our experience. It is this very sense of emptiness which, in itself, underlies the idea of a point of contact. We are aware that something is missing. We may not be able to put a name to it. We may not be able to do anything about it. But the Christian gospel is able to interpret our sense of longing, our feeling of unfulfilment, as an awareness of the absence of God – and thus to prepare the way for its fulfilment. Once we realize that we are incomplete, that we lack something, then we begin to wonder if that spiritual emptiness could be filled. It is this impulse which underlies the human quest for religious fulfilment – a quest which the gospel turns upside down through its declaration that we have been sought out by the grace of God.

It is precisely this idea which lies behind the famous words of Augustine: 'You have made us for yourself, and our hearts are restless until they rest in you.'[43] The doctrines of creation and redemption combine to interpret this sense of dissatisfaction and lack of fulfilment as a loss – a loss of fellowship with God – which can be restored. They yield a picture of a broken human nature, which still possesses an ability to be aware of its loss, and to hope that it might be restored. There is a natural point of contact for the gospel, grounded in the frustration of human nature to satisfy itself by its own devices. Augustine captured this idea perfectly when he spoke of the 'loving memory'[44] of God. It is a *memory* of God, in that it is grounded in the doctrines of creation and redemption, which affirm that we have partially *lost* something through sin – and are somehow made aware of that loss through grace. It is a *loving* memory, in that it is experienced as a sense of divine nostalgia, of spiritual wistfulness. There is a thirst to have more of that which we already have only in part.

The point of contact is thus an awareness or consciousness of the past presence of God and the present impoverishment of that presence, sufficient to stir us to will to recollect it in its totality, through the grace of God. It is a trigger, a stimulus, a foretaste of what is yet to come, and a disclosure of the inadequacy and poverty of what we now have. To use Augustine's vocabulary, the point of contact is a latent memory of God, reinforced by an encounter with his creation, which possesses the potential to point us to the source through which its sense of bitter-sweet longing may be satisfied.

Here, then, is a definite interpretative framework, firmly grounded in Scripture and the Christian tradition, which aims to make sense of much of human religious experience. A fundamental impulse which seems to lie behind religious experience – the quest for the transcendent – can be accounted for within the framework of Christian theology. It is not my intention to develop this point further, simply because space does not permit. But my basic contention is that the gospel itself enables us to understand why the various religious traditions of humanity exist, and why there might well be at least some degree of convergence among them in relation to a search for fulfilment. That degree of convergence can be *theologically justified*, and must be *apologetically exploited*.

So what approach may be adopted to the salvific place of Christianity within the world religious situation? The most helpful starting-point is to consider the notion of 'salvation' itself. The Christian notion of 'salvation' is complex and highly nuanced. The controlling images which are used in the New Testament to articulate its various aspects include terms and concepts drawn from personal relationships, physical healing, legal transactions and ethical transformation. Yet amid this rich diversity of understandings of the nature of salvation, one factor remains constant: however salvation is to be understood, it is grounded in the life, death and resurrection of Jesus Christ.[45]

Salvation is a possibility only on account of Jesus Christ. The early Christians had no hesitation in using the term 'saviour' (Greek: *sōtēr*) to refer to Jesus Christ, despite the fact that this term was already widely used within the complex and diverse religious context in which the gospel first emerged. For the New Testament writers, Jesus was the only saviour of humanity. On the basis of the evidence available to the New Testament writers, this conclusion seemed entirely proper and necessary. The evidence concerning Jesus needed to be interpreted in this direction, and was thus interpreted.

This does not, however, mean that the first Christians thought that Jesus as *sōter* offers the same *sōtēria* as others who bore this title before him. In classical Greek religion, Poseidon and the Dioskouroi were all acclaimed as *sōtēres*;[46] yet the 'salvation' in question appears to have been conceived in terms of temporal deliverance from a present threat, rather than any notion of eternal salvation.

The New Testament thus affirms the *particularity* of the redemptive act of God in Jesus Christ.[47] The early Christian tradition, basing itself upon the New Testament, reaffirmed this particularity. While allowing that God's revelation went far beyond Jesus Christ (in that God made himself known to various extents through such means as the natural order of creation, and human conscience and civilization), the general knowledge of God was not understood to entail universal salvation. John Calvin stated the various styles of knowledge of God available to humanity when he drew his celebrated distinction between a 'knowledge of God the creator' and a 'knowledge of God the redeemer'.[48] The former was universally available, mediated through nature and (in a fuller and more coherent manner) Scripture; the latter, which alone constituted a distinctively Christian knowledge of God, was made known only through Jesus Christ, as he is revealed in Scripture. Thus Calvin would have had no problems in allowing, for example, both Jews and Muslims to have access to a knowledge of God as creator; the particular and distinctively Christian understanding of God relates to knowing him as redeemer, rather than as creator alone.

Calvin here expresses a longstanding consensus within Christian theology that knowledge of God may be had outside the Christian tradition. Within the Reformed tradition, the general position of Calvin has been maintained, despite the vigorous challenge of Karl Barth, who insisted that no knowledge of God was available or possible outside Christ, thus shifting from a Christocentric to a Christomonist position. The strong tradition of natural theology within the Reformed tradition points to a belief, grounded in Scripture, that God has not left himself without witnesses in the world, whether in nature itself, classical philosophy, or other religions.[49] For example, Romans 1:18-32 clearly implies that divine revelation took place in human history, culture and experience prior to the coming of Jesus Christ, and indicates that this may be regarded as a preparation for the gospel (*praeparatio evangelica*) itself.

The same general principle is maintained in Lutheran dogmatics, and is often expressed in terms of the distinction between *Deus absconditus* and *Deus revelatus*. As Carl E. Braaten points out, the Lutheran tradition recognizes a twofold structure within the revelation of God: the hidden God of creation and law (*Deus absconditus*) and the revealed God of covenant and gospel (*Deus revelatus*).[50] A similar approach is also associated with the Second Vatican Council.[51] In allowing knowledge of God outside the specifically Christian community, I am not saying anything new, remarkable or particularly controversial but merely reiterating a longstanding consensus within Christian theology.

Nevertheless, some correctives must immediately be added, as follows.

1. The Christian tradition bears witness to a particular understanding of 'God', and cannot be merged into the various

concepts of divinity found in other religions. To allow that something may be known of God in non-Christian religions is not to say that every aspect of their understandings of God is consistent with Christianity, or that every aspect of the Christian understanding of God is found in other religions. We are talking about 'points of contact' and occasional convergences, not identity nor even fundamental consistent agreement.

2. In the Christian understanding, factual or cognitive knowledge of God is not regarded as saving in itself. As Søren Kierkegaard pointed out in his *Unscientific Postscript*, it is perfectly possible to know about the Christian understanding of God without being a Christian.[52] Knowledge of God is one thing; salvation is another. To allow that something may be known of God in non-Christian religions is not to imply that 'salvation', in the Christian understanding of that term, is available through them.

3. Furthermore, the notion of 'salvation' varies considerably from one religion to another. In the native religions of west Africa in particular, for example, there is often no discernible transcendent element associated with their notions of salvation. A certain laziness in dealing with English translations of the religious writings of other faiths, especially those originating from India and China, has allowed the rise of the assumption that all religions share common ideas of 'salvation'. In fact, the English term 'salvation' is often used to translate Sanskrit or Chinese terms with connotations and associations quite distinct from the Christian concept. These divergences are masked by the process of translation, which often suggests a degree of convergence which is absent in reality. So important are these points that they will be explored in more detail.

The Christian understanding of 'God'

There was a period when there was some sympathy for the idea that mutual understanding among the world's religions would be enhanced if Christians accepted a kind of 'Copernican revolution' in which they stopped regarding Jesus Christ as of central importance, and instead began to focus their attention on God. Being God-centred, we were assured, would be more helpful than being Christ-centred. The attraction of this model has since diminished substantially, as the relative poverty of both its intellectual foundations and its practical consequences has become increasingly clear. John Hick once argued that all religions should be seen as planets orbiting the sun.[53] However, writing from an Indian perspective, Raimundo Panikkar criticizes this notion, and argues for a total displacement of 'God' or 'the absolute' from such a centre. Instead, each religion is to be viewed as a galaxy in its own right, turning reciprocally around other such galaxies.[54] In other words, each religion is distinctive.

In the end, an incarnational Christology is now seen as a serious barrier to inter-religious understanding only in the sense that the Qur'an is also a barrier. Both are integral to the faiths in question. To eliminate them would be radically to alter these faiths, assisting inter-faith reconciliation only to the extent that it destroyed the distinctiveness of the religions in question. But what authority does the pluralist have to take such an abusive approach, which inflicts violence upon the integrity of these systems? This may be a hypothetical possibility in academic seminar rooms; in the real world, we must learn to live with conflicts between such defining and distinctive characteristics of faiths, rather than attempt to smooth them down. The religions are not putty to be moulded by pluralist ideologues, but living realities which demand respect and honour.

It is a simple matter of fact that traditional Christian theology is strongly resistant to the homogenizing agenda of religious pluralists, not least on account of its high Christology.[55] The suggestion that all religions are more or less talking about vaguely the same 'God' finds itself in difficulty in relation to certain essentially Christian ideas – most notably, the doctrines of the incarnation and the Trinity. For example, if God is Christ-like, as the doctrine of the divinity of Christ affirms in uncompromising terms, then the historical figure of Jesus, along with the witness to him in Scripture, becomes of foundational importance to Christianity. Such distinctive doctrines are embarrassing to those who wish to debunk what they term the 'myth of Christian uniqueness', who then proceed to demand that Christianity should abandon doctrines such as the incarnation, which imply a high profile of identification between Jesus Christ and God, in favour of various 'degree Christologies', which are more amenable to the reductionist programme of liberalism. In much the same way, the idea that God is in any sense disclosed or defined Christologically is set to one side, on account of its theologically momentous implications for the identity and significance of Jesus Christ – which liberal pluralism finds an embarrassment. Let us turn to consider these two points.

First, the idea of the incarnation is rejected, often dismissively, as a myth.[56] Thus John Hick and his collaborators reject the incarnation on various logical and common-sense counts – yet fail to deal with the question of why Christians should have developed this doctrine in the first place.[57] There is an underlying agenda to this dismissal of the incarnation, and a central part of that agenda is the elimination of the sheer *distinctiveness* of Christianity. A sharp distinction is thus drawn between the historical person of Jesus Christ, and the principles which he is alleged to represent. Paul Knitter is but one of many pluralist writers concerned to drive a wedge between the 'Jesus-event' (unique to Christianity) and the 'Christ-principle' (accessible to all religious traditions, and expressed in their own distinctive, but equally valid, ways).

It is fair, and indeed necessary, to enquire concerning the pressure for such developments, for a hidden pluralist agenda appears to govern the outcome of this Christological assault – a point made in a highly perceptive critique of Hick's incarnational views from the pen of Wolfhart Pannenberg. 'Hick's proposal of religious pluralism as an option of authentically Christian theology hinges on the condition of a prior demolition of the traditional doctrine of the incarnation.' Hick, Pannenberg notes, assumes that this demolition has already taken place, and chides him for his excessive selectivity – not to mention his lack of familiarity with recent German theology! – in drawing such a conclusion.[58]

It is also highly significant that the pluralist agenda forces its advocates to adopt heretical views of Christ in order to meet its needs. In an effort to fit Jesus into the mould of the 'great religious teachers of humanity' category, the Ebionite heresy has been revived, and made politically correct. Jesus is one of the religious options available among the great human teachers of religion.

Second, the idea that God is in some manner made known through Christ has been dismissed. Captivated by the image of a 'Copernican revolution' (probably one of the most overworked and misleading phrases in recent writings in this field), pluralists demand that Christians move away from a discussion of Christ to a discussion of God – yet fail to recognize that the 'God of the Christians' (Tertullian) might be rather different from other divinities, and that the doctrine of the Trinity spells out the nature of that distinction. The loose and vague talk about 'God' or 'Reality' found in much pluralist writing is not a result of theological sloppiness or confusion. It represents a deliberate rejection of authentically and distinctive Christian insights into God, in order to suggest that Christianity, to rework a phrase of the English deist writer Matthew Tindal (1656–1733), is simply the republication of the religion of nature.[59] It is thus a considered response to the recognition that for Christians to talk about the Trinity is to speak about a specific God (not just 'deity' in general), who has chosen to make himself known in a highly particular manner in and through Jesus Christ. An essential part of the agenda of prescriptive pluralism is the elimination of any distinctiveness in relation to the Christian understanding of the nature, purposes and person of God.

Yet human religious history shows that natural human ideas of the number, nature and character of the gods are notoriously vague and muddled. The Christian emphasis is upon the need to worship, not gods in general (Israel's strictures against Canaanite religion being especially important here), but a God who has chosen to make himself known. As Robert Jenson has persuasively argued, the doctrine of the Trinity is an attempt to spell out the identity of this God, and to avoid confusion with rival claimants to this title.[60] The doctrine of the Trinity defines and defends the particularity and distinctiveness and ultimately the *uniqueness* of the 'God of the Christians'. The New Testament gives a further twist to this development through its language about 'the God and Father of our Lord Jesus Christ', locating the identity of God in the actions and passions of Jesus Christ. To put it bluntly: for Christians, God is Christologically disclosed.

This point is of considerable importance. Most western religious pluralists appear to work with a concept of God which is shaped by the Christian tradition, whether this is openly acknowledged or not. For example, appeal is often made to the notion of a gracious and loving God by pluralists. Yet this is a distinctively Christian notion of God, which is ultimately grounded and substantiated in Jesus Christ. There is no such thing as a 'tradition-independent notion of God'. Even Kant's idea of God, allegedly purely rational in character and hence independent of culture, is actually ethnocentric. It has been deeply shaped by implicit Christian assumptions which were ingrained into Kant's social matrix. As Gavin D'Costa has pointed out, John Hick's concept of God, which plays such a significant role in his pluralist worldview, has been decisively shaped (whether he realizes or is prepared to admit this) by Christological considerations. 'How credibly', he asks, 'can Hick expound a doctrine of God's universal salvific will if he does not ground this crucial truth in the revelation of God in Christ, thereby bringing Christology back onto centerstage?'[61]

Pluralists have driven a wedge between God and Jesus Christ, as if Christians were obliged to choose between one or the other. As the pendulum swings towards a theocentric approach (assuming that the 'god' in question is common to all religious traditions), the Christology of the religious pluralists becomes reduced to negligible proportions. Only the lowest possible Christology within the Christian tradition is deemed to be worthy of acceptance in the modern period (the awkward fact that this Christology had been rejected as heretical by the early church being passed over). If the pluralists have some infallible source of knowledge about the nature and purposes of God apart from Christ, then what is the point of the gospel? And what kind of God is it who can be known apart from Christ? Are we talking about 'the God and Father of our Lord Jesus Christ' (1 Pet. 1:3) at all – or about some different deity? An idea of God can be allowed to be 'Christian' only if it is subjected to the standard of God's self-disclosure through Jesus Christ, as is made known to us through Scripture.

229

What is the relevance of this point to our theme? Salvation, in the Christian understanding of the notion, involves an altered relation with God, whether this is understood personally, substantially, morally or legally. But which God are we talking about? Old Testament writers were quite clear that 'salvation', as they understood it, was about a new relationship, not with any of the gods of Canaan, Philistia or Assyria, but with the one and only covenant God of Israel, whom they knew by the distinguishing personal title of 'the Lord'. For Christianity, the notion of salvation explicitly includes and centres upon a relationship, inaugurated in time and to be consummated beyond time, with none other than the 'God and Father of our Lord Jesus Christ'. We are thus dealing with a highly particularized notion of salvation, as will become clear later in this section.

The place of Jesus Christ in salvation

We have already touched upon the importance of Jesus Christ in relation to the Christian understanding of God, and the pluralist tendency which ends up, as the Harvard theologian Harvey Cox puts it, 'soft-pedalling the figure of Jesus himself'. For Cox – once regarded as one of the most radical theologians of the 1960s – the most appropriate way for Christians to engage in meaningful interfaith dialogue is to begin by recognizing that 'Jesus is, in some ways the *most* particularistic element of Christianity'.[62] Cox here makes the point that there is a need to begin from something concrete and historical, rather than some abstract symbol. And for Christians, this particularistic element is Jesus Christ. Christian theology, spirituality and above all Christian worship are strongly Christ-focused.

The New Testament, which endorses and legitimates this Christocentrism, does not merely regard Jesus Christ as *expressive* of a divine salvation, which may be made available in other forms. He is clearly understood to be *constitutive* of that salvation. In the Christian tradition, Jesus is viewed as more than *Rasul* ('the sent one', to use the fundamental Muslim definition of the sequence of prophets culminating in Muhammed). He is seen as the one who establishes as much as the one who is sent – a prophet and a saviour. Pluralists have a number of options here, from declaring that the New Testament is simply mistaken on this point (which precludes a serious claim to be Christian), to suggesting that the New Testament affirmations may be true for Christians, but have no binding force in this respect *extra muros ecclesiae* (outside the bounds of the church).[63] Yet the New Testament clearly regards Jesus Christ as, at least potentially, the saviour of the world, not simply of Christians, thus pointing to the strongly universal character of his saving work.

The nature of salvation

In an important study, John Hick has argued that there is a common core structure to all religions, which 'are fundamentally alike in exhibiting a soteriological structure. That is to say, they are all concerned with salvation/liberation/enlightenment/fulfilment.'[64] However, it may reasonably be observed that these concepts of salvation are conceived in such radically different ways, and are understood to be established or attained in such different manners, that only someone who was doggedly determined, as a matter of principle, to treat them as aspects of the same greater whole would have sufficient intellectual flexibility to do so. Do Christianity and Satanism really have the same understandings of salvation? My Satanist acquaintances certainly do not think so. In fact, Satanists accept that there is a God, but choose to worship his antithesis. This dualism hardly bodes well for a pluralist theory of the religions.

A more neutral observer, relieved from the necessity of insisting that all religions of the world are basically the same, might reasonably suggest that they do not merely offer different ways of achieving and conceptualizing salvation; they offer different 'salvations' altogether. The Rastafarian vision of a paradise in which blacks are served by menial whites; the Homeric notion of Tartaros; the old Norse concept of Valhalla; the Buddhist vision of *nirvana*; the Christian hope of resurrection to eternal life – all are obviously different. How can all the routes to salvation be equally 'valid' when the goals to be reached in such different ways are so obviously quite unrelated?

As noted above, there is enormous variation within the religions in relation to the nature of salvation. Christian conceptions of salvation focus on the establishment of a relationship between God (in the Christian sense of the term) and his people, and use a variety of images to articulate its various aspects. Underlying these convergent images of salvation is the common theme of 'salvation in and through Christ' – that is to say, that salvation is a possibility only on account of the life, death and resurrection of Jesus Christ, and that salvation is shaped in his likeness. As Joseph A. Di Noia, OP, comments, when Christians attempt to explain what the word 'salvation' includes,

> . . . we find ourselves talking about the triune God; the incarnation, passion, death and resurrection of Jesus Christ; grace, sin and justification; transfiguration and divinization; faith, hope and charity; the commandments and the moral virtues; and many other characteristically Christian things as well. We should not be surprised if, in trying to answer a cognate question, a member of another religious tradition, say a Buddhist, should also become very specific about Nirvana and all that bears on its attainment. We should not be surprised, furthermore, if the descriptions of salvation and Nirvana do not coincide . . . salvation has a specific content for Christians. It entails an interpersonal communion, made possible by Christ, between human persons and the Father, Son and Holy Spirit. At least at first sight, this seems to be something very different from what Buddhists can be supposed to be seeking when they follow the Excellent Eightfold Path that leads them on the way to realizing enlightenment and the extinction of self in Nirvana. At least on the face of things, what Buddhists mean by 'Nirvana' and what Christians mean by 'salvation' do not seem to coincide.[65]

Differences between notions of salvation are also reflected in the worship of religious communities. Those who are attracted to the Buddhist notion of salvation (or, more accurately, one of the many such options available within the various Buddhist traditions) will hardly want to become Christians, in that Christian theology, worship and prayer are closely interwoven with a definite series of beliefs concerning both the person and work of Jesus Christ. Christian worship reflects particular beliefs concerning the nature of both salvation and the saviour. Geoffrey Wainwright and others have emphasized the way in which theology and doxology are closely interconnected,[66] making it impossible to graft, for example, a Buddhist idea of salvation on to a Christian worshipping community. In a related context, Muslims continue to be at best highly sceptical, and more generally intensely critical, of the defining Christian practice of worshipping Jesus Christ. (This practice is generally seen as an instance of the heresy of *ittakhadha*, by which Jesus is acknowledged to be the physical Son of God.)

Pluralist writers occasionally point to the idea of 'kitten salvation' within Hinduism as an indication that the notion of grace is not distinctively Christian. The distinction between 'kitten salvation' and 'monkey salvation' within the *bhakti marga* tradition of Hinduism rests on the fact that a mother tigress carries her cubs, whereas baby monkeys have to hang on to their mothers. The idea of 'kitten salvation', specific to this form of Hinduism, is often appealed to as an indication of the 'convergence' of the religions over the grace of God.

Yet the situation is not as simple as this analysis might suggest. The concept is not found in any of the foundational documents of Hinduism, dating from the vedic period (2000–600 BC, in which a synthesis between the polytheistic sacrificial religion of the Aryans and the pantheistic monism of the Upanishads took place), nor during the pantheistic period (600 BC – AD 300). It emerged during the puranic period (AD 300–1200), during which Syrian forms of Christianity became established in the southern regions of India, and is especially associated with the medieval writer Sri Ramanuja (c. 1050–1137).[67] The assumption that 'kitten salvation' points to an inherent similarity between Hinduism and Christianity is dangerously simplistic; it might equally well illustrate the well-known tendency of some Hindu writers to 'borrow' ideas from Christianity.[68] Similarities may reflect the kind of borrowing associated with the strongly syncretistic tendencies of some forms

233

of Hinduism; they need not reflect fundamental convergence.

With these points in mind, let us address the question: 'Is salvation possible outside Christianity?' As a result of the writings of Ludwig Wittgenstein, theologians have become acutely sensitive to the need to establish the context in which words are used.[69] For Wittgenstein, the *Lebensform* ('form of living') within which a word was used was of decisive importance in establishing the meaning of that word. The Christian *Lebensform* is thus of controlling importance in understanding what the Christian concept of salvation implies, presupposes and expresses.

As Wittgenstein himself pointed out, the same word can be used in a large number of senses. One way of dealing with this might be to invent a totally new vocabulary, in which the meaning of each word was tightly and unequivocally defined. But this is not a real option. Languages, like religions, are living entities, and cannot be forced to behave in such an artificial way. A perfectly acceptable approach, according to Wittgenstein, is to take trouble to define the particular sense in which a word should be understood, in order to avoid confusion with its many other senses. This involves a careful study of its associations and its use in the 'form of living' to which it relates.[70] This point seems to be appreciated by Paul Knitter, who, noting that 'all knowledge is theory-laden', concludes that 'each religion is speaking within its own language-game'.[71] This use of a Wittgensteinian concept clearly indicates an awareness of the need to identify the use of words in 'language-games' to ascertain their specific meaning *within the tradition which employs them*. 'Salvation' is clearly a case in point. Its use and associations within the Christian tradition, especially in worship, point to a distinctive understanding of what the Christian faith is understood to confer upon believers, its ultimate basis, and the manner in which this comes about.[72]

If the term 'salvation' is understood to mean 'some benefit conferred upon or achieved by members of a community, whether individually or corporately', all religions offer 'salvation'. All – and by no means only religions – offer *something*. However, this is such a general statement that it is devoid of significant theological value. All religions, along with political theories such as Marxism and psychotherapeutic schools such as Rogerian therapy – may legitimately be styled 'salvific'.[73]

The statement 'all religions offer salvation' is thus potentially little more than a tautology. Only by using the most violent of means can all religions be said to offer the same 'salvation'. Respect for the integrity of the world's religions demands that 'salvation' be particularized – that is to say, that the distinctive morphology of a religion's understanding of salvation (including its basis, its mode of conveyance and appropriation, and its inherent nature) must be respected, and not coercively homogenized to suit the needs of some particular pressure group within the academy.

The distinctive character of each religion may and must be affirmed: Buddhism offers one style of 'salvation', just as Christianity offers another. It is no criticism of Buddhism to suggest that it does not offer a specifically Christian salvation, just as it is not in the least imperialist to state that the Christian vision of salvation is not the same as the Buddhist. These differences reflect the simple fact that Christianity is not Buddhism. It is essential to respect and honour differences here, and to resist the ever-present temptation to force them all into the same mould.

In the light of this approach, the following three statements may be set out.

1. Christianity has a particular understanding of the nature, grounds and means of obtaining salvation.[74] And the Christian understanding of salvation, like the Christian notion of God, is Christologically determined. Just as it is illegitimate to use the term 'God' in a vague and generic sense, allowing it to be understood that all religions share this same divinity, so it is improper to use the term 'salvation' as if it were common to all religions.

It should be noted that inadequate English translations of the foundational writings of other religions often contribute to the homogenizing agenda of prescriptive pluralism. The English word 'salvation' is often used to translate Greek, Hebrew, Arabic, Sanskrit and Chinese terms of considerably greater complexity than is appreciated. As a result, vastly different concepts are often translated by the same English word, suggesting an affinity between the writings of the religions which is actually absent in their original languages and contexts, in which the words take on specific overtones which prohibit them from designating the same concept in each case. 'Salvation' is a particularity, not a universality. There is an urgent need to pay more attention to the vocabulary and associations of 'salvation' across the religions, rather than allowing verbal vagueness to generate theological confusion.

2. Christianity is the only religion to offer salvation *in the Christian sense of that term*. This verbally clumsy, yet theologically precise, sentence acknowledges the point, stressed by Wittgenstein, that there is a vital need to make clear the associations of a term, and the particular sense in which it is being used. In that the word 'salvation' is meaningless unless its context is identified, it is necessary to establish the 'form of living' which gives the word its distinctive meaning – in this case, the Christian world of doctrine, worship and hope, going back to the New Testament and consolidated in the Christian tradition.

3. Salvation, in the Christian sense of that term, is proclaimed as a real and attractive possibility for those who are presently outside the Christian community. The entire enterprise of evangelism, now recognized to be of such vital importance to the Christian churches throughout the world, is directed towards the proclamation of this good news to the world.

Christian salvation and the world religions

With these three points in mind, let us return to the question of salvation in the religions. All religions are salvific in their own terms, in that they offer a particular conception of salvation. Yet I have stressed that there is a specifically Christian understanding of salvation, which is grounded uniquely in the life, death and resurrection of Jesus Christ. To affirm that there is a distinctively Christian understanding of salvation is not to deny that other faiths offer 'salvation' in their own terms; it is simply to note that the 'salvation' in question differs from one faith to another. In this sense, it is particular, not universal. It is perfectly legitimate for the Christian to wish to share his or her experience of and hopes concerning salvation with others; to do so is not to belittle others, but to wish to share the specifically *Christian* experience of salvation. In a free market of ideas, the attractiveness and relevance of the Christian understanding of salvation will determine whether others wish to embrace this understanding of salvation, and by doing so, become Christians.

Salvation, in its Christian sense, is thus available universally through the church. The Christian proclamation is that salvation is a universal possibility, which is not bounded by any geographical, cultural or social divide. It is not necessary to join a Christian denomination to receive God's salvation; it is by receiving that salvation that one enters the church – not in the sense of a physical building, or even a denomination, but in the sense of the community of believers down the ages. In no way does Christianity declare that salvation is a possibility only for those inside its bounds. The church may indeed be thought of as the company of the redeemed; nevertheless, those outside its bounds are invited to share in the wedding banquet, on condition that they dress accordingly (Mt. 22:1–12). None are coerced into attending; the invitation is nonetheless universal. The particularity of that invitation (in that it rests upon the person and work of Christ) does not in any way conflict with its universal proclamation and appeal.

Alongside the unequivocal affirmation of the particularity of God's act of redemption in Jesus Christ, the New Testament states the universality of God's saving will. It is God's wish that all people shall be saved and come to a knowledge of the truth (1 Tim. 2:4). God intends to have mercy upon all (Rom. 11:32). God does not want anyone to perish, but wants everyone to come to repentance (2 Pet. 3:9). A responsible Christian theology must be able to accommodate itself within the creative tension which results from the simultaneous New Testament affirmation of the particularity of the person and work of Christ, and the universality of the scope of his mission.[75]

This tension cannot be dissolved simply by adopting a universalist route, declaring that all will be saved in the end.[76] This approach has its attractions, not least because it appears to be more faithful to the theme of a loving God.[77] Yet the idea that all will be saved requires the inclusion of a number of additional beliefs, including that all will *consent* to be saved. What if some, wishing to exercise their God-given faculty of freedom, choose to refuse that offer, preferring to go their own way? In such a situation, the doctrine of universalism asks us to envisage a situation in which God imposes salvation upon individuals. It is a small step from the optimistic affirmation that 'all will be saved' to the authoritarian pronouncement that 'all *must* be saved, whether they like it or not'.

The Christian understanding of the love of God is that of a vulnerable love, which is offered to us through Christ. God offers us himself, in the knowledge that we may refuse him. Universalism denies humanity the right to say 'no' to God. Despite its initial attractions, it turns out to have its decidedly darker side, in effect declaring that all are predestined to be saved – raising precisely the same problems relating to divine sovereignty and human responsibility associated with the approach of John Calvin, an approach which is not usually regarded with any great enthusiasm by pluralists.

Religious Stalinism? Pluralism and the agenda of modernity

The prescriptive pluralism which we have been exploring in this chapter is itself dependent upon and a direct consequence of the modernist agenda. This form of pluralism is little more than an intellectual satellite of the Enlightenment, inextricably linked with its totalizing and homogenizing agenda. Earlier, in exploring the intellectual contours of modernism (see pp. 163–188), we noted that two central themes of modernism are the following:

1. a 'totalizing' urge, which insists that everything must be seen as an aspect of a grand theory or 'metanarrative';

2. a desire to master raw material – cultural, intellectual or physical – to fit in with the desires of humanity.

Both these themes can be discerned within the pluralist agenda. All religions are, we are told, to be viewed from the pluralist perspective, which alone allows them to be seen in their proper light. And where religions do not happen to fit in with the assumptions of this particular paradigm, they are forced to conform

– in the case of Christianity, by being placed under pressure to abandon its defining traditional beliefs in the resurrection and divinity of Jesus Christ, and the doctrine of the Trinity. This is tantamount to intellectual Stalinism. In making this assertion, I am deliberately pointing up the common modernist agenda and roots which underlie prescriptive pluralism, Nazism and Stalinism. All three are intellectual colonies of modernism, governed by the same rules and presumptions, even if they may vary in relation to matters of local detail.

In the end, therefore, the criticisms directed by postmodernity against modernity apply with equal, if not greater, force to prescriptive religious pluralism: it is actually potentially profoundly oppressive, failing to take seriously the integrity of the religions. The belief that all religions are ultimately expressions of the same transcendent reality is at best illusory and at worst oppressive – illusory because it lacks any substantiating basis, and oppressive because it involves the systematic imposition of the agenda of those in positions of intellectual power on the religions and those who adhere to them. The illiberal imposition of this pluralistic metanarrative on religions is ultimately a claim to *mastery* – both in the sense of having a Nietzschean authority and power to mould material according to one's own will, and in the sense of being able to relativize all the religions by having access to a privileged standpoint. As Terry Eagleton pointed out, 'post-modernism signals the end of such metanarratives whose secretly terroristic function was to ground and legitimate the illusion of a "universal" human history. We are now in the process of awakening from the nightmare of modernity, with its manipulative reason and fetish of the totality, into the laid-back pluralism of the post-modern, that heterogeneous range of life-styles and language games which has renounced the nostalgic urge to totalize and legitimate itself.'[78] Perhaps prescriptive pluralism ought to confront these questions, and ask itself whether it is prepared to allow Christianity to be Christianity, and not simply force it to be one manifestation of an unknown and unknowable, yet nevertheless totalizing, universal reality.

The attraction of pluralism lies not so much in its claims to truth (which are increasingly conceded to be remarkably elusive and shallow), but in its claim to foster tolerance among the religions. Yet this claim was also made by modernity, as in, for example, Lessing's parable *Nathan the Wise*. For Lessing, such an ideology would foster the toleration of the religions;[79] yet for Stalin, that same ideology held the key to their ultimate suppression and elimination. Prescriptive pluralism runs precisely the same risk. Toleration is much more likely to result from showing respect to other religions, than from forcing them into an artificial framework which suppresses their distinctiveness in an attempt to make observation conform to theory.

Conclusion

Evangelicalism thus recognizes that Christianity exists in the midst of a plurality of religions, and in some regions of the world within a culture which wishes to treat all religions on an equal political footing. But it sees no need to withdraw or retreat from any of the core convictions of the Christian faith on account of these factors. Indeed, it would regard such moves as a totally improper capitulation to cultural pressures. Evangelicalism affirms the particularity of the Christian faith, and asks that its integrity should be respected, and that cultural pressures to homogenize its beliefs and claims should be resisted. As the Enlightenment mindset becomes increasingly distant, there are excellent reasons for insisting that the distinctiveness and particularity of Christianity should be publicly affirmed and acted upon.

conclusion

There is now no doubt that evangelicalism is of major importance
to the future of global Christianity.[1] To outsiders, its spiritual
dynamism and activism, coupled with the intense commitment
which is so characteristic of individual evangelical believers and
churches, are strongly indicative of significant long-term growth
within the movement. Evangelicals themselves, however, would
single out their total commitment to the gospel as the most
fundamental reason for their present success and future potential.
They argue that they remained faithful to the gospel during a
period in western culture when others capitulated to social
pressures to accommodate Christianity to the ideas and values of a
secular worldview. Their passion for the truth of the gospel can
now be seen to be justified. They are now reaping the rewards of
their faithfulness.

Perhaps such a response is a little simplistic. Part of the
argument of this book has been that evangelicals did, as a matter of
fact, allow their secular context to affect their thinking, as can be
seen so clearly in the way in which Charles Hodge and Benjamin
B. Warfield allowed the theory of language associated with 'Scottish
realism' to influence their understanding of biblical authority (pp.
168–171). Other examples could doubtless be given. Nevertheless,
the fundamental evangelical conviction has been that it is
imperative to remain faithful to the gospel of Jesus Christ, and to
allow no ideas or values from outside Christianity to exercise a
normative role within its thought or life.

The present work has explored the issue of the intellectual

coherence and academic credibility of evangelicalism. If 'academic' is understood to refer to the cultural norms and values which have come to prevail in many western academic institutions, evangelicalism will have no interest in adopting or defending 'academic' significance. Evangelicalism has been too busy pursuing its evangelistic and pastoral ministries to have much time for this kind of 'academic' concern. Yet in many quarters, the term 'academic' continues to refer to intellectual coherence and plausibility, linked with a strong commitment to scholarship. It has been the concern of this work to show that, in this older sense of the term, evangelicalism has every reason to think of itself, and to be thought of, as 'academic'.

For some evangelicals, this will be an irrelevance. Who cares whether evangelicalism carries any intellectual weight? Surely the important thing is to win people for the Lord, and care for their souls. There is enormous wisdom in this comment, and it must be respected and honoured. It reminds us that evangelicalism must never be allowed to lose sight of the great challenges and joys of gospel ministry, or of the importance of ministering to and caring for ordinary people who love the Lord, yet have no interest in anything intellectual. It is, however, not inconsistent with this vision to suggest that evangelicalism also has a remarkably high degree of intellectual coherence, especially in the face of its rivals in the contemporary academic world. But why does it matter to point this out? What conceivable value can it have?

Appreciating the merits and potential sophistication of evangelicalism in this respect is of considerable importance for several reasons. A simple point concerns the role of universities and colleges in western culture. The stereotypes of evangelicalism which are often offered by such establishments portray evangelicalism as unthinking, anti-intellectual and devoid of significance for thinking people. The popular success and influence of the movement are therefore misinterpreted in some influential academic circles as a direct indication of its lack of intellectual merit and sophistication. As a result, the social élite of tomorrow has often been saturated during its formative phase with anti-evangelical stereotypes. While protest by evangelicals against such stereotypes must continue, this should be supplemented by an increasingly vigorous assertion and demonstration of the intellectual sophistication of the movement.

The evangelical voice thus must be heard in academia, with courses on 'evangelical theology' and 'evangelical spirituality' being allowed to find their legitimate place in the teaching of mainline seminaries and colleges. Evangelicals need to appreciate this sophistication for themselves before they can persuade others. The present work has attempted to encourage this process of confidence-building within the movement, so that potential future evangelical leaders and thinkers need not feel under any legitimate pressure to abandon their evangelical faith on account of its alleged irrationalism.

Perhaps the greatest challenge to evangelicalism in the next generation is to develop an increasing intellectual commitment without losing its roots in the life and faith of ordinary Christian believers. The strongly negative associations of the term 'academic' are a constant warning of the dangers of formulating a sophisticated theology or worldview without engaging firmly with the agenda and concerns of the church. It is the easiest thing in the world to aspire to intellectual erudition; developing this while remaining firmly in touch with the realities of the common Christian life is a somewhat more daunting task.

Yet it remains a task which must be undertaken. Evangelicalism, especially in North America, has deeply populist roots. While this secure grounding in popular culture prevents evangelicalism from indulging itself in the business of academic scholarship for its own sake, it nevertheless means that the movement runs a serious risk of becoming as intellectually and spiritually ephemeral and shallow as that culture. Theology, understood as a positive and sustained engagement with the riches and resources of the Christian faith, offers evangelicalism the opportunity of supplementing its dynamic and activist populism by sinking deep roots, capable of nourishing and sustaining the movement in heart and mind.

The 'scandal of the evangelical mind' (Mark Noll) lies in the fact that, in the recent past, evangelicals have failed to allow their faith to shape their understanding of the world.[2] In part, the present work has aimed to correct this deficiency by reassuring evangelicals of the coherence and viability of their beliefs. To construct an edifice, one must first be assured of the reliability of its foundations. This book has aimed to secure the public acceptance of the intellectual adequacy and sufficiency of evangelicalism, in terms both of its own internal criteria and of the alternatives in the modern western world.

No longer need evangelicals feel unduly vulnerable, defensive or apologetic about their distinctive beliefs. They can now begin to apply them, and to consolidate and extend the great advances made in the last generation. The evangelical passion for truth must become a passion for the evangelical mind. Evangelicalism has made major contributions to shaping and renewing the life of the Christian church; the task of shaping and renewing the life of the Christian mind now awaits it.

notes

Introduction

1. London: Hodder & Stoughton, 1994, and Downers Grove, IL: InterVarsity Press, 1995.

2. See the important and influential analysis by Mark Noll, *The Scandal of the Evangelical Mind* (Grand Rapids, MI: Eerdmans, and Leicester: Inter-Varsity Press, 1994), which highlights the recent failure of evangelicalism to address such issues. On the notion of a 'Christian mind', see Harry Blamires, *The Christian Mind: How Should a Christian Think?* (London: SPCK, 1963). For further useful comments, see Arthur Holmes, *Contours of a Christian Worldview* (Grand Rapids, MI: Eerdmans, 1983); *idem, The Idea of a Christian College* (rev. edn., Grand Rapids, MI: Eerdmans, 1987); Edith L. Blumhofer and Joel A. Carpenter, *Twentieth Century Evangelicalism: A Guide to the Sources* (New York: Garland Publishing, 1990), pp. 187-239.

3. It should also be noted that Australian evangelicalism has maintained a strong commitment to academic theology without in any way losing sight of its evangelistic and pastoral roles. The role of Moore Theological College, Sydney, in this development should be noted. See Stephen Judd and Kenneth Cable, *Sydney Anglicans* (Sydney: Anglican Information Office, 1987), pp. 286-291.

4. The definitive study remains George Marsden, *Fundamentalism and American Culture: The Shaping of Twentieth Century Evangelicalism 1870-1925* (New York: Oxford University Press, 1980). See also George M. Marsden, *Reforming Fundamentalism: Fuller Seminary and the New Evangelicalism* (Grand Rapids, MI: Eerdmans, 1987); Bradley J. Longfield, *The Presbyterian Controversy: Fundamentalists, Modernists and Moderates* (New York: Oxford University Press, 1991); Martin E. Marty, 'What is Fundamentalism? Theological Perspectives', in H. Küng and J. Moltmann (eds.), *Fundamentalism as an Ecumenical Challenge* (*Concilium* 1992/3, London: SCM, 1992), pp. 3-13.

5. See the kind of considerations set out recently in George Marsden, *The Soul of the American University: From Protestant Establishment to Established Non-Belief* (New York: Oxford University Press, 1994) and Douglas Sloan, *Faith and Knowledge: Mainline Protestantism and American Higher Education* (Louisville, KY: Westminster/John Knox, 1994).

6. Note the perceptive comment on evangelicalism within the Church of England during the 1940s: 'Evangelicals inclined to the view that they were excused culture, scholarship and intellectual exercise on religious grounds': Randle Manwaring, *From Controversy to Co-existence: Evangelicals in the Church of England, 1914–1980* (Cambridge: Cambridge University Press, 1985), p. 55.

7. David F. Wells, *No Place for Truth; or, Whatever Happened to Evangelical Theology?* (Grand Rapids, MI: Eerdmans, 1993; Leicester: Inter-Varsity Press, 1995).

8. Wells, *No Place for Truth*, p. 101.

9. For a definitive guide to evangelical theology during the twentieth century, see Walter A. Elwell (ed.), *Handbook of Evangelical Theologians* (Grand Rapids, MI: Baker, 1993).

10. Note the perceptive comment of John E. Smith, *The Spirit of American Philosophy* (New York: Oxford University Press, 1963), p. vii: 'It is no exaggeration to say that in American intellectual life, irrelevant thinking has always been considered to be the cardinal sin.' The importance of the instrumentalism of John Dewey (1859–1952) should be noted here. See also the excellent account of Cornel West, *The American Evasion of Philosophy: A Genealogy of Pragmatism* (Madison, WI: University of Wisconsin Press, 1989), p. 5. On the significance of popular religion for evangelicalism, see Richard J. Mouw, *Consulting the Faithful: What Christian Intellectuals can learn from Popular Religion* (Grand Rapids, MI: Eerdmans, 1994), pp. 1–14; 23–42.

11. Ninian Smart, *The Science of Religion and the Sociology of Knowledge* (Princeton, NJ: Princeton University Press, 1973), pp. 6–7.

12. For reflections on this theme with specific reference to Anglicanism, see Alister E. McGrath, *The Renewal of Anglicanism* (London: SPCK, 1993).

13. For documentation and reflection, see B. Murchland (ed.), *The Meaning of the Death of God* (New York: Vintage, 1967).

14. Cited in A. M. Ramsey, *The Christian Priest Today* (London: SPCK, 1972), p. 21.

15. See John B. Boles, *The Great Revival, 1787–1805: The Origins of the Southern Evangelical Mind* (Lexicon, KY: University Press of Kentucky, 1972); Terry D. Bilhartz, *Urban Religion and the Second Great Awakening* (Rutherford, NJ: Fairleigh Dickinson University Press, 1986).

16. See Noll, *The Scandal of the Evangelical Mind*, pp. 60–64. Noll points in particular to the influence of George Whitefield in shaping such attitudes, as brought out in the recent study by Harry S. Stout, *The Divine Dramatist: George Whitefield and the Rise of Modern Evangelicalism* (Grand Rapids, MI: Eerdmans, 1991).

17. The most widely read criticism remains Allan Bloom, *The Closing of the American Mind* (New York: Simon & Schuster, 1987). This should be supplemented by more recent studies, such as Dinesh D'Souza, *Illiberal Education: The Politics of Race and Sex on Campus* (New York: Free Press, 1991) and Arthur Schlesinger, *The Disuniting of America* (New York: Norton, 1992).

18. For both a personal narrative and a critique of this trend, see Paul C. McGlasson, *Another Gospel: A Confrontation with Liberation Theology* (Grand Rapids, MI: Baker, 1994). See especially his comments on 'theological fascism' (pp.

80–84), which reflect his own experience at one American seminary.

19. For example, see the argument that liberalism is 'basically a brief against belief and conviction': Stanley Fish, *There's No Such Thing as Free Speech* (New York: Oxford University Press, 1994), p. 296.

20. It is thus perfectly permissible to refer to Calvin's sixteenth-century reformation at Geneva in terms of 'secularization', in that responsibility for social tasks formerly undertaken by the church was handed over to the city council.

21. See Paul V. Mankowski, SJ, 'Academic Religion', in *First Things* 21, May 1992, pp. 31–37; quote at p. 34.

22. Charles Newman, *The Post-Modern Aura: The Act of Fiction in an Age of Inflation* (Evanston, IL: Northwestern University Press, 1985).

23. See the analysis of Lawrence L. Habermehl, *The Counterfeit Wisdom of Shallow Minds* (Bern/Frankfurt: Peter Lang, 1995).

24. Antonio Gramsci, *Gli intellettuali e l'organizzazione della cultura* (8th edn., Turin: Einaudi, 1964). More generally, see Alberto Caracciolo, *La città futura: saggi sulla figura e il pensiero di Antonio Gramsci* (Milan: Feltrinelli, 1976); Giuseppe Fiori, *Vita di Antonio Gramsci* (Bari: Editori Laterza, 1989).

25. See the pertinent comments of Robert Scholes, *Protocols of Reading* (New Haven, CT: Yale University Press, 1989), pp. 92–93.

26. See the comments of David W. Bebbington in his review of W. A. Elwell (ed.), *Handbook of Evangelical Theologians*, in *Christianity Today*, 12 September 1994, pp. 73–74.

27. I hope to do this myself in a three-volume work now in preparation, entitled *A Theology of the Cross*, which will explore the critical and foundational theological role played by the cross for evangelicals. These volumes will not focus purely on matters of theology, but will deal with the impact of the cross on every aspect of Christian thinking and living, including the increasingly important issue of spirituality.

28. See Blumhofer and Carpenter, *Twentieth Century Evangelicalism*; K. S. Kantzer and C. F. H. Henry, *Evangelical Affirmations* (Grand Rapids, MI: Zondervan, 1990), pp. 27–38; George Marsden, 'The Evangelical Denomination', in *Evangelicalism and Modern America* (Grand Rapids, MI: Eerdmans, 1984), pp. vii–xix; David W. Bebbington, *Evangelicalism in Modern Britain* (London: Unwin Hyman, 1989), pp. 2–17; Douglas A. Sweeney, 'The Essential Evangelicalism Dialectic: The Historiography of the Early Neo-Evangelical Movement and the Observer-Participant Dilemma', *Church History* 60 (1991), pp. 70–84. For further discussion, see D. F. Wells and J. D. Woodbridge (eds.), *The Evangelicals* (Nashville, TN: Abingdon, 1975); D. G. Bloesch, *The Essentials of Evangelical Theology* (2 vols., San Francisco: Harper & Row, 1978–79); David Dockery (ed.), *Are Southern Baptists Evangelicals?* (Nashville, TN: Broadman, 1993); Millard J. Erickson, *The Evangelical Mind and Heart* (Grand Rapids, MI: Baker, 1993), pp. 13–14; Alister E. McGrath, *Evangelicalism and the Future of Christianity* (London: Hodder & Stoughton, 1994, and Downers Grove, IL: InterVarsity Press, 1995).

29. Ludwig Wittgenstein, *Philosophical Investigations* (Oxford: Blackwell, 1968), pp.

31–32. Wittgenstein's analysis merits careful study at this point.
30. N. H. Keeble and Geoffrey F. Nuttall (eds.), *Calendar of the Correspondence of Richard Baxter* (2 vols., Oxford: Clarendon, 1991), vol. 1, p. 226.

Chapter 1

1. See John Stott's discussion of the uniqueness of Christ in *The Contemporary Christian* (Leicester: Inter-Varsity Press, 1992), pp. 296–320.
2. Stephen Neill, *Crises of Belief* (London: Hodder & Stoughton, 1984), p. 23; published in the United States as *Christian Faith and Other Faiths* (Downers Grove, IL: InterVarsity Press, 1984). A similar Christological affirmation underlies Martin Luther's famous declaration concerning the doctrine of justification by faith as the 'article by which the church stands or falls'. See Ernst Wolf, 'Die Rechtfertigungslehre als Mitte und Grenze reformatorischer Theologie', *Evangelische Theologie* 9 (1949–50), pp. 298–308. For further analysis, see Alister E. McGrath, 'The Article by which the Church Stands or Falls', *Evangelical Quarterly* 58 (1986), pp. 207–228; *idem*, 'Der articulus iustificationis als axiomatischer Grundsatz des christlichen Glaubens', *Zeitschrift für Theologie und Kirche* 81 (1984), pp. 383–394; *idem*, 'Karl Barth and the *articulus iustificationis*. The Significance of his Critique of Ernst Wolf within the Context of his Theological Method', *Theologische Zeitschrift* 39 (1983), pp. 349–361; *idem*, 'Karl Barth als Aufklärer? Der Zusammenhang seiner Lehre vom Werke Christi mit der Erwählungslehre', *Kerygma und Dogma* 30 (1984), pp. 273–283.
3. Aloysius Pieris, in J. Hick and P. Knitter (eds.), *The Myth of Christian Uniqueness* (Maryknoll, NY: Orbis, 1988), p. 171. The title of this volume is seriously misleading; the editors indicate that they have no intention of denying Christian uniqueness; their concern is to 'interpret it anew'. See Paul Knitter, 'Preface', *The Myth of Christian Uniqueness*, p. vii. Note also John Mbiti's emphatic assertion that, in an African context, the 'uniqueness of Christianity is in Jesus Christ': John Mbiti, *African Religions and Philosophy* (London: Heinemann, 1969), p. 277.
4. Even Clark Pinnock, who would be regarded by some as perhaps the most 'inclusive' of modern evangelical theologians, mounts a devastating critique of 'pluralist' approaches to the significance of Christ. See Clark H. Pinnock, *A Wideness in God's Mercy: The Finality of Jesus Christ in a World of Religions* (Grand Rapids, MI: Zondervan, 1992), pp. 49–80.
5. For this trend, see John D. Barrow, *Theories of Everything: The Quest for Ultimate Explanation* (Oxford: Clarendon, 1991). Barrow notes the dependency of such quests on 'the Platonic emphasis upon timeless universals as more important to the nature of things than the world of particulars that we observe and experience' (p. 30). The rediscovery of the priority of the particular is of major importance to the emergence of postliberalism in more recent theological reflections.
6. On the theological aspects, see D. Z. Phillips, *Faith after Foundationalism*

(London: Routledge, 1988). For the more general phenomenon, see Stephen Crook, *Modernist Radicalism and its Aftermath: Foundationalism and Anti-foundationalism in Radical Social Theory* (London: Routledge, 1991).

7. Thus writers such as Charles Hodge appeal to the Scottish 'common-sense' philosophy in the defence of their theology. For the dangers which this raises, see pp. 166–174. Some evangelicals, such as Carl F. H. Henry and R. C. Sproul, are foundationalist in their approaches, once more apparently for apologetic reasons; this does not, however, mean that evangelicalism as a whole is foundationalist in its methodology. For some thoughtful reflections on this general issue, with particular reference to Henry's *God, Revelation and Authority* (6 vols., Waco, TX: Word, 1976–83), see Richard R. Topping, 'The Anti-Foundationalist Challenge to Evangelical Apologetics', *Evangelical Quarterly* 63 (1991), pp. 45–60.

8. A characteristic insight of John's gospel: see Ignace de La Potterie, *La verité dans Saint Jean* (2 vols., Rome: Editrice Pontificio Instituto Biblico, 1977).

9. The theological dimensions of this theme are fully explored in Wolfhart Pannenberg, *Jesus – God and Man* (London: SCM, 1968), pp. 53–108.

10. Iris Murdoch, *The Sovereignty of the Good* (London: Routledge & Kegan Paul, 1970), p. 80.

11. G. E. Lessing, 'Über den Beweis des Geistes und der Kraft', in *Gotthold Ephraim Lessings sämtlichen Schriften*, vol. 13, ed. Karl Lachmann (Berlin: Göschen'sche Verlagshandlung, 1897), 4.11 – 8.20.

12. For the way in which Enlightenment presuppositions governed the interpretation of both Scripture and Jesus Christ, see Hans Frei, *The Identity of Jesus Christ* (Philadelphia: Fortress, 1975), p. xvi.

13. Ben F. Meyer, *The Aims of Jesus* (London: SCM, 1979), p. 15.

14. On which see Georges Benrekassa, *La politique et sa mémoire: la politique et l'historique dans la pensée des lumières* (Paris: Payot, 1983).

15. Quoted in David Gill, 'The Faith of the Founding Fathers', in *One Nation Under God* (Waco, TX: Word, 1975), p. 41.

16. George Tyrrell, *Christianity at the Cross-Roads* (1909; repr. London: Faber, 1963), p. 49.

17. Albert Schweitzer, *The Quest of the Historical Jesus* (3rd edn., London: A. & C. Black, 1954), p. 4.

18. On narcissism, see Christopher Lasch, *The Culture of Narcissism* (London: Abacus, 1980); Neville Symington, *Narcissism: A New Theory* (London: Carnac Books, 1993).

19. For a survey of recent evangelical scholarship and theological reflection, see Douglas Jacobsen and Frederick Schmidt, 'Behind Orthodoxy and Beyond It: Recent Developments in Evangelical Christology', *Scottish Journal of Theology* 45 (1993), pp. 515–541.

20. Jeffrey Stout, *The Flight from Authority: Religion, Morality and the Quest for Autonomy* (Notre Dame, IN: University of Notre Dame Press, 1981), pp. 2–3.

21. On the literary significance of Prometheus, see Raymond Trousson, *Le thème de Prométhée dans le littérature européene* (Geneva: Droz, 1976); Linda M. Lewis, *The*

Promethean Politics of Milton, Blake and Shelley (London: University of Missouri Press, 1992). On Prometheus in Attic culture, see Paola Pisi, *Prometo nel culto attico* (Rome: Edizioni dell'Ateno, 1994); on the parallels between Adam and Prometheus, see Larry J. Kreitzer, *Prometheus and Adam: Enduring Symbols of the Human Situation* (Lanham, MD: University of America Press, 1994).

22. Ludwig Feuerbach, *The Essence of Christianity*; in *Gesammelte Werke*, ed. W. Schuffenhauer (Berlin: Akademie Verlag, 1973), vol. 5, pp. 46–47. See further Max Wartofsky, *Feuerbach* (Cambridge: Cambridge University Press, 1982); W. I. Brazall, *The Young Hegelians* (New Haven, CT and London: Yale University Press, 1970); James Bradley, 'Across the River and Beyond the Trees: Feuerbach's Relevance to Modern Theology', in S. W. Sykes and D. Holmes (eds.), *New Studies in Theology* (London: Duckworth, 1980), pp. 139–161.

23. This is an extremely difficult notion to analyse in English, not least on account of the subtle interaction between the two German words Marx uses (*Entäusserung* and *Entfremdung*) to describe the phenonmenon. The reader is referred to Bertell Ollman, *Alienation: Marx's Conception of Man in Capitalist Society* (Cambridge: Cambridge University Press, 1977) for an analysis.

24. Karl Marx, *Theses on Feuerbach* (1845); in *Marx–Engels Gesamtausgabe*, vol. 1, part 5, ed. A. Adoratskii (Berlin: Marx-Engels Verlag, 1932), 533.14 – 555.35.

25. Romano Guardini, *Letters from Lake Como: Explorations in Technology and the Human Race* (1923; repr. Grand Rapids, MI: Eerdmans, 1994), pp. 16–17. On issues raised by the rise of technology, see Jacques Ellul, *The Technological Society* (New York: Knopf, 1964); Albert Borgman, *Technology and the Character of Contemporary Life: A Philosophical Inquiry* (Chicago: University of Chicago Press, 1984).

26. Guardini, *Letters from Lake Como*, p. 44.

27. Guardini, *Letters from Lake Como*, p. 46.

28. This is the position of Neil Postman, *Technopoly: The Surrender of Culture to Technology* (New York: Vintage, 1993), quote at p. 71. See also the views of the Canadian writer George Grant, *Technology and Empire* (Toronto: Anansi, 1986).

29. See Roger Lundin, *The Culture of Interpretation* (Grand Rapids, MI: Eerdmans, 1993).

30. For some of the issues this raises in relation to 'transvaluation', see James S. Hans, *The Question of Value* (Carbondale, IL: Southern Illinois University Press, 1989).

31. See Martin Kähler, *Der sogenannte historische Jesus und der geschichtliche, biblische Christus*, ed. E. Wolf (1892; repr. Munich: Kaiser Verlag, 1953), pp. 40–45.

32. For an excellent discussion of this point, see David J. Hesselgrave and Edward Rommen, *Contextualization: Meanings, Methods and Models* (Grand Rapids, MI: Baker, 1989).

33. 'The Theological Clarification of the Present State of the German Evangelical Churches (1934)', sections 1, 3; in W. Niesel (ed.), *Bekenntnisschiften und Kirchenordnungen der nach Gottes Wort reformierten Kirche* (Zurich: Evangelischer Verlag, 1938), 335.25–31; 335.46 – 336.10.

34. For example, see James Barr, *Old and New in Interpretation* (London: SCM, 1966), pp. 83–102; F. G. Downing, *Has Christianity a Revelation?* (London: SCM, 1964).

35. This point is made clearly by Wolfhart Pannenberg, 'Revelation in Early Christianity', in G. R. Evans (ed.), *Christian Authority* (Oxford: Oxford University Press, 1988), pp. 76–85. For biblical concepts of revelation see Rolf Rendtorff, *Canon and Theology: Overtures to an Old Testament Theology* (Minneapolis, MN: Fortress, 1993), pp. 114–124, and especially the lucid survey provided by John Goldingay, *Models for Scripture* (Grand Rapids, MI: Eerdmans, 1994), pp. 287–347.

36. For an exploration, see M. N. A. Bockmuehl, *Revelation and Mystery* (Tübingen: Mohr, 1990); D. Lührmann, *Das Offenbarungsverständnis bei Paulus und in den paulinischen Gemeinden* (Neukirchen and Vluyn: Neukirchener Verlag, 1965).

37. For a useful survey, see J. Glaser, 'Towards a Mutual Understanding of Christian and Islamic Concepts of Revelation', *Themelios* 7 (1982), pp. 16–22.

38. The term 'Qur'an' literally means 'reading' or perhaps 'reading aloud'. Evangelicals have resisted a direct identification of 'revelation' with 'Scripture', partly on account of a fear that it will lead to bibliolatry: see Donald G. Bloesch, *Essentials of Evangelical Theology* (San Francisco: Harper & Row, 1982), vol. 1, pp. 52–53. As will become clear from our analysis, it is not Scripture, but Jesus Christ, who is to be worshipped as God. Martin Luther's discussion of this point in the 1525 work *De servo arbitrio* is of importance here. Note especially his comment that 'God and the Scripture of God are two things, no less than the creator and his creature are two things': *D. Martin Luthers Werke: Kritische Gesamtausgabe*, vol. 18 (Weimar: Böhlau, 1885), p. 606.

39. Islam recognizes a small number of 'sayings of God' (*ahadith qudsiyya*) which are not included in the Qur'an.

40. *D. Martin Luthers Werke: Kritische Gesamtausgabe*, vol. 40 (Weimar: Böhlau, 1911), 602.18 – 603.13; 607.19 – 609.14.

41. Ludwig Feuerbach, *Das Wesen des Christentums*, in *Gesammelte Werke*, ed. W. Schuffenhauer (Berlin: Akademie Verlag, 1973), vol. 5, pp. 46–47.

42. See the perceptive comments of Wolfhart Pannenberg, *Jesus – God and Man* (Philadelphia: Westminster, 1968), pp. 38–39, 47–48.

43. See Karl Marx, 'Thesen über Feuerbach' (1845) in *Marx-Engels Gesamtausgabe*, vol. 1, part 5, ed. A. Adoratskii (Berlin: Marx-Engels Verlag, 1932), 533.14 – 555.35.

44. Stout, *The Flight from Authority*, pp. 2–3.

45. The two formulae occur together at Gal. 2:20–21. The 'giving up' formula (see Rom. 4:5; 8:32; Gal. 1:4; 2:20) can have the sense of 'Christ being given up by God' (that is, as an action of God) or of 'Christ giving himself up' (that is, an act of obedient self-giving on the part of Christ). Martin Hengel comments that the phrase 'Christ died for us' (see Rom. 5:6, 8; 14:9; 1 Cor. 8:11; 15:3; 2 Cor. 5:14–15; Gal. 2:21; 1 Thes. 5:10) is 'the most frequent and most important confessional statement in the Pauline epistles and at the same time in the primitive Christian

tradition'. Martin Hengel, *The Atonement: The Origins of the Doctrine in the New Testament* (London: SCM, 1981), p. 37.

46. It is, however, interesting to note that some evangelical approaches to the nature of revelation seem to come close to the Islamic notion of a propositional revelation from God, rather than the Christian concept of a personal revelation of God in Christ. In part, this development seems to have been a reaction against the neo-orthodox notion of a 'contentless revelation' or 'revelation as presence' (see pp. 106–108). All evangelicals affirm that Jesus Christ is the self-revelation of God. Yet Jesus is a *person*, not a proposition or simply a source of propositions. A purely propositional approach to revelation impoverishes the biblical notion of revelation, and replaces it with a diluted concept which owes far more to Enlightenment rationalism and the concept of truth associated with Spinoza and Descartes than to the biblical revelation itself. For evangelicalism, Jesus Christ *is* the self-revelation of God; he *is* God, and not merely the vehicle of transmission of propositions concerning God. This important point is certainly envisaged in Bernard Ramm's argument that revelation must be both propositional *and* personal: Bernard Ramm, *Special Revelation and the Word of God* (Grand Rapids, MI: Eerdmans, 1961), *passim*.

47. For examples, see C. H. Cosgrove, 'Justification in Paul: A Linguistic and Theological Reflection', *Journal of Biblical Literature* 106 (1987), pp. 653–670; David Hill, *Greek Words and Hebrew Meanings: Studies in the Semantics of Soteriological Terms* (Cambridge: Cambridge University Press, 1967); R. P. Martin, *Reconciliation: A Study of Paul's Theology* (Atlanta, GA: John Knox, 1981); Leon Morris, *The Apostolic Preaching of the Cross* (3rd edn., London: Inter-Varsity Press, 1965).

48. See Charles B. Cousar, *A Theology of the Cross* (Minneapolis, MN: Fortress, 1990), pp. 82–87; J. Driver, *Understanding the Atonement for the Mission of the Church* (Scottdale, PA: Herald, 1986).

49. See Ulrich Luz, '*Theologia Crucis* als Mitte der Theologie im Neuen Testament', *Evangelische Theologie* 34 (1974), pp. 116–141. On Paul in general, see Ernst Käsemann, 'The Saving Significance of the Death of Jesus in Paul', in *Perspectives on Paul* (Philadelphia: Fortress, 1971), pp. 32–59; H. W. Kuhn, 'Jesus als Gekreuzigter in der frühchristichen Verkündigung', *Zeitschrift für Theologie und Kirche* 72 (1975), pp. 1–46; Cousar, *A Theology of the Cross*.

50. Paul Knitter, *No Other Name? A Critical Survey of Christian Attitudes Towards the World Religions* (Maryknoll, NY: Orbis, 1985), pp. 171–204.

51. For an excellent survey of pluralist responses to traditional orthodox Christologies, including that of Knitter, see Clark H. Pinnock, *A Wideness in God's Mercy: The Finality of Jesus Christ in a World of Religions* (Grand Rapids, MI: Zondervan, 1992), pp. 49–80.

52. On the idea of *mimēsis* in Plato, see Maria Kardaun, *Der Mimesisbegriff in der griechischen Antike* (Amsterdam: North Holland, 1993).

53. Charles Gore, 'Our Lord's Human Example', *Church Quarterly Review* 16 (1883), pp. 282–313; quote at p. 298.

54. For an excellent analysis of these points, see O. M. T. O'Donovan,

Resurrection and Moral Order (2nd edn., Leicester: Apollos, and Grand Rapids, MI: Eerdmans, 1994).

55. For a more detailed analysis of this point, see Alister E. McGrath, 'Christian Ethics', in R. Morgan (ed.), *The Religion of the Incarnation: Anglican Essays in Commemoration of Lux Mundi* (Bristol: Bristol Classical Press, 1989), pp. 189–204. On the general point at issue, see John B. Webster, 'Christology, Imitability and Ethics', *Scottish Journal of Theology* 39 (1986), pp. 309–326.

56. A point stressed by H. D. Betz, *Nachfolge und Nachahmung Jesu Christi im Neuen Testament* (Tübingen: Mohr, 1967). Note especially the suggestion (p. 186) that Paul understands the Christian life as 'Mimesis Christi'.

57. See Beverly Gaventa, 'Galatians 1 and 2: Autobiography as Paradigm', *Novum Testamentum* 28 (1986), pp. 309–326; Victor Paul Furnish, *Theology and Ethics in Paul* (Nashville, TN: Abingdon, 1968).

58. L. Gregory Bloomquist, *The Function of Suffering in Philippians* (Sheffield: Sheffield Academic Press, 1993); Scott J. Hafemann, *Suffering and Ministry in the Spirit: Paul's Defense of His Ministry in 2 Corinthians 2:14 – 3:3* (Grand Rapids, MI: Eerdmans, 1990).

59. This point has been given considerable prominence in theological discussion of the last two decades, as may be seen from works such as Geoffrey Wainwright, *Doxology: The Praise of God in Worship, Doctrine and Life* (New York: Oxford University Press, 1980) and Aidan Kavanagh, *On Liturgical Theology* (New York: Pueblo, 1984).

60. James I. Packer, 'An Introduction to Systematic Spirituality', *Crux* 26/1 (March 1990), pp. 2–8; quote at p. 6.

61. On this point, see Richard J. Bauckham, 'The Worship of Jesus in Apocalyptic Christianity', *New Testament Studies* 27 (1980–81), pp. 322–341; Richard T. France, 'The Worship of Jesus: A Neglected Factor in Christological Debate?', in H. H. Rowdon (ed.), *Christ the Lord* (Leicester: Inter-Varsity Press, 1982), pp. 17–36.

62. Pliny, Epistle X, 96; see further Ralph P. Martin, *Carmen Christi: Philippians 2:5–11 in Recent Interpretation and in the Setting of Early Christian Worship* (Cambridge: Cambridge University Press, 1967), pp. 1–9.

63. See the useful survey by Ralph P. Martin, 'Hymns in the New Testament: An Evolving Pattern of Worship Responses', *Ex Auditu* 8 (1992), pp. 33–44. For an older and fuller assessment, see R. Deichgräber, *Gotteshymnus und Christushymnus in der frühen Christenheit* (Göttingen: Vandenhoeck & Ruprecht, 1967).

64. The thesis of P. Maurice Casey, *From Jewish Prophet to Gentile God* (Cambridge: James Clarke, 1991).

65. See L. W. Hurtado, *One God, One Lord: Early Christian Devotion and Ancient Jewish Monotheism* (Philadelphia: Fortress, 1988).

66. The hymns of William Cowper and Charles Wesley are excellent examples. See J. Richard Watson, 'Cowper's Olney Hymns', in *Essays and Reviews* 38 (1985), pp. 45–65; J. E. Rattenbury, *The Evangelical Doctrines of Charles Wesley's Hymns* (3rd edn., London: Epworth, 1954).

67. For the full context, see Martin Kähler, *Der sogenannte historische Jesus und der*

geschichtliche, biblische Christus, ed. E. Wolf (1892; repr. Munich: Kaiser Verlag, 1953), pp. 40–45.

68. See the remarkable analysis in Paul Tillich, *Systematic Theology* (3 vols., Chicago: University of Chicago Press, 1978), vol. 2, pp. 113–114.

69. For an analysis, see Alister E. McGrath, *The Making of Modern German Christology* (2nd edn., Leicester: Apollos, and Grand Rapids, MI: Zondervan, 1994), pp. 155–173.

70. For a careful analysis of this issue, see Miikka Ruokanen, *Hermeneutics as an Ecumenical Method in the Theology of Gerhard Ebeling* (Helsinki: Luther-Agricola-Gesellschaft, 1982), pp. 162–189.

71. See N. Walter, 'Paul and the Early Christian Jesus-Tradition', in A. J. M. Wedderburn and C. Wolff (eds.), *Paul and Jesus* (Sheffield: JSOT, 1989), pp. 51–80; David Wenham, 'Paul's Use of the Jesus Tradition', in D. Wenham (ed.), *Gospel Perspectives 5: The Jesus Tradition outside the Gospels* (Sheffield: JSOT, 1984), pp. 7–37. Most recently, see the excellent analysis in David Wenham, *Paul: Follower of Jesus or Founder of Christianity?* (Grand Rapids, MI: Eerdmans, 1995), especially pp. 71–103.

72. See J. I. H. McDonald, *Kerygma and Didache: The Articulation and Structure of the Earliest Christian Message* (Cambridge: Cambridge University Press, 1980).

73. C. H. Mounce, *The Essential Nature of New Testament Preaching* (Grand Rapids, MI: Eerdmans, 1960), p. 84. See also Peter Stuhlmacher, 'The Pauline Gospel', in P. Stuhlmacher (ed.), *The Gospel and the Gospels* (Grand Rapids: Eerdmans, 1991), pp. 149–172.

74. See especially William J. Abraham, 'A Theology of Evangelism', *Interpretation* 48 (1994), pp. 117–130.

75. For the moment, the most helpful theological analysis of evangelism from an evangelical perspective remains William J. Abraham, *The Logic of Evangelism* (Grand Rapids, MI: Eerdmans, 1989). See also his article 'A Theology of Evangelism', *Interpretation* 48 (1994), pp. 117–130.

76. I have chosen to use this form of words at this stage in the argument to allow for the possibility of both ontological and functional Christologies. However, it will become clear that, rightly understood, they are interconnected and inseparable.

77. *Institutes*, III.ii.6; *cf.* II.ix.3. For an excellent example of the application of this principle, see Thomas F. Torrance, *Preaching Christ Today* (Grand Rapids, MI: Eerdmans, 1994), pp. 1–40.

78. See the collection of essays in Wenham (ed.), *Gospel Perspectives 5: The Jesus Tradition outside the Gospels*; more briefly, R. T. France, *The Evidence for Jesus* (London: Hodder & Stoughton, 1986), pp. 19–85.

79. John Newton, *Works* (6 vols., Edinburgh: Banner of Truth, 1984), vol. 2, p. 18.

Chapter 2

1. For an excellent account of the incident, see Roland H. Bainton, *Here I Stand: A Life of Martin Luther* (Nashville, TN: Abingdon, 1950), p. 185.

2. Westminster Confession, I, 6; in E. F. K. Müller (ed.), *Die Bekenntnisschriften der reformierten Kirche* (Leipzig: Böhme, 1903), 545.11–20.

3. For details of the interpretation of the *sola Scriptura* principle, see Alister E. McGrath, *Reformation Thought: An Introduction* (2nd edn., Oxford and Cambridge, MA: Blackwell, 1993), pp. 140–155. For the high view of Scripture associated with the Reformation heritage, see the excellent study of W. Robert Godfrey, 'Biblical Authority in the Sixteenth and Seventeenth Centuries', in D. A. Carson and J. D. Woodbridge (eds.), *Scripture and Truth* (Grand Rapids, MI: Zondervan, 1983), pp. 225–250.

4. *D. Martin Luthers Werke. Kritische Gesamtausgabe: Tischreden*, vol. 2 (Weimar: Böhlau, 1883–), p. 439.

5. *D. Martin Luthers Werke. Kritische Gesamtausgabe: Deutsche Bibel* vol. 8 (Weimar: Böhlau, 1883–), p. 12.

6. *Ioannis Calvini opera quae supersunt omnia* (59 vols., Brunschweig and Berlin: Schwetschke, 1863–1900), vol. 9, p. 815. There are some thoughtful explorations of related themes to be found in John D. Morrison, 'John Calvin's Christological Assertion of Word Authority in the Context of Sixteenth Century Ecclesiological Polemics', *Scottish Journal of Theology* 45 (1993), pp. 465–486. For the Christocentric orientation of the Reformation doctrine of Scripture in general, see J. K. S. Reid, *The Authority of Scripture* (New York: Harper & Row, 1957), pp. 29–72; Brian A. Gerrish, 'The Word of God and the Words of Scripture: Luther and Calvin on Biblical Authority', in *The Old Protestantism and the New* (Chicago: University of Chicago Press, 1982), pp. 51–68.

7. Abraham Kuyper, *The Work of the Holy Spirit* (New York: Funk & Wagnalls, 1900), p. 397. Similarly, Herman Bavinck (1854–1921) affirmed that the object of Christian faith is Jesus Christ, as he is attested by Scripture.

8. See the important discussion in Donald G. Bloesch, *Essentials of Evangelical Theology* (San Francisco: Harper & Row, 1982), vol. 1, pp. 52–56.

9. Kuyper, *The Work of the Holy Spirit*, p. 399.

10. For a discussion, see Peter Jensen, 'The Spirit of Revelation', in B. G. Webb (ed.), *Spirit of the Living God (Explorations 6*; Homebush West, NSW: Lancer, 1992), pp. 1–18.

11. Karl Barth, *Church Dogmatics* (14 vols., Edinburgh: Clark, 1936–75), II/2, pp. 52–54.

12. See, among others, John Wenham, *Christ and the Bible* (2nd edn., Leicester: Inter-Varsity Press, 1984).

13. John Barton, *People of the Book?* (London: SPCK, 1988), p. 83.

14. See David Wenham (ed.), *Gospel Perspectives 5: The Jesus Tradition outside the Gospels* (Sheffield: JSOT, 1984); more briefly, R. T. France, *The Evidence for Jesus* (London: Hodder & Stoughton, 1986), pp. 19–85.

15. Stephen Neill, *The Supremacy of Jesus* (London: Hodder & Stoughton, 1984), pp. 9–17. Perhaps his finest popular exploration of this theme is to be found in *The Challenge of Jesus Christ* (Madras: SPCK India, 1944).

16. This point is noted by Francis Schüssler Fiorenza, 'The Crisis of Scriptural

Authority', *Interpretation* 44 (1990), pp. 353–368.

17. See the careful studies of Paul de Vooght, *Les sources de la doctrine chrétienne d'après les théologiens du XIVe siècle* (Paris, 1954), and Hermann Schüssler, *Der Primät der Heiligen Schrift als theologisches und kanonistisches Problem im Spätmittelalter* (Wiesbaden, 1977). More generally, see Alister E. McGrath, *The Intellectual Origins of the European Reformation* (Oxford: Blackwell, 1987), pp. 122–174; George Tavard, *Holy Writ or Holy Church* (New York: Harper & Row, 1959), pp. 22–23.

18. For the exploration of the direct and indirect influence of Scripture at this time, see Beryl Smalley, *The Study of the Bible in the Middle Ages* (3rd edn., Oxford: Blackwell, 1983).

19. Don Cupitt, *Taking Leave of God* (London: SCM, 1980), p. 9.

20. See the often-cited study of Allan Bloom, *The Closing of the American Mind* (New York: Simon & Schuster, 1987).

21. On this, see R. A. Markus, *Saeculum: History and Society in the Theology of St Augustine* (Cambridge: Cambridge University Press, 1970); Jaroslav Pelikan, *The Mystery of Continuity: Time and History, Memory and Eternity in the Thought of St Augustine* (Charlottesville, VA: University of Virginia Press, 1986).

22. See Paul Althaus, *Die deutsche Stunde der Kirche* (Göttingen: Vandenhoeck & Ruprecht, 1933). For a vigorous critique of the theology which prioritized German history in this way, see Ernst Wolf, *Barmen: Kirche zwischen Versuchung und Gnade* (2nd edn., Munich: Kaiser Verlag, 1970).

23. For the text of this document, see Gerhard Niemöller, *Die erste Bekenntnissynode der Deutschen Evangelischen Kirche zu Barmen* (2 vols., Göttingen: Vandenhoeck & Ruprecht, 1959), vol. 1, pp. 142–146.

24. See the disquieting analysis of Robert P. Ericksen, *Theologians under Hitler: Gerhard Kittel, Paul Althaus, and Emanuel Hirsch* (New Haven, CT: Yale University Press, 1985). The case of Emanuel Hirsch (1888–1972), who openly supported the Nazis, is especially significant (see Ericksen, pp. 120–197). For further documentation, see the series *Arbeiten zur Geschichte des Kirchenkampfes* (Göttingen and Zurich: Vandenhoeck & Ruprecht).

25. Stanley Hauerwas and William H. Willimon, *Resident Aliens: Life in the Christian Colony* (Nashville, TN: Abingdon, 1989), pp. 24–25.

26. Wilfried Härle, 'Der Aufruf der 93 Intellektuellen und Karl Barths Bruch mit der liberalen Theologie', *Zeitschrift für Theologie und Kirche* 72 (1975), pp. 207–224. More generally, see Wolfgang Huber, 'Evangelische Theologie und Kirche beim Ausbruch des Ersten Weltkriegs', *Studien zur Friedensforschung* 4 (1970), pp. 148–215.

27. Karl Barth, *Evangelische Theologie im 19. Jahrhundert* (Zurich: Zollikon, 1957), p. 6. See further Härle, 'Der Aufruf der 93 Intellektuellen und Karl Barths Bruch mit der liberalen Theologie'.

28. For the post-Stalinist period, see Vladimir Shlapentokh, *Soviet Intellectuals and Political Power* (Princeton, NJ: Princeton University Press, 1990).

29. Further documentation of this point is impossible within the space available.

The kind of approach I would be inclined to follow is mapped out in Alister E. McGrath, 'Christian Ethics', in *The Religion of the Incarnation: Anglican Essays in Commemoration of Lux Mundi* (Bristol: Bristol Classic Press, 1989), pp. 189–204.

30. John Shelby Spong, *Rescuing the Bible from Fundamentalism* (San Francisco: HarperCollins, 1991).

31. *The Fundamentals: A Testimony of the Truth* (12 vols., Chicago: Testimony Publishing Company, 1910–15).

32. The definitive study remains George Marsden, *Fundamentalism and American Culture: The Shaping of Twentieth Century Evangelicalism 1870–1925* (New York: Oxford University Press, 1980).

33. Spong, *Rescuing the Bible from Fundamentalism*, pp. 108–25.

34. John Shelby Spong, *Born of a Woman: A Bishop Rethinks the Birth of Jesus* (San Francisco: HarperCollins, 1992).

35. N. T. Wright, *Who was Jesus?* (Grand Rapids, MI: Eerdmans, 1992), pp. 65–92.

36. Wright, *Who was Jesus?*, pp. 91–92.

37. Gordon Kaufman, *Essay on Theological Method* (Missoula, MT: Scholars Press, 1975), p. 15. See also his appeal to a concept of God rooted in western culture in *Theology for a Nuclear Age* (Philadelphia: Westminster, 1985), pp. 22–23.

38. See H. C. G. Matthew, *The Liberal Imperialists* (London: Oxford University Press, 1973).

39. See William A. Galston, *Liberal Purposes: Goods, Virtues, and Diversity in the Liberal State* (Cambridge: Cambridge University Press, 1990).

40. See, for example, Lawrence Kohlberg, *The Philosophy of Moral Development* (New York: Harper & Row, 1981).

41. See especially Carol Gilligan, *In a Different Voice: Psychological Theory and Women's Development* (Cambridge, MA: Harvard University Press, 1982); Albert Borgmann, *Crossing the Postmodern Divide* (Chicago: University of Chicago Press, 1992), pp. 53–54.

42. Peter L. Berger, *A Far Glory: The Quest for Faith in an Age of Credulity* (New York: Free Press, 1992), pp. 10–11.

43. Berger, *A Far Glory*, p. 12 (emphasis in original).

44. W. R. Inge, *Diary of a Dean* (London: Hutchinson, 1949), p. 12.

45. Eugene B. Borowitz, 'The Enduring Truth of Religious Liberalism', in N. J. Cohen (ed.), *The Fundamentalist Phenomenon* (Grand Rapids, MI: Eerdmans, 1990), pp. 230–247; quote at p. 231.

46. This is the central theme of his major work, *Die gegenwärtige geistige Lage im Spiegel philosophischer und theologischer Besinnung* (Göttingen: Vandenhoeck & Ruprecht, 1934), which was written in response to the events of 1933.

47. For a useful analysis, see Michael Oakeshott, *Experience and its Modes* (Cambridge: Cambridge University Press, 1933). The best general study, from a philosophical standpoint, is Wayne Proudfoot, *Religious Experience* (Berkeley, CA: University of California Press, 1985). For a more theological approach, see Nicholas Lash, *Easter in Ordinary: Reflections on Human Experience and the Knowledge of God* (London: SCM, 1988).

48. See Gerhard Ebeling, 'Die Klage über das Erfahrungsdefizit in der Theologie als Frage nach ihrer Sache', *Wort und Glaube III* (Tübingen: Mohr, 1975), pp. 3–28.

49. For a useful study, see C. Stephen Evans, *Subjectivity and Religious Belief* (Grand Rapids, MI: Christian University Press, 1976).

50. George Lindbeck, *The Nature of Doctrine* (Philadelphia: Westminster, 1984). For an assessment and critique, see Alister E. McGrath, *The Genesis of Doctrine* (Oxford: Blackwell, 1990), pp. 14–34, and especially pp. 136–161 of the present study.

51. Lindbeck, *Nature of Doctrine*, p. 32.

52. Lindbeck, *Nature of Doctrine*, p. 23.

53. Lindbeck, *Nature of Doctrine*, p. 17.

54. See the useful analysis of William P. Alston, 'Christian Experience and Christian Belief', in A. Plantinga and N. Wolterstorff (eds.), *Faith and Rationality: Reason and Belief in God* (Notre Dame, IN: University of Notre Dame Press, 1983), pp. 103–134.

55. Gerhard E. Spiegler, *The Eternal Covenant: Schleiermacher's Experiment in Cultural Theology* (New York: Harper & Row, 1967), pp. 136–156.

56. B. R. F. Lonergan, *Philosophy of God and Theology* (London: Darton, Longman & Todd, 1973), p. 50.

57. It must be noted at this point that Lonergan is heavily dependent upon the somewhat questionable conclusions (*e.g.* that the 'higher religions' derive from the same common core experience of transcendence) of the Chicago writer Friedrich Heiler.

58. See Alister E. McGrath, *Luther's Theology of the Cross* (Oxford: Blackwell, 1985), pp. 148–175.

59. For a penetrating account of the importance of 'conversion', see Paula Fredsen, 'Paul and Augustine', *Journal of Theological Studies* 37 (1986), pp. 3–34. Note especially the emphasis on a break or discontinuity with the past.

60. Fraser Watts and Mark Williams, *The Psychology of Religious Knowing* (Cambridge: Cambridge University Press, 1988), pp. 10–23. On the distinction between 'committed' and 'consensual', see R. O. Allen and B. Spilka, 'Committed and Consensual Religion', *Journal for the Scientific Study of Religion* 6 (1967), pp. 191–206.

61. Watts and Williams, *Psychology of Religious Knowing*, pp. 109–127.

62. Lindbeck, *Nature of Doctrine*, p. 128.

63. Many 'experiential-expressive' accounts of doctrine would presumably dismiss this anxiety as pointless, given their non-cognitive understanding of the concept of revelation: see Avery Dulles, *Models of Revelation* (Dublin: Gill & Macmillan, 1983), pp. 98–114. For a careful analysis of experience as a theological resource, see Lash, *Easter in Ordinary*.

64. See the letter to Eberhard Bethge, dated 16 July 1944, in Dietrich Bonhoeffer, *Letters and Papers from Prison*, ed. E. Bethge (New York: Macmillan, and London: SCM, 1971), pp. 359–361.

65. On the theme of the 'hidden God' in Luther's early theology, see John

Dillenberger, *God Hidden and Revealed* (Philadelphia: Fortress, 1953); McGrath, *Luther's Theology of the Cross*, pp. 161–175.

66. For what follows, see McGrath, *Luther's Theology of the Cross*. For the implications of this approach for Christian spirituality, see Alister McGrath, *Roots that Refresh: A Celebration of Reformation Spirituality* (London: Hodder & Stoughton, 1992); North American edition published as *Spirituality in an Age of Change* (Grand Rapids, MI: Zondervan, 1994).

67. Francis Schüssler Fiorenza, *Foundational Theology: Jesus and the Church* (New York: Crossroad Publishing Co., 1984), p. 283.

68. For other reflections on European theology, see Alister E. McGrath, 'The European Roots of Evangelicalism', *Anvil* 9 (1992), pp. 239–248.

69. On Calvin's understanding of the dialectic between theology and experience, see Wilhelm Balke, 'The Word of God and *Experientia* according to Calvin', in W. H. Neuser (ed.), *Calvinus Ecclesiae Doctor* (Kampen: Kok, 1978), pp. 19–31.

70. Søren Kierkegaard, *Unscientific Postscript* (London: Oxford University Press, 1941), pp. 169–224. *Cf.* P. L. Holmer, 'Kierkegaard and Religious Propositions', *Journal of Religion* 35 (1955), pp. 135–146.

71. *D. Martin Luthers Werke: Kritische Gesamtausgabe*, vol. 5 (Weimar: Böhlau, 1885), 163.28–29. For a full discussion, see McGrath, *Luther's Theology of the Cross*, pp. 148–152.

72. Plato, *Gorgias*, 493b–d.

73. Diogenes Allen, *The Traces of God* (Cambridge, MA: Cowley Publications, 1981), p. 19.

74. Augustine, *Confessions*, I.i.1. Citations are from the recent translation by Henry Chadwick (Oxford: Oxford University Press, 1991), p. 3.

75. For a superb presentation of Augustine's thoughts on this tension, see John Burnaby, *Amor Dei: A Study in the Religion of St Augustine* (London: Hodder & Stoughton, 1938), pp. 52–73.

76. *Confessions*, XII.xvi.23; Chadwick, p. 257.

77. C. S. Lewis, *Surprised by Joy* (London: Collins, 1959), p. 20.

78. Lewis, *Surprised by Joy*, p. 19.

79. C. S. Lewis, 'The Weight of Glory', in *Screwtape Proposes A Toast* (London: Collins, 1965), pp. 97–98.

80. Simone Weil, *Waiting for God* (New York: Putnam, 1951), p. 210.

81. Lewis, 'The Weight of Glory', p. 99.

82. C. S. Lewis, 'The Language of Religion', in *Christian Reflections* (London: Collins, 1981), p. 169.

83. Stanley Hauerwas, *The Peaceable Kingdom* (Notre Dame, IN: University of Notre Dame Press, 1983), p. xxi.

84. See Alister E. McGrath, *Bridge-Building: Effective Christian Apologetics* (Leicester: Inter-Varsity Press, 1992). North American edition published as *Intellectuals Don't Need God and Other Modern Myths* (Grand Rapids, MI: Zondervan, 1993).

85. On this, see Gabriel Fackre, 'The Scandals of Particularity and Universality',

Mid-Stream 22 (1983), pp. 32–52.
86. G. E. Lessing, 'Über den Beweis des Geistes und der Kraft', in *Gotthold Ephraim Lessings sämtlichen Schriften*, vol. 13, ed. Karl Lachmann (Berlin: Göschen'sche Verlagshandlung, 1897), 5.34–36.
87. Stephen Toulmin, *The Uses of Argument* (Cambridge: Cambridge University Press, 1958), p. 127.
88. See Lewis Carroll, 'What the Tortoise said to Achilles', *Mind* 4 (1895), pp. 278–280. For minor criticisms of this seminal paper, see J. Thomson, 'What Achilles should have said to the Tortoise', *Ratio* 3 (1960), pp. 95–105. The problem of circularity in rational deduction is explored fully in Susan Haack, 'The Justification of Deduction', *Mind* 85 (1976), pp. 112–119.
89. A useful introduction may be found in Gottfried Martin, *Kant's Metaphysics and Theory of Science* (Manchester: Manchester University Press, 1955), pp. 16–20.
90. R. M. Hare, *The Language of Morals* (Oxford: Oxford University Press, 1952). See the criticisms by Jeffrey Stout, *Ethics after Babel: The Languages of Morals and Their Discontents* (Princeton, NJ: Princeton University Press, 1988), pp. 60–81.
91. Toulmin, *Uses of Argument*, p. 183.
92. Alasdair MacIntyre, *Whose Justice? Which Rationality?* (Notre Dame, IN: University of Notre Dame, 1988), p. 6.
93. Hans-Georg Gadamer, *Truth and Method* (London: Sheed & Ward, 1975), p. 271.
94. Paul K. Feyerabend, *Science in a Free Society* (London: Verso, 1983), p. 82. For a more restrained exposition of such points, see his *Against Method* (3rd edn., London: Verso, 1993). The collection of essays entitled *Farewell to Reason* (London: Verso, 1987) is also of importance.
95. See Thomas Aquinas, *Summa Theologia*, Ia q. 1 aa. 1, 8.
96. The 'quest of the historical Jesus' is an excellent example of the influence of rationalism, in which rationalist preconceptions about what Jesus must have been like are allowed to exercise a controlling influence over the interpretation of the New Testament.
97. See the careful and insightful analysis by Nicholas Wolterstorff, *Reason within the Bounds of Religion* (2nd edn., Grand Rapids, MI: Eerdmans, 1984).
98. See Alister E. McGrath, *The Intellectual Origins of the European Reformation* (Oxford: Blackwell, 1987), pp. 140–151.
99. James I. Packer, *'Fundamentalism' and the Word of God* (Leicester: Inter-Varsity Press, and Grand Rapids, MI: Eerdmans, 1958; reissued, Inter-Varsity Press, 1996), p. 48. For further reflections on the positive role of tradition for evangelicalism, see James I. Packer, 'The Comfort of Conservatism', in M. J. Horton (ed.), *Power Religion* (Chicago: Moody Press, 1992), pp. 283–299.
100. *Epitome*, 1–8; in *Die Bekenntnisschriften der evangelisch-lutherischen Kirche* (2nd edn., Göttingen: Vandenhoeck & Ruprecht, 1952), 767.14 – 769.34.
101. See John Milbank, 'The Name of Jesus: Incarnation, Atonement, Ecclesiology', *Modern Theology* 7 (1991), pp. 311–333.
102. David L. Edwards with John Stott, *Essentials: A Liberal–Evangelical Dialogue*

(London: Hodder & Stoughton, 1988), p. 73. The discussion of evangelical beliefs in this book is especially illuminating.

103. I. Howard Marshall is a case in point, through his study *Biblical Inspiration* (London: Hodder & Stoughton, 1982). For some other discussions of inspiration from an evangelical viewpoint, see Packer, *'Fundamentalism' and the Word of God*. For other discussions of biblical inspiration which are helpful from an evangelical perspective, see P. J. Achtemeier, *The Inspiration of Scripture* (Philadelphia: Westminster, 1980); W. J. Abraham, *The Divine Inspiration of Holy Scripture* (Oxford: Oxford University Press, 1981); K. R. Trembath, *Evangelical Theories of Biblical Inspiration* (Oxford: Oxford University Press, 1987).

104. William Barclay, writing at a popular level, was a fine scholar who rationalized the miracles. Gerd Theissen at least hints at such rationalization in his splendid book *The Shadow of the Galilean* (London: SCM, 1987), p. 120. For evangelical scholarly discussion of such miracles, see David Wenham and Craig Blomberg (eds.), *Gospel Perspectives 6: The Miracles of Jesus* (Sheffield: JSOT Press, 1986).

105. On the two-source theory, see among others E. P. Sanders and M. Davies, *Studying the Synoptic Gospels* (London: SCM, 1989); on the parables, see Craig L. Blomberg, *Interpreting the Parables* (Leicester: Inter-Varsity Press, 1990).

106. Walter Wink, *Transforming Bible Study* (Nashville, TN: Abingdon, 1980), p. 155.

107. W. Robertson Smith, *Answer to the Form of Libel* (Edinburgh: Douglas, 1878), p. 21.

108. See the discussion in Kierkegaard, *Unscientific Postscript*, pp. 169–224.

109. For the phrase, see James Houston, *The Transforming Friendship* (Oxford: Lion Publishing, 1993). More generally, see Alister E. McGrath, *The Genesis of Doctrine* (Oxford: Blackwell, 1990), pp. 78–80. For a consideration of the relation of Scripture and doctrine, see pp. 52–66.

110. See John Sandys-Wunsch and Laurence Eldredge, 'J. P. Gabler and the Distinction between Biblical and Dogmatic Theology', *Scottish Journal of Theology* 33 (1980), pp. 133–158; Magne Saebo, 'Johann Philip Gablers Bedeutung für die Biblische Theologie', *Zeitschrift für Alttestamentlichen Wissenschaft* 99 (1987), pp. 1–16.

111. For a detailed survey, see Hans-Joachim Kraus, *Die Biblische Theologie: Ihre Geschichte und Problematik* (Neukirchen and Vluyn: Neukirchener Verlag, 1970); at a more popular level, see Krister Stendahl, 'Biblical Theology, Contemporary', in *The Interpreter's Dictionary of the Bible* (New York: Abingdon, 1961), vol. 1, pp. 418–432.

112. For an excellent discussion of this point, see David J. Hesselgrave and Edward Rommen, *Contextualization: Meanings, Methods and Models* (Grand Rapids, MI: Baker, and Leicester: Apollos, 1989).

113. David F. Wells, 'The Nature and Function of Theology', in R. K. Johnston (ed.), *The Use of the Bible in Theology: Evangelical Options* (Atlanta, GA: John Knox, 1985), p. 177.

114. For an important analysis, see N. T. Wright, *The New Testament and the People of God* (Minneapolis, MN: Fortress, 1992), pp. 139–143; also his earlier essay 'How can the Bible be Authoritative?', *Vox Evangelica* 21 (1991), pp. 7–32.

115. Hans Frei, *The Eclipse of Biblical Narrative* (New Haven, CT: Yale University Press, 1974). For a discussion of the three main approaches which developed during the eighteenth century, see pp. 255–266. There is also useful material to be found in John Rogerson, *Old Testament Criticism in the Nineteenth Century* (London: SPCK, 1984).

116. Frei, *Eclipse of Biblical Narrative*, p. 2. See also Brevard Childs, 'The *Sensus Literalis* of Scripture: An Ancient and Modern Problem', in H. Donner *et al.* (eds.), *Beiträge zur alttestamentlichen Theologie* (Göttingen: Vandenhoeck & Ruprecht, 1977), pp. 80–93.

117. Brevard Childs, 'Critical Reflections on James Barr's Understanding of the Literal and Allegorical', *Journal for the Study of the Old Testament* 46 (1990), pp. 3–9; quote at p. 8. This article was a reply to James Barr, 'The Literal, the Allegorical and Modern Biblical Scholarship', *Journal for the Study of the Old Testament* 44 (1989), pp. 3–17.

118. See R. Lischer, 'Luther and Contemporary Preaching', *Scottish Journal of Theology* 36 (1983), pp. 487–504. See also his subsequent article 'The Limits of Story', *Interpretation* 38 (1984), pp. 26–38.

119. Frei, *Eclipse of Biblical Narrative*, pp. 141–142.

120. Andrew Fox, 'The Intellectual Consequences of the Sixteenth-Century Religious Upheaval and the Coming of a Rational World View', *Sixteenth Century Journal* 18 (1987), pp. 63–80.

121. Sidney A. Ahlstrom, 'The Scottish Philosophy and American Theology', *Church History* 24 (1955), pp. 257–272.

122. For the general point, see Alister E. McGrath, 'Geschichte, Überlieferung und Erzählung: Überlegungen zur Identität und Aufgabe christlicher Theologie', *Kerygma und Dogma* 32 (1986), pp. 234–253. More generally, see Gabriel Fackre, 'Narrative Theology: An Overview', *Interpretation* 37 (1983), pp. 340–352, and particularly the idea of 'rendering', as explored in Dale Patrick, *The Rendering of God in the Old Testament* (Philadelphia: Fortress, 1981), and subsequently in Hugh C. White, *Narration and Discourse in the Book of Genesis* (Cambridge: Cambridge University Press, 1991). On the distinctive features of narrative in general, see Robert Scholes and Robert Kellogg, *The Nature of Narrative* (New York: Oxford University Press, 1966).

123. This point is made with particular clarity by Walter Brueggemann, who points out that the standard historico-critical approach to the Old Testament methodologically excludes everything which evoked the sense of *wonder* with which Israel recounted its history: see Walter Brueggemann, *Abiding Astonishment: Psalms, Modernity and the Making of History* (Louisville, KY: Westminster/John Knox, 1991), pp. 37–38.

124. See David F. Ford, *Barth and God's Story* (Frankfurt: Peter Lang, 1985). A similar approach can be seen in Robert W. Jenson, 'The Triune God', in C. E.

Braaten and R. W. Jenson (eds.), *Christian Dogmatics* (2 vols., Philadelphia: Fortress, 1984), vol. 1, pp. 87–92.

125. H. Richard Niebuhr, *The Meaning of Revelation* (New York: Macmillan, 1960), pp. 32–66.

126. What follows is an abbreviated account of a more substantial discussion found in Alister E. McGrath, *The Genesis of Doctrine* (Oxford: Blackwell, 1990), pp. 52–66.

127. For this theme in the writings of Karl Barth, see David F. Ford, 'Barth's Interpretation of the Bible', in S. W. Sykes (ed.), *Karl Barth: Studies of his Theological Method* (Oxford: Oxford University Press, 1979), pp. 55–87.

128. A. E. Harvey, 'Christian Propositions and Christian Stories', in A. E. Harvey (ed.), *God Incarnate: Story and Belief* (London: SPCK, 1981), pp. 1–13.

129. For explorations of this insight from an evangelical perspective, see Clark Pinnock, *Tracking the Maze* (San Francisco: Harper & Row, 1990), pp. 153–154; Stanley J. Grenz, *Revisioning Evangelical Theology* (Downers Grove, IL: InterVarsity Press, 1993), p. 78.

130. Colin E. Gunton, '*Christus Victor* Revisited: A Study in Metaphor and the Transformation of Meaning', *Journal of Theological Studies* 36 (1985), pp. 129–145.

131. See D. E. de Clerck, 'Droits du démon et nécessité de la rédemption', *Recherches de Théologie Ancienne et Médiévale* 14 (1947), pp. 32–64.

132. Alister E. McGrath, *Iustitia Dei: A History of the Christian Doctrine of Justification* (2 vols., Cambridge: Cambridge University Press, 1986), vol. 1, pp. 55–62.

133. Rowan D. Williams, *Arius: Heresy and Tradition* (London: Darton, Longman & Todd, 1987), pp. 117–157 and references therein.

134. Williams, *Arius*, p. 231.

135. For the significance of Christian worship in the shaping of early Christian doctrine, see Maurice F. Wiles, *The Making of Christian Doctrine* (Cambridge: Cambridge University Press, 1967), pp. 62–93. On the place of doxology in theology in general, see Geoffrey Wainwright, *Doxology: The Praise of God in Worship, Doctrine and Life* (New York: Oxford University Press, 1980).

136. Robert W. Jenson, *The Triune Identity* (Philadelphia: Fortress, 1982), pp. 1–56.

137. See Richard B. Hays, *The Faith of Jesus Christ: An Investigation of the Narrative Substructure of Galatians 3:1 – 4:11* (Chico, CA: Scholars Press, 1983), especially pp. 193–246.

138. See McGrath, *Luther's Theology of the Cross*, pp. 148–181.

139. For a full analysis, see McGrath, *Luther's Theology of the Cross*, pp. 95–181.

140. On Aristotle's idea, see D. W. Hamlyn, 'Aristotle's God', in G. J. Hughes (ed.), *The Philosophical Assessment of Theology* (Tunbridge Wells: Search Press, 1987), pp. 15–33.

141. For example, see James D. G. Dunn, 'The Authority of Scripture according to Scripture', *Churchman* 96 (1982), pp. 104–123, 201–225.

142. These norms derive from an Enlightenment-type of common-sense philosophy, to be considered in more detail at pp. 166–173. See, for example,

Sidney E. Ahlstrom, 'The Scottish Philosophy and American Theology', *Church History* 24 (1955), pp. 257–272.

Chapter 3

1. The classic evangelical critique of liberalism remains J. Gresham Machen, *Christianity and Liberalism* (1923; reprinted Grand Rapids, MI: Eerdmans, 1994). This work was based on a 1921 lecture entitled 'Liberalism or Christianity', published in *Princeton Theological Review* 20 (1922), pp. 93–117.
2. Writings which illustrate this approach include Hans Frei, *The Identity of Jesus Christ* (Philadelphia: Fortress, 1975); Paul Holmer, *The Grammar of Faith* (New York: Harper & Row, 1978); David Kelsey, *The Uses of Scripture in Recent Theology* (Philadelphia: Fortress, 1975); *idem*, 'The Bible and Christian Theology', *Journal of the American Academy of Religion* 48 (1980), pp. 358–402; George Lindbeck, *The Nature of Doctrine: Religion and Theology in a Postliberal Age* (Philadelphia: Westminster, 1984).
3. A point noted by Brevard Childs, *The New Testament as Canon* (Philadelphia: Fortress, 1984), p. 541.
4. See Stanley Hauerwas, *Against the Nations* (Minneapolis, MN: Winston Press, 1985); *idem*, *A Community of Character: Toward a Constructive Christian Social Ethic* (Notre Dame, IN: University of Notre Dame Press, 1981); William C. Placher, *Unapologetic Theology: A Christian Voice in a Pluralistic Conversation* (Louisville, KY: Westminster/John Knox, 1989); Ronald E. Thiemann, *Revelation and Theology: The Gospel as Narrated Promise* (Notre Dame, IN: University of Notre Dame Press, 1985).
5. For general overviews, see William C. Placher, 'Postliberal Theology', in D. F. Ford (ed.), *The Modern Theologians* (2 vols., Oxford and Cambridge, MA: Blackwell, 1989), vol. 2, pp. 115–128; Sheila Greeve Davaney and Delwin Brown, 'Postliberalism', in A. E. McGrath (ed.), *The Blackwell Encyclopaedia of Modern Christian Thought* (Oxford and Cambridge, MA: Blackwell, 1993), pp. 453–456.
6. William C. Placher, 'Paul Ricoeur and Postliberal Theology: A Conflict of Interpretations', *Modern Theology* 4 (1987), pp. 35–52.
7. See Alasdair MacIntyre, *After Virtue* (2nd edn., Notre Dame, IN: University of Notre Dame Press, 1984). For perceptive readings of this text and its programme, see Richard J. Bernstein, 'Nietzsche or Aristotle? Reflections on Alasdair MacIntyre's *After Virtue*', *Soundings* 67 (1984), pp. 14–15; L. Gregory Jones, 'Alasdair MacIntyre on Narrative, Community and the Moral Life', *Modern Theology* 4 (1987), pp. 53–69.
8. For excellent accounts, see Kenneth Cauthen, *The Impact of American Religious Liberalism* (Lanham, MD: University Press of America, 1962); William R. Hutchinson, *The Modernist Impulse in American Protestantism* (New York: Oxford University Press, 1976).
9. See B. K. Martin, *French Liberal Thought in the Eighteenth Century* (2nd edn., London: Turnstile Press, 1954).
10. Madame de Staël was followed into exile in Switzerland by her lover, Benjamin

Constant, whose writings during this period are particularly significant statements of liberal principles. See Stephen Holmes, *Benjamin Constant and the Making of Modern Liberalism* (New Haven, CT: Yale University Press, 1984).

11. For the development of the term, see Guido de Ruggiero, *History of European Liberalism* (London: Oxford University Press, 1927).

12. Cited in F. W. Knickerbocker, *Free Minds: John Morley and His Friends* (Cambridge, MA: Harvard University Press, 1943), p. 163. On Victorian liberalism in general, see Ian Bradley, *The Optimists: Themes and Personalities in Victorian Liberalism* (London: Faber & Faber, 1980).

13. J. F. Bethune-Baker, *The Faith of the Apostles' Creed: An Essay in Adjustment of Belief and Faith* (London: Macmillan, 1918).

14. George Tyrrell, *Christianity at the Cross-Roads* (1909; repr. London: Black, 1963), p. 49.

15. See Brian J. Walsh, 'Liberal Tyranny', *Third Way* 15/6 (1992), pp. 26–30.

16. John Macquarrie, *Jesus Christ in Modern Thought* (London: SCM, 1990), p. 253.

17. For a survey of recent critiques of liberalism in the United States, see Ronald Beiner, *What's the Matter with Liberalism?* (Berkeley, CA: University of California Press, 1992); Barry Penn Hollar, *On Being the Church in the United States: Contemporary Theological Critiques of Liberalism* (New York and Berne: Peter Lang, 1994).

18. Stanley Fish, *There's No Such Thing as Free Speech* (New York: Oxford University Press, 1994), p. 296. Fish himself argues that there are no objective, universal standards for truth, in that all 'truth claims' are simply manipulations of language in order to achieve political or social power. Debates over 'truth' are thus in reality nothing other than power games.

19. Alasdair MacIntyre, *Whose Justice? Which Rationality?* (Notre Dame, IN: University of Notre Dame Press, 1988), p. 335.

20. It is important, however, to note that some more recent defences of liberalism are non-foundational: for a non-foundational approach to liberalism, see Richard Rorty, 'The Priority of Democracy to Philosophy', in G. Outka and J. P. Reeder (eds.), *Prospects for a Common Morality* (Princeton, NJ: Princeton University Press, 1993), pp. 254–278.

21. For example, see his *On Theology* (San Francisco: Harper & Row, 1986).

22. For example, see Gordon Kaufman, *Essay on Theological Method* (Missoula, MT: Scholars Press, 1975); *idem*, *Theology for a Nuclear Age* (Philadelphia: Westminster, 1985).

23. See A. Plantinga and N. Wolterstorff (eds.), *Faith and Rationality: Reason and Belief in God* (Notre Dame, IN: University of Notre Dame Press, 1983).

24. Jacques Ellul, *Violence* (New York: Seabury Press, 1969), p. 28.

25. Wade Clark Roof and William McKinney, *American Mainline Religion: Its Changing Shape and Future* (Brunswick, NJ: Rutgers University Press, 1987).

26. Roof and McKinney, *American Mainline Religion*, p. 242.

27. Michael Oakeshott, *On Human Conduct* (Oxford: Clarendon, 1975). A more sympathetic account of this point may be found in David R. Mappel, 'Civil

Association and the Idea of Contingency', *Political Theory* 18 (1990), pp. 392–410.
28. Ronald Dworkin, 'Liberalism', in S. Hampshire (ed.), *Public and Private Morality* (Cambridge: Cambridge University Press, 1978), p. 217. See a similar comment in John Rawls, *A Theory of Justice* (Cambridge, MA: Harvard University Press, 1971), p. 19; Bruce Ackermann, *Social Justice in the Liberal State* (New Haven, CT: Yale University Press, 1980), p. 11.
29. For an especially helpful assessment of the New Age, see Linda Christensen, 'The New Age', in Michael Green and Alister McGrath, *How Shall We Reach Them?* (Nashville, TN: Thomas Nelson, 1995), pp. 78–106.
30. Max L. Stackhouse and Dennis P. McCann, 'Public Theology after the Collapse of Socialism', *Christian Century*, 16 January 1991, pp. 45–47. Other writers sympathetic to this 'public theology' include Robert Benne, David Hollenbach, SJ, and Robin Lovin. For an example of the approach adopted, see Robert Benne, *The Paradoxical Vision: A Public Theology for the Twenty-First Century* (Minneapolis, MN: Fortress, 1995).
31. Reinhold Niebuhr, *Leaves from the Notebook of a Tamed Critic* (New York: Meridian, 1957), p. 16.
32. Os Guinness, 'Tribespeople, Idiots or Citizens? Evangelicals, Religious Liberty and a Public Philosophy for the Public Square', in K. S. Kantzer and C. F. H. Henry (eds.), *Evangelical Affirmations* (Grand Rapids, MI: Zondervan, 1990), pp. 457–497; quote at p. 471.
33. Lesslie Newbigin, *Truth to Tell: The Gospel as Public Truth* (Grand Rapids, MI: Eerdmans, 1991), p. 49.
34. On the theological aspects, see D. Z. Phillips, *Faith after Foundationalism* (London: Routledge, 1988). For the more general phenomenon, see Stephen Crook, *Modernist Radicalism and its Aftermath: Foundationalism and Anti-foundationalism in Radical Social Theory* (London: Routledge, 1991); John E. Thiel, *Nonfoundationalism* (Minneapolis, MN: Fortress, 1994).
35. Mary Midgley, *Beast and Man* (New York: Meridian, 1980), p. 306.
36. This point is made, although in different ways, in Holmer, *The Grammar of Faith*; Frei, *The Eclipse of Biblical Narrative*, and Lindbeck, *Nature of Doctrine*.
37. Lindbeck, *Nature of Doctrine*, p. 129.
38. I think it is fair to point out that postliberal writers are not themselves entirely free from such dependence on extrabiblical foundations. For example, in his *Nature of Doctrine*, George Lindbeck clearly depends upon the kind of cultural analysis provided by Clifford Geertz, in his major essay 'Religion as a Cultural System', in D. R. Cutler (ed.), *The Religious Situation* (Boston, MA: Beacon, 1968), pp. 639–688; while in his *Community of Character*, Stanley Hauerwas seems to rely on the analysis of Yves Simon regarding 'political authority', as stated in *Philosophy of Democratic Government* (Chicago: University of Chicago Press, 1951).
39. See David F. Ford, 'The Best Apologetics is a Good Systematics: A Proposal About the Place of Narrative in Christian Systematic Theology', *Anglican Theological Review* 67 (1985), pp. 232–253; William Werphehowski, 'Ad Hoc Apologetics', *Journal of Religion* 66 (1986), pp. 282–301; Benno van den Toren, 'A

New Direction in Christian Apologetics', *European Journal of Theology* 2 (1993), pp. 49–64.

40. See Lindbeck, *Nature of Doctrine*, p. 131. A similar point is made by Hans Frei, who notes that it is legitimate to 'borrow' from other disciplines in order to explain the subject matter of Christianity. Hans Frei, 'An Afterword: Eberhard Busch's Biography of Karl Barth', in H. M. Rumscheidt (ed.), *Karl Barth in Re-Review* (Pittsburg, PA: Pickwick Publications, 1981), pp. 95–116, especially p. 114.

41. This is the approach which I adopt and justify elsewhere, on the basis of assumptions drawn directly from the evangelical tradition. See Alister E. McGrath, *Bridge-Building: Effective Christian Apologetics* (Leicester: Inter-Varsity Press, 1992); published in North America as *Intellectuals Don't Need God and Other Modern Myths: Building Bridges to Faith Through Apologetics* (Grand Rapids, MI: Zondervan, 1993).

42. Stanley Hauerwas and William H. Willimon, *Resident Aliens: Life in the Christian Colony* (Nashville, TN: Abingdon, 1989), p. 18.

43. The use of this Wittgensteinian term is significant: see Paul Holmer, 'Wittgenstein: Saying and Showing', *Neue Zeitschrift für systematische Theologie und Religionsphilosophie* 33 (1980), pp. 222–235.

44. Holmer, *Grammar of Faith*, p. 23.

45. See Gordon J. Michaelson, Jr, 'The Response to Lindbeck', *Modern Theology* 4 (1988), pp. 107–120.

46. Lindbeck, *Nature of Doctrine*, p. 16.

47. Lindbeck, *Nature of Doctrine*, p. 21. This would certainly correspond to the popular stereotype of evangelicalism, although I would not have expected to find such wooden stereotypes in such a work.

48. It might also reasonably be pointed out that it pays inadequate attention to what it means to suggest that religious claims are 'cognitive' in the first place: an excellent discussion of this point (published too late to be available to Lindbeck) may be found in James Kellenberger, *Cognitivity of Religion: Three Views* (London: Macmillan, 1985).

49. Lindbeck, *Nature of Doctrine*, p. 47. But compare the concessions on pp. 80, 105.

50. A point noted by Brian A. Gerrish, 'The Nature of Doctrine', *Journal of Religion* 68 (1988), pp. 87–92, especially pp. 87–88.

51. On this, see J. M. Parent, 'La notion de dogme au XIIIe siècle', in *Etude d'histoire litteraire et doctrinaire du XIIIe siècle* (Paris, 1932), pp. 141–163.

52. Gillian R. Evans, *Alan of Lille: The Frontiers of Theology in the Later Twelfth Century* (Cambridge: Cambridge University Press, 1983), pp. 64–80.

53. For example, see Bede's careful discussion of various different modes and levels of representation, *tropoi* (such as metaphor, catachresis, metalepsis, anadiplosis and metonymia) and *schemata* (such as anaphora, prolepsis and zeugma). Bede, *De schematibus et tropis*; J. P. Migne, *Patrologia Latina*, 90.175A-B.

54. For example, see Evans, *Alan of Lille*, pp. 33–36. A recent work which attempts a similar clarification of the word 'God' in such a manner is Theodore

W. Jennings, *Beyond Theism: A Grammar of God-Language* (New York: Oxford University Press, 1985), especially pp. 59–74.

55. For an exploration of the relation between cognitive statements and experience, see Alister E. McGrath, 'Theology and Experience: Reflections on Cognitive and Experiential Approaches to Theology', *European Journal of Theology* 2 (1993), pp. 65–74.

56. Lindbeck makes a related point in connection with Hamlet and Denmark: *Nature of Doctrine*, p. 65.

57. C. S. Lewis, *Surprised by Joy* (London: Collins, 1959), p. 17. It is, of course, debatable whether this is the experience Longfellow had intended to convey; discussion of this question must, however, lie beyond the present study.

58. For an excellent study focusing on Calvin, see Benoît Girardin, *Rhétorique et théologique. Calvin: le commentaire de l'épître aux Romains* (Paris: Gallimard, 1979), pp. 205–273.

59. The rhetorical figures of analogy and metaphor are of supreme importance in this respect: see Sallie McFague, *Metaphorical Theology: Models of God in Religious Language* (Philadelphia: Fortress, 1985); Janet Martin Soskice, *Metaphor and Religious Language* (Oxford: Clarendon, 1985), pp. 118–161.

60. See Fraser Watts and Isaac Williams, *The Psychology of Religious Knowing* (Cambridge: Cambridge University Press, 1988), pp. 59–74.

61. Jonathan Wordsworth, *William Wordsworth: The Borders of Vision* (Oxford: Oxford University Press, 1982), pp. 1–35. The same theme is explored with reference to the idea of 'liminality' by John R. Watson, *Wordsworth's Vital Soul: The Sacred and Profane in Wordsworth's Poetry* (London: Maacmillan, 1982). These ideas cannot be dismissed simply as outmoded nineteenth-century Romanticism. Many seminal ideas of English Romanticism have been appropriated and creatively developed in twentieth-century English religious and literary writings. Thus Owen Barfield and J. R. R. Tolkien exploit Coleridge's doctrine of the creative imagination; while C. S. Lewis, Charles Williams and Tolkien all affirm that 'romantic' experiences (such as *Sehnsucht*) are, or can become, religious experiences. See R. J. Reilly, *Romantic Religion* (Athens, GA: Georgia State University Press, 1971).

62. C. S. Lewis, 'The Weight of Glory', in *Screwtape Proposes A Toast* (London: Collins, 1965), pp. 97–98.

63. On this concept in the literature of late German Romanticism, see Adalbert Elschenbroich, *Romantische Sehnsucht und Kosmogonie* (Tübingen: Niemeyer, 1971).

64. Evelyn Waugh, *Brideshead Revisited* (Harmondsworth: Penguin, 1983), p. 288.

65. See the important analysis offered by F. D. E. Schleiermacher, *The Christian Faith* (Edinburgh: T. & T. Clark, 1928), pp. 78–83.

66. Gerrish, 'Nature of Doctrine', p. 92.

67. For this point in relation to the writings of Schillebeeckx, see L. Dupré, 'Experience and Interpretation: A Philosophical Reflection on Schillebeeckx' *Jesus and Christ*', *Theological Studies* 43 (1982), pp. 30–51.

68. A point stressed by John R. Carnes, *Axiomatics and Dogmatics* (Belfast:

Christian Journals, 1982), pp. 10–15. See also the earlier study of Norbert R. Hanson, *Perception and Discovery* (San Francisco: Freeman and Cooper, 1969); idem, *Observation and Explanation* (New York: Harper & Row, 1971).

69. Gerhard Ebeling, 'Die Klage über das Erfahrungsdefizit in der Theologie als Frage nach ihrer Sache', in *Wort und Glaube III* (Tübingen: Mohr, 1975), pp. 3–28.

70. See Eberhard Jüngel, *God as the Mystery of the World* (Edinburgh: T. & T. Clark, 1983), p. 32.

71. Clifford Geertz, 'Religion as a Cultural System', in D. R. Cutler (ed.), *The Religious Situation* (Boston, MA: Beacon, 1968), pp. 639–88.

72. It would seem that Lindbeck's philosophical stances must be related to the longstanding English-language debate concerning 'Wittgensteinian fideism': see Kai Nielsen, 'Wittgensteinian Fideism', *Philosophy* 42 (1967), pp. 191–209. The continuing use of this term has been severely criticized by Fergus Kerr, *Theology after Wittgenstein* (Oxford: Blackwell, 1985), pp. 28–31. It is one of the many merits of Lindbeck's work to attempt to respond to Wittgenstein, both in the rejection of 'cognitive' models of doctrine and in the affirmation of the value of a 'cultural-linguistic' approach.

73. See Lindbeck, *Nature of Doctrine*, pp. 32–41; quote at p. 33.

74. Lindbeck, *Nature of Doctrine*, p. 65.

75. For Hans Frei's discussion of the relation of 'fact-likeness' to 'factuality', see Frei, *The Eclipse of Biblical Narrative*, p. 187.

76. Lindbeck, *Nature of Doctrine*, p. 114. Lindbeck argues that an 'extratextual' approach characterizes the propositionalist and experiential-expressive approach. For further discussion of this point, see T. W. Tilley, 'Incommensurability, Intratextuality, and Fideism', *Modern Theology* 5 (1989), pp. 87–111.

77. Holmer, *Grammar of Faith*, p. 203.

78. Holmer, *Grammar of Faith*, p. 20.

79. F. D. E. Schleiermacher, *Brief Outline of the Study of Theology* (Richmond, VA: John Knox, 1966), p. 71.

80. Lindbeck, *Nature of Doctrine*, p. 106. See also pp. 66–67.

81. On this point, see D. Z. Phillips, 'Lindbeck's Audience', *Modern Theology* 4 (1988), pp. 133–154.

82. Lindbeck, *Nature of Doctrine*, p. 65. For views similar to Lindbeck's, yet articulated from an evangelical perspective, see Stanley J. Grenz, *Revisioning Evangelical Theology* (Downers Grove, IL: InterVarsity Press, 1993), p. 15; Clark Pinnock, *Tracking the Maze* (San Francisco: Harper & Row, 1990), p. 186.

83. Bruce Marshall, 'Aquinas as a Postliberal Theologian', *The Thomist* 53 (1984), pp. 353–401. See also his 'Absorbing the World: Christianity and the Universe of Truths', in B. Marshall (ed.), *Theology and Dialogue: Essays in Conversation with George Lindbeck* (Notre Dame, IN: University of Notre Dame Press, 1990), pp. 69–102.

84. Lindbeck, *Nature of Doctrine*, p. 19.

85. Lindbeck, *Nature of Doctrine*, pp. 92–96.

86. Lindbeck, *Nature of Doctrine*, p. 94. For the suggestion that Lindbeck is not

merely dependent upon Bernard Lonergan at this point, but actually misunderstands him, see Stephen Williams, 'Lindbeck's Regulative Christology', *Modern Theology* 4 (1988), pp. 173–186.

87. As pointed out by Williams, 'Lindbeck's Regulative Christology', p. 178.

88. Rowan Williams, 'Trinity and Revelation', *Modern Theology* 2 (1986), pp. 197–212.

89. See Alister E. McGrath, *The Making of Modern German Christology* (2nd edn., Leicester: Apollos and Grand Rapids, MI: Zondervan, 1994), pp. 145–198.

90. Ronald Thiemann would appear to represent a critic of this approach, at least in respect of the referent of theological language. Focusing on the concept of 'promise', Thiemann argues that the character of the gospel as promise points to a reality beyond the world of human language, and points to the realm of eschatology as the sphere in which questions of 'truth' or 'reference' are ultimately resolved: Thiemann, *Revelation and Theology*, pp. 153–156.

91. For example, see Alister E. McGrath, *Evangelicalism and the Future of Christianity* (London: Hodder & Stoughton, 1994, and Downers Grove, IL: InterVarsity Press, 1995).

92. See the sophisticated 'critical realist' approach to Scripture developed by N. T. Wright, *The New Testament and the People of God*, vol. 1: *Christian Origins and the Question of God* (Minneapolis, MN: Fortress, 1992), pp. 47–80.

93. Hauerwas, *Community of Character*, p. 56.

94. Hauerwas, *Community of Character*, pp. 65–66. Note that Hauerwas is not denying that Scripture may be used and interpreted in other spheres; he is simply pointing out that the *proper* sphere for such use and interpretation is the life of the church.

95. See the helpful discussion in John Sykes, 'Narrative Accounts of Biblical Authority: The Need for a Doctrine of Revelation', *Modern Theology* 5 (1989), pp. 327–342; L. Gregory Jones, 'A Response to Sykes: Revelation and the Practices of Interpreting Scripture', *Modern Theology* 5 (1989), pp. 343–348.

96. Carl F. H. Henry, 'Theology and Biblical Authority: A Review Article', *Journal of the Evangelical Theological Society* 19 (1976), pp. 315–323.

97. For a survey of evangelical opinion on this issue, see Kern Robert Trembath, *Evangelical Theories of Biblical Inspiration* (New York: Oxford University Press, 1987).

98. For the issues which lie behind my formulation, see Brevard Childs, *Biblical Theology in Crisis* (Philadelphia: Westminster, 1970), p. 102; Frei, *Eclipse of Biblical Narrative*, p. 133.

99. The best (and probably the most sympathetic) analysis is to be found in George Hunsinger, 'Hans Frei as Theologian: The Quest for a Generous Orthodoxy', *Modern Theology* 8 (1992), pp. 103–128. Note especially the extended discussion at note 13, pp. 124–126.

100. Hunsinger, 'Hans Frei as Theologian', p. 123.

101. For the argument, see Frei, *Eclipse of Biblical Narrative*, p. 315.

102. See Wolfhart Pannenberg, *Jesus – God and Man* (Philadelphia: Westminster,

1968). For reflections on Pannenberg's methodological analysis, see Alister E. McGrath, 'Christology and Soteriology: A Response to Wolfhart Pannenberg's Critique of the Soteriological Approach to Christology', *Theologische Zeitschrift* 42 (1986), pp. 222–236.

103. A. B. Ritschl, *The Christian Doctrine of Justification and Reconciliation* (Edinburgh: T. & T. Clark, 1900), vol. 3, p. 591.

104. Ritschl, *Justification and Reconciliation*, vol. 3, p. 465.

105. See the excellent analysis in Stefan Scheld, *Die Christologie Emil Brunners* (Wiesbaden: Franz Steiner, 1981), especially pp. 111–115.

106. For this phrase, see Frei, *Identity of Jesus Christ*, p. 4.

107. Frei, *Identity of Jesus Christ*, p. 56.

108. For the phrase, see Frei, *Identity of Jesus Christ*, p. 143.

109. See Ernst Käsemann, 'Blind Alleys in the Jesus of History Controversy', in *New Testament Questions of Today* (London: SCM, 1969), pp. 23–66; Joachim Jeremias, *New Testament Theology* (London: SCM, 1975), vol. 1; Günther Bornkamm, *Jesus of Nazareth* (London: Hodder & Stoughton, 1960); Reinhard Slenczka, *Geschichtlichkeit und Personsein Jesu Christi* (Göttingen: Vandenhoeck & Ruprecht, 1967).

110. See McGrath, *Making of Modern German Christology*, pp. 145–198, and references therein.

111. See Wolfgang Grieve, 'Jesus und Glaube: Das Problem der Christologie Gerhard Ebelings', *Kerygma und Dogma* 22 (1976), pp. 163–180.

112. For an analysis, see David V. Way, *The Lordship of Christ: Ernst Käsemann's Interpretation of Paul's Theology* (Oxford: Clarendon, 1991).

113. For a survey of related issues, see Douglas Jacobsen and Frederick Schmidt, 'Behind Orthodoxy and Beyond It: Recent Developments in Evangelical Christology', *Scottish Journal of Theology* 45 (1993), pp. 515–541.

114. A point stressed to me by George Lindbeck at the 1995 Evangelical–Postliberal Dialogue at Wheaton College, Illinois.

Chapter 4

1. See Alister E. McGrath, 'Religion', in J. W. Yolton (ed.), *The Blackwell Companion to the Enlightenment* (Oxford and Cambridge, MA: Blackwell, 1992), pp. 447–452.

2. Leslie Houlden, in J. Hick (ed.), *The Myth of God Incarnate* (London: SCM, 1977), p. 125.

3. On these general themes, see Diogenes Allen, *Christian Belief in a Postmodern World* (Louisville, KY: Westminster/John Knox, 1989); Thomas C. Oden, *After Modernity . . . What? Agenda for Theology* (Grand Rapids, MI: Zondervan, 1990).

4. Details may be found in Matei Calinescu, *Five Faces of Modernity* (Durham, NC: Duke University Press, 1987); Terry Eagleton, *The Ideology of the Aesthetic* (Oxford: Blackwell, 1990); Kevin Hart, *The Trespass of the Sign* (Cambridge: Cambridge University Press, 1989); David Harvey, *The Condition of Postmodernity*

(Oxford: Blackwell, 1989); Christopher Norris, *What's Wrong with Postmodernism?* (Baltimore, MD: Johns Hopkins University Press, 1990).

5. On this earlier relation, see Alister E. McGrath, *The Intellectual Origins of the European Reformation* (Oxford: Blackwell, 1987), pp. 32–68.

6. Louis Dumont, *Essays on Individualism: Modern Theory in Anthropological Perspective* (Chicago: University of Chicago Press, 1986), p. 25.

7. Harvey, *The Condition of Postmodernity*, p. 12.

8. G. W. F. Hegel, 'Über die Religion der Griechen und Römer', in J. Hoffmeister (ed.), *Dokumente zu Hegels Entwicklung* (Stuttgart: Fromanns Verlag, 1936), pp. 43–48.

9. See C. G. Hempelmann, 'Keine ewige Wahrheiten, als unaufhörlich zeitlich: Hamanns Kontroverse mit Kant über Sprache und Vernunft', *Theologische Beiträge* 18 (1987), pp. 5–33.

10. See A. Plantinga and N. Wolterstorff (eds.), *Faith and Rationality: Reason and Belief in God* (Notre Dame, IN: University of Notre Dame Press, 1983); Nicholas Wolterstorff, *Reason within the Bounds of Religion* (2nd edn., Grand Rapids, MI: Eerdmans, 1984).

11. For the full text, see *Le Livre du Recteur de l'Academie de Genève, 1559–1878* (6 vols., Geneva: Droz, 1964–1980), vol. 1, pp. 61–64 and 67–77.

12. See Hugh Trevor-Roper, 'The Religious Origins of the Enlightenment', in *Religion, The Reformation and Social Change* (London: Macmillan, 1967), pp. 1–45.

13. For a general survey of the regional variants of the Enlightenment, see R. Porter and M. Teich (eds.), *The Enlightenment in National Context* (Cambridge: Cambridge University Press, 1981).

14. See Franco Venturi, *Italy and the Enlightenment* (London: Longman, 1972); Dino Carpaneto and Giuseppe Ricuperati, *Italy in the Age of Reason, 1685–1789* (London: Longman, 1987); David Goodman, 'Science and the Clergy in the Spanish Enlightenment', *History of Science* 21 (1983), pp. 111–140.

15. See Anand C. Chitnis, *The Scottish Enlightenment* (London: Croom Helm, 1976); Henry F. May, *The Enlightenment in America* (Oxford: Oxford University Press, 1976).

16. Richard Sher, *Church and University in the Scottish Enlightenment* (Princeton, NJ: Princeton University Press, 1985). For an important discussion of the spread of the influence of the philosophy, see Michael Gauvreau, 'The Empire of Evangelicalism: Varieties of Common Sense in Scotland, Canada, and the United States', in M. A. Noll, D. W. Bebbington and G. A. Rawlyk (eds.), *Evangelicalism: Comparative Studies of Popular Protestantism in North America, the British Isles, and Beyond* (New York: Oxford University Press, 1994), pp. 219–252, with extensive documentation.

17. This development has been documented in some detail by Mark Noll, *Princeton and the Republic, 1768–1822* (Princeton, NJ: Princeton University Press, 1989), pp. 28–58.

18. As argued persuasively by Sidney E. Ahlstrom, 'The Scottish Philosophy and American Theology', *Church History* 24 (1955), pp. 257–272.

19. See May, *The Enlightenment in America*.

20. Ahlstrom, 'The Scottish Philosophy', p. 266.

21. George Marsden, *Fundamentalism and American Culture* (New York: Oxford University Press, 1980), pp. 111–112.

22. For a particularly interesting analysis, see John C. Vander Stelt, *Philosophy and Scripture: A Study in Old Princeton and Westminster Theology* (Marlton, NJ: Mack, 1978), pp. 166–184; Jack B. Rogers and Donald K. McKim, *The Authority and Interpretation of the Bible* (San Francisco: Harper & Row, 1979), pp. 323–351. For H. Evan Runner, this trend led to a 'rationalistic *rigor mortis*' setting in within Reformed evangelicalism: H. Evan Runner, *The Relation of the Bible to Learning* (Rexdale, Ontario: Association for Reformed Scientific Studies, 1967), pp. 81–83.

23. Kern Robert Trembath, *Evangelical Theories of Biblical Inspiration* (New York: Oxford University Press, 1987), p. 18.

24. Trembath, *Evangelical Theories of Biblical Inspiration*, p. 19; Rogers and McKim, *The Authority and Interpretation of the Bible*, p. 291.

25. Trembath, *Evangelical Theories of Biblical Inspiration*, p. 20.

26. Donald G. Bloesch, *Essentials of Evangelical Theology* (2 vols., San Francisco: Harper & Row, 1979), vol. 2, pp. 267–268.

27. Carl F. H. Henry, *God, Revelation and Authority* (6 vols., Waco, TX: Word, 1976–83), vol. 3, p. 476.

28. Henry, *God, Revelation and Authority*, vol. 1, p. 232. For criticism of this approach from an evangelical perspective, see Stuart C. Hackett, *The Reconstruction of the Christian Revelation Claim* (Grand Rapids, MI: Baker, 1984).

29. Bernard Ramm, *Special Revelation and the Word of God* (Grand Rapids, MI: Eerdmans, 1961), p. 68.

30. Tertullian, *De praescriptione haereticorum*, 7; in *Sources chrétiennes*, vol. 46, ed. R. F. Refoulé (Paris: Editions du Cerf, 1957), 96.4 – 99.3.

31. For documentation of this trend, see Millard J. Erickson, *The Evangelical Mind and Heart* (Grand Rapids, MI: Baker, 1993), pp. 102–104.

32. See Carl F. H. Henry, 'Narrative Theology: An Evangelical Appraisal', *Trinity Journal* 8 (1987), pp. 3–19, which takes a critical stance. Note the brief response from Hans Frei, 'Response to Narrative Theology: An Evangelical Appraisal', *Trinity Journal* 8 (1987), pp. 21–24.

33. Henry, *God, Revelation and Authority*, vol. 3, p. 453. For comments on this type of approach, see Kevin J. Vanhoozer, 'The Semantics of Biblical Literature', in D. A. Carson and J. D. Woodbridge (eds.), *Hermeneutics, Authority and Canon* (Grand Rapids, MI: Zondervan, 1986), pp. 49–104, especially pp. 67–75. For a more recent defence of the need to be sensitive to the literary styles within Scripture, see Kevin J. Vanhoozer, 'From Canon to Concept: Same and Other in the Relation between Biblical and Systematic Theology', *Scottish Bulletin of Evangelical Theology* 12 (1994), pp. 96–124.

34. For important surveys, see Robert Grant, *Gods and the One God: Christian Theology in the Graeco-Roman World* (London: SPCK, 1986); Henry Chadwick, *Early Christian Thought and the Classical Tradition* (Oxford: Clarendon, 1966).

35. This is the style of approach found in the apologetic writings of Justin Martyr. See *Apologia*, I.xlvi.2–3; II.x.2–3; II.xiii.4–6; in *Saint Justin: Apologies*, ed. A. Wartelle (Paris: Etudes Augustiniennes, 1987), 160.6–9; 210.3–7; 216.11–18. A more developed form of the approach is associated with Clement of Alexandria, *Stromata*, I.v.28; in *Die griechischen christlichen Schriftsteller der erste Jahrhunderte. Clemens Alexandrinus: Zweiter Band. Stromata Buch I–VI*, ed. O. Stählin and L. Früchtel (Berlin: Akademie Verlag, 1985), pp. 17.31 – 18.5.

36. Tertullian, *De praescriptione haereticorum*, 7.

37. Hans Frei, *The Eclipse of Biblical Narrative: A Study in Eighteenth and Nineteenth Century Biblical Hermeneutics* (New Haven, CT: Yale University Press, 1977). For the new interest in narrative theology, see Ronald F. Thiemann, *Revelation and Theology: The Gospel as Narrated Promise* (Notre Dame, IN: University of Notre Dame Press, 1985); Garrett Green, *Scriptural Authority and Narrative Interpretation* (Philadelphia: Fortress, 1987).

38. Frei, *The Eclipse of Biblical Narrative*, p. 9. Locke's epistemology is known to have been significant in relation to laying the foundations of later English deism. For the difficulties associated with the term 'deism', see R. E. Sullivan, *John Toland and the Deist Controversy* (Cambridge, MA: Harvard University Press, 1982).

39. Gabriel Fackre, 'Narrative Theology in Evangelical Perspective', in *Ecumenical Faith in Evangelical Perspective* (Grand Rapids, MI: Eerdmans, 1993), pp. 123–146.

40. See Dale Patrick, *The Rendering of God in the Old Testament* (Philadelphia: Fortress, 1981).

41. For an analysis, and the development of approaches which avoid such restrictions, see Alister E. McGrath, *Beyond the Quiet Time* (London: SPCK, and Grand Rapids, MI: Baker, 1995).

42. On secular concepts of truth, especially those conditioned by the Enlightenment, see Michael Dummett, *Truth and Other Enigmas* (London: Duckworth, 1978); Leszek Kolakowski, 'Marx and the Classical Definition of Truth', in *Marxism and Beyond* (London: Pall Mall Press, 1969), pp. 59–87; J. R. Lucas, 'True', *Philosophy* 44 (1969), pp. 175–186.

43. For what follows, see G. J. Botterweck and H. Ringgen (eds.), *Theologisches Wörterbuch zum Alten Testament* I/3 (Stuttgart: Verlag Kohlhammer, 1971), cols. 333–341; M. E. J. Richardson (ed.), *Hebrew and Aramaic Lexicon of the Old Testament* (4 vols., Leiden: Brill, 1994), vol. 1, pp. 68–69.

44. On which see especially D. Michel, 'Ämät: Untersuchung über Wahrheit im Hebräische', *Archiv für Begriffsgeschichte* 12 (1968), pp. 30–57; Anthony Thiselton, 'Truth', in C. Brown (ed.), *The New International Dictionary of New Testament Theology* (Grand Rapids, MI: Eerdmans, 1978), vol. 3, pp. 874–902.

45. See H. Hommel, 'Wahrheit und Gerechtigkeit: Zur Geschichte und Deutung eines Begriffspaars', *Antike und Abendland* 15 (1969), pp. 159–186, and the extension of this study in Alister E. McGrath, *Iustitia Dei: A History of the Christian Doctrine of Justification* (2 vols., Cambridge: Cambridge University Press, 1986), vol. 1, pp. 4–16.

46. Søren Kierkegaard, *Unscientific Postscript* (London: Oxford University Press, 1941), pp. 169-224. *Cf.* P. L. Holmer, 'Kierkegaard and Religious Propositions', *Journal of Religion* 35 (1955), pp. 135–146.

47. John Mackay, *The Presbyterian Way of Life* (Englewood Cliffs, NJ: Prentice-Hall, 1960), pp. 9–10.

48. On the distinction between 'modern' and 'postmodern' theologies, see Nancey Murphy and James Wm. McClendon, Jr, 'Distinguishing Modern and Postmodern Theologies', *Modern Theology* 5 (1989), pp. 191–214.

49. Alan Wilde, *Horizons of Assent: Modernism, Postmodernism and the Ironic Imagination* (Baltimore, MD: Johns Hopkins University Press, 1981), p. 131.

50. Os Guinness, *Fit Bodies, Fat Minds* (London: Hodder & Stoughton, 1994), p. 105.

51. See especially Zygmunt Bauman, *Modernity and the Holocaust* (Cambridge: Polity Press, 1989). There are also some useful comments in Stephen Toulmin, *Cosmopolis: The Hidden Agenda of Modernity* (New York: Free Press, 1990).

52. Jean-François Lyotard, *The Postmodern Condition: A Report on Knowledge* (Manchester: Manchester University Press, 1984), p. xxv. For an excellent evangelical response to postmodern notions of 'truth', see J. Richard Middleton and Brian J. Walsh, *Truth is Stranger than it Used to Be* (Downers Grove, IL: InterVarsity Press, 1995). Other evangelical responses of note include Roger Lundin, *The Culture of Interpretation* (Grand Rapids, MI: Eerdmans, 1993), and Gene Edward Veith, *Postmodern Times: A Christian Guide to Contemporary Thought and Culture* (Wheaton, IL: Crossway, 1994).

53. For an excellent illustrated survey of the rise of modernism, see Harvey, *The Condition of Postmodernity*, pp. 260–283. For some of the ideas which lay behind its architectural styles, see Walter Gropius, *The Scope of Total Architecture* (New York: Collier, 1966).

54. See Leonardo Benevolo, *A History of Modern Architecture* (London: Routledge & Kegan Paul, 1971); Kenneth Frampton, *Modern Architecture, 1851-1945* (New York: Rizzoli, 1983).

55. Cited in Howard Harris and Alan Lipman, 'Viewpoint: A Culture of Despair. Reflections on Post-Modern Architecture', *Sociological Review* 34 (1986), pp. 837–854; quote at p. 838. Milton Keynes is a postwar new town in Bedfordshire, England, planned on severely modernist lines. The themes concerned can be more fully explored from works such as Alberto Perez Gomez, *Architecture and the Crisis of Modern Science* (Cambridge, MA: Massachussets Institute of Technology Press, 1983); James Hoston, *The Modernist City* (Chicago: University of Chicago Press, 1989).

56. Frederick Jameson, *Postmodernism, or the Cultural Logic of Late Capitalism* (London: Verso, 1992). For more extended reflections on some of these themes, see Sophie Watson and Katherine Gibson (eds.), *Postmodern Cities and Spaces* (Oxford: Blackwell, 1994).

57. Jean-François Lyotard, *Le postmodernism expliqué aux enfants* (Paris: Editions Galilée, 1986), p. 36.

58. See 'The Paradox of Morality: An Interview with Emmanuel Lévinas', in R. Bernesconi and D. Wood, *The Provocation of Lévinas: The Rethinking of the Other* (London: Routledge & Kegan Paul, 1988), p. 178.

59. For their theological significance, see Alister E. McGrath, *The Genesis of Doctrine* (Oxford: Blackwell, 1990), pp. 165–171.

60. Walter Benjamin, 'Theses on the Philosophy of History', in *Illuminations: Essays and Reflections* (London: Jonathan Cape, 1970), pp. 257–258.

61. See the analysis in Edith Wyschogrod, *Spirit in Ashes: Hegel, Heidegger and Man-made Mass Death* (New Haven, CT: Yale University Press, 1985).

62. Czeslaw Milosz, *Nobel Lecture* (New York: Farrar, Straus & Giroux, 1980), p. 14.

63. See Gregory Baum, 'Modernity: A Sociological Perspective', *Concilium* 6 (1992), pp. 3–9. Note especially the conclusion (p. 8): 'What has been named postmodern is a phase of modernity itself.'

64. The following works are helpful: Calinescu, *Five Faces of Modernity*; Eagleton, *The Ideology of the Aesthetic*; Hart, *The Trespass of the Sign*; Harvey, *The Condition of Postmodernity*; Norris, *What's Wrong with Postmodernism?*.

65. For some of the issues, see David Lodge, 'Modernism, Antimodernism, Postmodernism', in *Working with Structuralism* (London: Routledge & Kegan Paul, 1981), pp. 3–16. Michael Levenson's helpful *Genealogy of Modernism* (Cambridge: Cambridge University Press, 1984) tends towards the 'subjectivist' view that 'modernism' represents a rejection of a world which may be known objectively in favour of the view that it can be experienced only through individual consciousness.

66. Ihab Hassan, *The Dismemberment of Orpheus: Toward a Postmodern Literature* (New York: Oxford University Press, 1982), pp. 267–268. See also his 'Culture of Postmodernism', *Theory, Culture and Society* 2 (1985), pp. 119–132, especially pp. 123–124.

67. See Ferdinand de Saussure, *Course in General Linguistics* (New York: McGraw-Hill, 1966); Umberto Eco, *A Theory of Semiotics* (Bloomington, IN: Indiana University Press, 1976).

68. For reflections, see Mark Gottdiener, *Postmodern Semiotics: Material Culture and the Forms of Postmodern Life* (Oxford: Blackwell, 1995), pp. 3–53.

69. On this, see Paul de Man, *Allegories of Reading* (New Haven, CT: Yale University Press, 1979); J. Hillis Millar, *The Ethics of Reading* (New York: Columbia University Press, 1987), and especially Christopher Norris, *Deconstruction and the Interests of Theory* (London: Pinter Publishers, 1988).

70. For a close reading of the presuppositions and implications of this approach, see Christopher Norris, 'Kant Disfigured: Ethics, Deconstruction and the Text Sublime', in *The Truth about Postmodernism* (Oxford: Blackwell, 1993), pp. 182–256.

71. For an excellent analysis of this trend, see David Lehman, *Signs of the Times* (London: André Deutsch, 1991).

72. Lyotard, *Le postmodernism expliqué aux enfants*, pp. 121–122. See also his

arguments for a 'war on totality': Lyotard, *The Postmodern Condition*, p. 82. For related arguments, see Stanley Fish, *There's No Such Thing as Free Speech* (New York: Oxford University Press, 1994). Fish argues that all 'truth claims' are simply veiled attempts to achieve political or social power. Debates over 'truth' are thus in reality nothing other than power games. For this reason, Fish argues against the cardinal North American virtue of freedom of speech, seeing this as the freedom to oppress and manipulate.

73. A point stressed by Kenneth L. Gergen, *The Saturated Self: Dilemmas of Identity in Contemporary Life* (New York: Basic Books, 1991), p. 252. See also the general survey provided by Gary J. Percesepe, 'The Unbearable Lightness of Being Postmodern', *Christian Scholar's Review* 20 (1992), pp. 118–135.

74. Terry Eagleton, 'Awakening from Modernity', *The Times Literary Supplement*, 20 February 1987.

75. See the excellent survey of Gordon R. Lewis, *Testing Christianity's Truth Claims: Approaches to Christian Apologetics* (Chicago: Moody Press, 1976).

76. John Caputo, *Radical Hermeneutics* (Bloomington, IN: Indiana University Press, 1987), p. 156. For penetrating discussions of the tensions within this approach to 'truth', see J. L. Marsh, J. D. Caputo and M. Westphal, *Modernity and Its Discontents* (New York: Fordham University Press, 1992), pp. 89–92, 168–177.

77. Allen, *Christian Belief in a Postmodern World*, pp. 5–6.

78. Allan Bloom, *The Closing of the American Mind* (New York: Simon & Schuster, 1987), pp. 25–26.

79. Stanley Hauerwas, *A Community of Character* (Notre Dame, IN: University of Notre Dame Press, 1981), p. 1.

80. Allen, *Christian Belief in a Postmodern World*, p. 1.

81. Lewis, *Testing Christianity's Truth Claims*.

82. Bloom, *The Closing of the American Mind*, p. 26. For an account of the British decision to abolish this practice, see Stephen Neill, *A History of Christianity in India, 1707–1858* (Cambridge: Cambridge University Press, 1985), pp. 157–158. Regulation XVII of the Bengal Code (1829) declared that 'the practice of suttee, or of burning or burying alive the widows of Hindus, is hereby illegal, and punishable by the criminal courts'.

83. Michael Mahon, *Foucault's Nietzschean Genealogy: Truth, Power, and the Subject* (Albany, NY: State University of New York Press, 1992).

84. The most important writings are his *Order of Things: An Archaeology of the Human Sciences* (New York: Vintage, 1973); *Power/Knowledge: Selected Interviews and Other Writings, 1972–1977* (New York: Pantheon, 1980); *Histoire de la folie à l'âge classique* (Paris: Gallimard, 1972).

85. This citation is taken from a late interview, published as 'The Ethic of Care for the Self as a Practice of Freedom', in James Bernauer and David Rasmussen (eds.), *The Final Foucault* (Cambridge, MA: Massachussets Institute of Technology Press, 1988), p. 20.

86. Stanley Rosen, *Hermeneutics as Politics* (Oxford: Oxford University Press, 1987), pp. 189–190.

87. Ben F. Meyer, 'The Philosophical Crusher', *First Things* 12, April 1991, pp. 9–11; quote at p. 10. See also Bernard Bergonzi, *Exploding English: Criticism, Theory, Culture* (Oxford: Clarendon, 1990).

88. Francis A. Schaeffer, *Trilogy* (Wheaton, IL: Crossway, and Leicester: Inter-Varsity Press, 1990), p. 58.

89. Schaeffer, *Trilogy*, p. 134.

90. Hélé Béji, 'La patrimoine de la cruauté', *Le débat* 73 (1993), p. 167.

91. I owe this lucid statement of this point to Robert S. Downie and Elisabeth Talfer, *Respect for Persons* (London: Allen & Unwin, 1969), p. 42.

92. Michael Walzer, 'The Politics of Michel Foucault', in David Couzens Hoy (ed.), *Foucault: A Critical Reader* (Oxford: Blackwell, 1986), pp. 51–68. Walzer's own position may be studied from his *Spheres of Justice: A Defence of Pluralism and Equality* (Oxford: Blackwell, 1983).

93. For a further exploration of this point, see Zygmunt Bauman, *Postmodern Ethics* (Oxford: Blackwell, 1993), especially pp. 37–61.

94. Richard Rorty, *Consequences of Pragmatism* (Minneapolis, MN: University of Minneapolis Press, 1982), p. xlii.

95. Rorty, *Consequences of Pragmatism*, p. xlii.

96. Lyotard, *The Postmodern Condition*, p. 66.

97. Lyotard, *The Postmodern Condition*, p. 60.

98. Steven Connor, *Postmodernist Culture: An Introduction to Theories of the Contemporary* (Oxford: Blackwell, 1989), p. 35.

99. For some promising indications at the apologetic level, see Richard R. Topping, 'The Anti-Foundationalist Challenge to Evangelical Apologetics', *Evangelical Quarterly* 63 (1991), pp. 45–60.

Chapter 5

1. Michael Green, *Acts for Today: First Century Christianity for Twentieth Century Christians* (London: Hodder & Stoughton, 1993), p. 38. For qualifications of these comments in relation to the early church as a whole, see Robert L. Wilken, 'Religious Pluralism and Early Christian Theology', *Interpretation* 44 (1988), pp. 379–391. Parts of the present chapter were originally published in the form of articles: see Alister E. McGrath, 'The Challenge of Pluralism for the Contemporary Christian Church', *Journal of the Evangelical Theological Society* 35 (1992), pp. 361–373; idem, 'The Christian Church's Response to Pluralism', *Journal of the Evangelical Theological Society* 35 (1992), pp. 487–501.

2. J. A. Di Noia, OP, 'Christian Universalism: The Nonexclusive Particularity of Salvation in Christ', in C. E. Braaten and R. W. Jenson (eds.), *Either/Or: The Gospel or Neopaganism* (Grand Rapids, MI: Eerdmans, 1995), pp. 36–47, especially pp. 36–37.

3. John Hick, *Problems of Religious Pluralism* (London: Macmillan, 1985), p. 102.

4. Diogenes Allen, *Christian Belief in a Postmodern World* (Louisville, KY: Westminster/John Knox, 1989), p. 9.

5. Lesslie Newbigin, *The Gospel in a Pluralist Society* (Grand Rapids, MI: Eerdmans, 1989), p. 1.

6. Justin Martyr's discussion of 'Christianity before Christ' shows the sensitivity of early Christian writers to the continuing presence of pagan religions in the region. See especially *Apologia*, I.xlvi.1-3; in A. Wartelle (ed.), *Saint Justin: Apologies* (Paris: Etudies Augustiniennes, 1987), 160.1-10.

7. The literature is huge. On the Arab context, see Robert B. Betts, *Christians in the Arab East* (Atlanta, GA: John Knox, 1989). The situation in India has been surveyed in a masterly manner by Stephen Neill, *A History of Christianity in India* (2 vols., Cambridge: Cambridge University Press, 1984-85).

8. See the excellent survey in P. J. Marshall and G. Williams (eds.), *The Great Map of Mankind: British Perceptions of the World in the Age of Enlightenment* (London: Dent, 1982).

9. Inevitably, the picture is more complex than these generalizations suggest. See, for example Djavad Hadidi, *Voltaire et l'Islam* (Paris: Publications Orientalistes de France, 1974).

10. There is a huge literature, of which the following is typical: *Economic and Social Impact of Immigration* (Ottawa: Economic Council of Canada, 1991); Leon F. Bouvier, *Peaceful Invasions: Immigration and Changing America* (Washington, DC: Center for Immigration Studies, 1992); James Jupp and Marie Kabala, *The Politics of Australian Immigration* (Canberra: AGPS, 1993).

11. David Tracy, *Plurality and Ambiguity* (San Francisco: Harper & Row, 1987), p. 90.

12. John Milbank, 'The End of Dialogue', in G. D'Costa (ed.), *Christian Uniqueness Reconsidered: The Myth of a Pluralistic Theology of Religions* (Maryknoll, NY: Orbis, 1990), pp. 174-191; quote at p. 176. This essay merits detailed reading.

13. Ninian Smart, 'Truth and Religions', in J. Hick (ed.), *Truth and Dialogue: The Relationship between World Religions* (London: Sheldon, 1974), p. 57.

14. John B. Cobb, Jr, 'Beyond Pluralism', in D'Costa (ed.), *Christian Uniqueness Reconsidered*, p. 84.

15. Anthony Giddens, *Sociology* (Oxford: Polity Press, 1989), p. 452.

16. Paul Knitter, in J. Hick and P. Knitter (eds.), *The Myth of Christian Uniqueness* (Maryknoll, NY: Orbis, 1988), p. 184.

17. See Arnulf Camps, *Partners in Dialogue* (Maryknoll, NY: Orbis, 1983), p. 30.

18. Paul Griffiths and Delmas Lewis, 'On Grading Religions, Seeking Truth, and Being Nice to People: A Reply to Professor Hick', *Religious Studies* 19 (1983), p. 78. The issue is explored at greater depth in Paul J. Griffiths, *An Apology for Apologetics: A Study in the Logic of Interreligious Dialogue* (Maryknoll, NY: Orbis, 1991).

19. John V. Taylor, 'The Theological Basis of Interfaith Dialogue', in J. Hick and B. Hebblethwaite (eds.), *Christianity and Other Religions* (Philadelphia: Fortress, 1981), p. 212.

20. On this, see Michael C. Stokes, *Plato's Socratic Conversations: Drama and Dialectic in Three Dialogues* (London: Athlone, 1986). For the application of the

method in therapy, see Tullio Marandhao, *Therapeutic Discourse and Socratic Dialogue* (Madison, WI: University of Wisconsin Press, 1986).

21. John Hick, 'Towards a Philosophy of Religious Pluralism', *Neue Zeitschrift für systematische Theologie und Religionsphilosophie* 22 (1980), p. 135.

22. Newbigin, *The Gospel in a Pluralist Society*, pp. 9–10.

23. Ninian Smart, 'Truth and Religions', in Hick (ed.), *Truth and Dialogue*, p. 55.

24. See Phra Khantipalo, *Tolerance: A Study of Buddhist Sources* (London: Rider, 1964), p. 154.

25. See Newbigin, *Gospel in a Pluralist Society*, pp. 159–161, 168–170. For a penetrating and devastating philosophical critique of the position associated with Cantwell Smith and Hick, see Keith Ward, *Religion and Revelation: A Theology of Revelation in the World's Religions* (Oxford: Clarendon, 1994), pp. 310–317.

26. Kathryn Tanner, 'Respect for Other Religions: A Christian Antidote to Colonialist Discourse', *Modern Theology* 9 (1993), pp. 1–18.

27. Tanner, 'Respect for Other Religions', p. 2.

28. Tanner, 'Respect for Other Religions', p. 2. See also John Apczynski, 'John Hick's Theocentrism: Revolution or Implicitly Exclusive?', *Modern Theology* 8 (1992), pp. 39–52.

29. Sura 4:157. For further exploration of this matter, see Geoffrey Parrinder, *Jesus in the Qur'an* (London: Sheldon, 1965).

30. See Malik Ghulam Farid (ed.), *The Holy Qur'an with English Translation and Commentary* (Rabwah, Pakistan: Oriental and Religious Publishing Co, 1969), p. 232. As the editor comments (n. 697), this translation does not deny that Jesus was placed on a cross; it does, however, explicitly deny that he died on the cross.

31. See the foundational work by Mizra Ghulam Ahmad (the founder of the Ahmadiyya movement), *Jesus in India* (Tilbury: Islam International, 1989). The Ahmadi tract *Jesus in Kashmir* (London: London Mosque, 1977) should also be noted.

32. Note especially the comments of Parrinder, *Jesus in the Qur'an*, p. 116.

33. Muhammad Zafrulla Khan, *Deliverance from the Cross* (London: London Mosque, 1978), p. 89.

34. Hans Küng, *Christianity: Its Essence and History* (London: SCM, 1995), p. 36. See also his more general emphasis on the importance of Jesus Christ and Scripture, p. xxiii.

35. See the remarkable essay of Wilfred Cantwell Smith, 'Conflicting Truth Claims: A Rejoinder', in Hick (ed.), *Truth and Dialogue*, pp. 156–162, which interprets 'truth' in such an experimental and elastic manner that contradiction is virtually excluded as a matter of principle.

36. Jacob Neusner, *Telling Tales: The Urgency and Basis for Judeo-Christian Dialogue* (Louisville, KY: Westminster/John Knox, 1993).

37. Gilles Kepel, *La revanche de Dieu: chrétiens, juifs et musulmans à la reconquête du monde* (Paris: Seuil, 1991).

38. Richard Rorty, *The Consequences of Pragmatism* (Minneapolis, MN: University of Minnesota Press, 1982), p. 166.

39. Islam, like Christianity, is a missionary religion, which is actively seeking to expand its influence in the West through conversion (*da'wah*) and territorial expansion (*dâr al-islâm*): see Larry Poston, *Islamic Da'wah in the West: Muslim Missionary Activity and the Dynamics of Conversion to Islam* (New York: Oxford University Press, 1992).

40. Happily, there are promising developments on offer. See, for example, Paul Varo Martinson, *A Theology of World Religions* (Minneapolis, MN: Augsburg, 1987); Allen, *Christian Belief in a Postmodern World*, pp. 185–196; Carl E. Braaten, *No Other Gospel! Christianity among the World's Religions* (Minneapolis, MN: Fortress, 1992), pp. 83–102.

41. Braaten, *No Other Gospel!*, p. 71.

42. See David Cairns, *The Image of God in Man* (London: Collins, 1973).

43. Augustine, *Confessions*, I.i.1. See the translation by Henry Chadwick (Oxford: Oxford University Press, 1991), p. 3.

44. *Confessions*, VII.xvii.23; Chadwick, pp. 126–127: 'I carried with me only a loving memory and a desire for that of which I had the aroma but which I had not yet the capacity to eat.'

45. See Alister E. McGrath, 'Christology and Soteriology: A Response to Wolfhart Pannenberg's Critique of the Soteriological Approach to Christology', *Theologische Zeitschrift* 42 (1986), pp. 222–236.

46. See Walter Burkert, *Greek Religion* (Oxford: Blackwell, 1975), pp. 137, 213, and references therein.

47. See Lesslie Newbigin, *The Finality of Christ* (Richmond, VA: John Knox, 1969); more recently, Clark H. Pinnock, *A Wideness in God's Mercy: The Finality of Jesus Christ in a World of Religions* (Grand Rapids, MI: Zondervan, 1992), pp. 49–80.

48. See Edward A. Dowey, *The Knowledge of God in Calvin's Theology* (New York: Columbia University Press, 1952).

49. On this point, see John Platt, *Reformed Thought and Scholasticism: The Arguments for the Existence of God in Dutch Theology, 1575–1650* (Leiden: Brill, 1982). See also the important study of Michael L. Czapky Sudduth, 'The Prospects for Mediate Natural Theology in John Calvin', *Religious Studies* 31 (1995), pp. 53–68.

50. Carl E. Braaten, 'Christ is God's Final, Not the Only, Revelation', in Braaten, *No Other Gospel*, pp. 65–82; quote at p. 68.

51. Mikka Ruokanen, *The Catholic Doctrine of Non-Christian Religions According to the Second Vatican Council* (Leiden: Brill, 1992). For the primary source, see Vatican II, *Nostra Aetate*, 28 October 1965; in *Vatican II: Conciliar and Postconciliar Documents*, ed. Austin Flannery, OP (Northport, NY: Costello Publishing Company, and Dublin: Dominican Publications, 1975), pp. 738–742.

52. Søren Kierkegaard, *Unscientific Postscript* (London: Oxford University Press, 1941), pp. 169–224. *Cf.* P. L. Holmer, 'Kierkegaard and Religious Propositions', *Journal of Religion* 35 (1955), pp. 135–146.

53. John Hick, *God and the Universe of Faiths* (London: Macmillan, 1973), pp. 120–132.

54. Raimundo Panikkar, in Hick and Knitter (eds.), *The Myth of Christian Uniqueness*, p. 109.

55. The same point applies to Islam, which strongly resists attempts to homogenize or relativize the teaching of the Qur'an.

56. Perhaps most notably in J. Hick (ed.), *The Myth of God Incarnate* (London: SCM, 1977).

57. See Alister E. McGrath, 'Resurrection and Incarnation: The Foundations of the Christian Faith', in A. Walker (ed.), *Different Gospels* (2nd edn., London: SPCK, 1993), pp. 27–42.

58. Wolfhart Pannenberg, 'Religious Pluralism and Conflicting Truth Claims', in D'Costa (ed.), *Christian Uniqueness Reconsidered*, p. 100.

59. Tindal's chief work is entitled *Christianity as Old as Creation, or the Gospel a Republication of the Religion of Nature* (1730). On this, see Peter A. Byrne, *Natural Religion and the Religion of Nature* (London: Routledge, 1989).

60. Robert Jenson, *The Triune Identity* (Philadelphia: Fortress, 1982), pp. 1–20.

61. Gavin D'Costa, *John Hick's Theology of Religions* (New York: University Press of America, 1987), p. 103.

62. Harvey Cox, *Many Mansions* (Boston, MA: Beacon, 1988), pp. 5–6.

63. For a survey and criticism of these options, see Pinnock, *A Wideness in God's Mercy*, pp. 64–74.

64. John Hick, *The Second Christianity* (London: SCM, 1983), p. 86.

65. Di Noia, 'Christian Universalism', pp. 41, 44.

66. Geoffrey Wainwright, *Doxology: The Praise of God in Worship, Doctrine and Life* (New York: Oxford University Press, 1980). For a more recent discussion, see Aidan Kavanagh, *On Liturgical Theology* (New York: Pueblo, 1984). The Latin formula *lex orandi, lex credendi* is often used to summarize this inter-relationship.

67. The best study remains J. B. Carman, *The Theology of Ramanuja* (New Haven, CT: Yale University Press, 1974).

68. The nineteenth-century writer Ramohun Roy is a case in point. See the useful material assembled by Dermot Killingley, *Ramohun Roy in Hindu and Christian Tradition* (Newcastle-upon-Tyne: Grevatt & Grevatt, 1993).

69. A theme explored with considerable skill in Fergus Kerr, *Theology after Wittgenstein* (Oxford: Blackwell, 1988).

70. Ludwig Wittgenstein, *Lectures and Conversations on Aesthetics, Psychology and Religious Belief* (Oxford: Blackwell, 1966), p. 2: 'If I had to say what is the main mistake made by philosophers . . . I would say that it is that when language is looked at, what is looked at is a form of words and not the use made of the form of words.' There is an interesting parallel here with Barth's statement that the expressions which make up the 'spoken matter of proclamation' in the Christian faith 'acquire their meaning from the associations and contexts in which they are used': Karl Barth, *Church Dogmatics* (13 vols., Edinburgh: Clark, 1936–75), vol. I/1, p. 86.

71. Paul Knitter, in Hick and Knitter (eds.), *Myth of Christian Uniqueness*, p. 183.

72. Such a conclusion is defended, although for what seem to be different reasons,

in Joseph-Augustine Di Noia, *The Diversity of Religions: A Christian Perspective* (Washington, DC: Catholic University of America Press, 1992).

73. Note especially the subtitle of the significant study by E. Brooks Holifield, *A History of Pastoral Care in America: From Salvation to Self-Realization* (Nashville, TN: Abingdon, 1983). See also Philip Rieff, *The Triumph of the Therapeutic* (Chicago: University of Chicago Press, 1967).

74. On the third point, the importance of the doctrine of justification by faith through grace must be noted. See Alister E. McGrath, *Iustitia Dei: A History of the Christian Doctrine of Justification* (2 vols., Cambridge: Cambridge University Press, 1986).

75. Ignatius, *To the Smyrnaeans*, 7. See J. Stevenson (ed.), *A New Eusebius* (London: SPCK, 1957), p. 48.

76. Cyprian of Carthage, *De catholicae ecclesiae unitate*, 5–7; in *Corpus Christianorum: Series Latina* vol. 3, ed. M. Bévenot (Turnholt: Brepols, 1972), 252.117 – 254.176.

77. For useful historical background, see Hans Küng, *The Church* (New York: Sheed & Ward, 1967), pp. 313–319.

78. In their very different ways, the theologies of Karl Rahner and Karl Barth can be seen as attempts to resolve the tension at this point.

79. On this approach in Karl Barth, see Alister E. McGrath, 'Karl Barth als Aufklärer? Der Zusammenhang seiner Lehre vom Werke Christi mit der Erwählungslehre', *Kerygma und Dogma* 30 (1984) pp. 273–283.

80. This is the position taken by John A. T. Robinson, *In the End, God* (London: Clark, 1950).

81. Terry Eagleton, 'Awakening from Modernity', *The Times Literary Supplement*, 20 February 1987.

82. For the parallels between Lessing and modern pluralist writers such as Paul Knitter, see Reinhold Bernhardt, 'Ein neuer Lessing? Paul Knitters Theologie der Religionen', *Evangelische Theologie* 49 (1989), pp. 516–528.

Conclusion

1. See the arguments put forward in Alister E. McGrath, *Evangelicalism and the Future of Christianity* (London: Hodder & Stoughton, 1994, and Downers Grove, IL: InterVarsity Press, 1995).

2. See the important and influential analysis by Mark Noll, *The Scandal of the Evangelical Mind* (Grand Rapids, MI: Eerdmans, and Leicester: Inter-Varsity Press,1994), already alluded to in the present study.

index